Soul Searching with Djwhal Khul, the Tibetan

By
Moriah Marston

airleaf.com

© Copyright 2006, Moriah Marston

All Rights Reserved.

No part of this book may be reproduced, stored in a retrieval system, or transmitted by any means, electronic, mechanical, photocopying, recording, or otherwise, without written permission from the author.

ISBN: 1-60002-220-0

Words of Praise

"I enjoyed reading *Soul Searching* tremendously! It is so powerful and loving told. The author's honesty and vulnerability—the richness that is there spiritually and otherwise—is breathtaking. The story, words and Higher understanding speaks volumes and connects me in deeper ways to wholeness, trust and faith."

—Terri C, New York City

"Moriah Marston's book, *Soul Searching with Djwhal Khul, the Tibetan*, is riveting! In this beautifully written autobiographical account of her spiritual journey, the author presents us with a synthesis of profound insights and channeled wisdom interwoven with the story of her emotional and spiritual healing on the path to becoming a conscious channel for an Ascended Master. Ms. Marston demonstrates a psychological acumen that imbues her autobiography with a credibility and perspective that enrich our understanding of her (and our own) struggles at this time in humanity's history.

The structure of *Soul Searching* reflects the richness and nonlinear nature of the spiritual and emotional paradigms which Ms. Marston describes. The book can be savored as a series of essays or (and this is my approach) you can dive in, read straight through and arrive with the realization that you've just been through a transformative experience. I strongly recommend that you obtain a copy of Soul Searching so that a few years down the road you can claim the privilege of having a first edition of this extraordinary work.

—Reviewed by Jennifer Torrey, Psychotherapist, Greenfield, MA

Table of Contents

DEDICATION vii
ACKNOWLEDGMENTS viii
INTRODUCTION ix

THE CALLING 1
   Voices of the Soul 1
   Razor's Edge 2

IN THE BEGINNING 5
   The Beginning 5
   Dream of Window with Curtains Blowing 10
   Madness 14
   The Quest for the Divine Mother 17
   After Mama Left 19
   Monadic Imprint 22

FROM THE EYES OF A CHILD 25
   Truth 25
   Selling Our Souls 30
   Cruelty 32
   The Wound Becomes the Gift 34
   Music 39
   The Sound Current 42
   The Mask 45
   Intelligence 47
   The Negative Pole 49

JOINING THE HUMAN RACE 53
   Dad's Death 53
   Entering the Real World 56

   Astrology 60
   Fate vs. Free Will 65
   Moon's Nodes: The Soul's Cutting Edge 68
   Ithaca 72
   Freedom! 73
   Spiritual Awakening 76

THE PRESENCE OF PAST LIVES 80
   Having It All 80
   Past Life Selves 83
   Life in the Barn 84
   Building the House in the Woods 88
   Power 91
   Past life Regression with Inger 101

THE WITCH AND THE TIBETAN: A LOVE STORY 107
   The Golden One 107
   Relationship with Djwhal Khul 108
   Protection 113
   Distrust 116
   Moving into the Mystery 117
   Dreams: The Gateway to the Unconscious 121
   The Descent Experience 127
   I'm a Witch! 130
   Past Life as a Witch 132
   Relationships with Invisible Beings 139
   Soul Emergence 142

THE ORACLE AND THE GOLDEN DISCS 147
   Greece Trip 147
   Tablets Revealed 150
   Greek Oracle Lifetime 154
   Chiron and the Virgo/Pisces Intercept 159

Sacrifice: Willing vs. Unwilling 162

"MAY THE FORCE BE WITH YOU" 167
    Tibetan Past Life 167
    Hungry Ghosts 172
    The Force 176
    Russia 181
    Grace 188

TRANSMUTING THE DARK FORCE 191
    Shamanic Healing and Egyptian Past Life 191
    The Cosmic Janitor 217
    Evil 223
    My Soul's Response to Letting Go of Evil 227

BREAKING THROUGH 229
    Resistance 229
    Striving 233
    Magnitude 237

GLOSSARY 240
MORIAH MARSTON AND THE SCHOOL OF THE GOLDEN DISCS 242
CREDITS 248

DEDICATION

This book is dedicated to the Masters who bring to humanity guidance, encouragement, vision, inspiration, renewed faith and profound love. Their devotion graces our path, furthers world evolution and dissolves the illusion of separation, reminding us that we are never alone.

ACKNOWLEDGMENTS

I wish to thank Marilyn Penney for mid-wiving this book into form with her excellent creative editing, sensitive attunement to the material and joyful collaboration; Nancy Howe for repeatedly reminding me of my destiny as a writer, especially during times of vision "blackouts" when the prospect of languaging my truth seemed impossible; Mary Arsenault for providing a powerful vehicle for bringing my writing to the world through her publication, *Wisdom* magazine and for encouraging me to go the distance; special appreciation to my soul family Heidi, Jeanne M., Nina S., Roger and Robbie, Jean F, Ellen and Michael E., Soldann G. and Dreya W. for your loving support and joyful connection.

Words cannot express my deepest gratitude to my soulmate and husband, Zayne, for his consistent positive focus that pulled me out of many vortexes of despair and unworthiness, for his countless hours of rewriting the book, helping to find just the right word when my mind was overloaded, for his vibrant excitement and passion for my emerging soul as it has revealed itself through writing this book, for his steadfast partnering in running the School of the Golden Discs, for sitting by my side grounding and protecting me during hundreds of hours of group channeling sessions, for his love and commitment to the Tibetan, and for his own accelerated evolution that inspires me to keep up with him as together we walk hand in hand through the Gateway of Awakening.

INTRODUCTION

Welcome to the world of the soul, with its many levels of memory and knowing. Suspend linear reality as you enter the expansive paradigm of multidimensionality. Allow yourself to travel beyond time and space into the energetic core that holds our essence.

Please accompany me on the quest to find understanding in a world of unanswerable questions. The impossibility of these questions carries the paradox of human experience. Making peace with this essential enigma extends us to embrace the greater core of paradox reflecting the interface between the human condition and the spiritual dimension. Let us sit within the Greater Mystery together and allow ourselves to be impacted by the universal passion of all life.

This book is a multidimensional story of my soul-alignment process. Soul alignment requires that we embrace all the voices of our inner life with awareness and acceptance. The process of writing this book has had a profound healing and integrative impact on my consciousness. The purpose of the story, in addition to furthering my own transformation, is to inspire the reader to open to his/her multi-dimensional being and to experience soul-integration. The work is to uncover and discover the domain of one's soul.

I am asking the reader to accept the paradigm of reincarnation. Allow your own memories, hunches, and intuitive flashes to be stimulated and to surface as you read. Soul-alignment lays the groundwork for one's own unique enlightenment process. To open to multidimensional reality is to accept that our present selves are the results of many lifetimes of human experience. As we look at any patterns in ourselves we need to explore their roots, some of which can be hundreds if not thousands of years old. To heal the soul through story is to incorporate all lifetimes into the present one, which brings us true wholeness and transformation.

Writing this book has been a cleansing process to release any blockages that would inhibit the flow of my awakening consciousness. Writing my story has grounded my intuition. The courage to share my deepest self has healed wounds around hiding my truth while enhancing my trust in the essential safety of this universe that we collectively inhabit. Let this be an inspiration to readers to allow their own soul memories to emerge, to share their stories with others and therefore, to serve as models that soul-integration is possible for everyone. We are all in this alchemical stew together, living each other's reality as if it were our own.

Please join me in viewing our human experience from the paradigm that we are all students attending earth school. Our lives are essentially a grand learning process. There are many human teachers available for guidance. In addition, the faculty of earth school includes a group of teachers on the spiritual plane called the Ascended Masters. These Masters work internally with humanity twenty-four hours a day, to teach, heal, and guide our evolution, often while we are sleeping.

Djwhal Khul, also called "the Tibetan," is one of these Ascended Masters. He is known as the Great Psychologist because of his extensive wisdom regarding the human psyche, based in part on his own soul's development through lifetimes on planet earth. His last human incarnation was in Tibet. At that time, in the early 1900's, he telepathically transmitted metaphysical knowledge to Alice Bailey who lived in England. She recorded these teachings in many volumes of books that became the foundation for the Arcane School.

The Arcane School is based on the paradigm of an emerging new level of advanced collective consciousness, described by Djwhal Khul as "the birth of a new cosmic day." Ushering in this new paradigm are groups of world servers dedicated to restoring the Divine Plan on earth. After his ascension onto the spirit plane, the Tibetan has continued to work energetically with thousands of students to accelerate their awakening so that they may assist in the Great Work of invoking this momentous evolutionary leap for humanity.

I have been a channel for Djwhal Khul since 1986. Channeling is the art of making contact, receiving through expanded awareness, with another vibration or energy field. It is like being a human radio station. We have energetic sensors that can pick up "stations" of higher vibrational frequencies. We often receive these frequencies through our heart center and/or through the top of our head (the crown chakra). We can tap into highly creative realms, wisdom, inventions, as well as guidance from beings who dwell on the spiritual plane.

Channeling Djwhal Khul has opened my awareness, accelerated my process, expanded my wisdom/intuition and augmented my service to my therapy/astrology clients. One of the purposes of this book is to demonstrate the natural phenomena of channeling and to substantiate that there truly **is** communication with the spirit plane available to all. Please be open to receiving the Tibetan's energy through his words. The Tibetan's wish is that this book will inspire readers to open their own channel. To be in channel is to accept our birthright of natural alignment with a greater reality.

I have written my story in chronological order and peppered it with past life memories as they surfaced in my current life. The book is written in vignettes that describe the puzzle pieces holding the mystery of who I am. To let each piece take center stage and to speak for itself is to gather the clues to the overall window on my soul. Each puzzle piece is a number on a combination lock that opens the safe door holding the treasure of expanded vision. Please digest each vignette, allowing it to add yet another layer to the unfolding of the bigger picture.

Allow this to be a model for your own detective work of uncovering all of self. This is an invitation for you to pioneer the frontier of the domain of your soul. May you be inspired to welcome all the different voices of your soul to come forward with their puzzle pieces, emissaries of the magnificent vista of your Higher Self's journey. Allow my story to be a healing platform for your process of total self-acceptance, unconditional self-love and transformation.

The Tibetan encourages:

The courage to touch all dimensions of one's soul opens the pathway to true magnitude. To embrace one's story of profound awakening is to find the Holy Grail of alignment with the Higher Self at long last. Do not allow false beliefs to convince self that this great work of integration can be postponed until a future lifetime when self is wiser, braver, stronger, or more mature. The time has arrived on planet earth to come forward in full disclosure of self's Essence. In that revelation self releases all judgments, not only about self, but about all beings.

Beyond judgment lies a world of great beauty and exquisite refinement. The student can then serve as a conduit for the rarefied Light pouring forth from higher levels of existence. May each student boldly shout out to the heavens all that their passions tell them is truth, so that humankind may recognize itself in each other and experience unification at long last.

Remember that the Masters encircle the earth plane, forming a holding environment of great love and appreciation for humankind's extraordinary endeavor to open their eyes to the true spiritual root of their being. We applaud all students who take responsibility to move through the veils of illusion and dare to touch the heart of their souls with frank honesty and humility. This place of trust is the gateway to true wisdom and understanding.

From this point of heightened integration the students can go forth to teach others about this opening process, reassuring them that it can indeed be done with effort and the intention to serve the Divine Plan. The more students there are who open their eyes, the greater the evolution of humankind as it eventually takes its rightful place in the universe. Finally the earth plane will be experienced as a world of exquisite richness, a realm that augments the divine through its concentration of Love and Light so beautifully expressed in the challenges of being human. We are greatly appreciative for the devotion, hard work, discipline and loving willingness reflected in the students' commitment to their awakening. This great soul labor of Love makes all things possible.

THE CALLING

Voices of the Soul

The great work of self-realization is to integrate all the internal voices into a coherent whole. While they don't have to get along harmoniously, they do have to be heard, expressed, resolved and woven together into a greater tapestry that is the Self. If even one small voice is left out, repressed, it makes its presence felt to the whole being just as a small splinter in the foot can prevent even the most athletic body from reaching its peak. This process involves uncovering, stimulating, encouraging, loving and healing all aspects of the soul, treasuring each as a precious gift. Patience, patience, patience and persistence, tolerance for ambiguity, paradox, chaos, confusion and not-knowing are the ingredients for this great labor of Love called soul-alignment. While this work creates a powerful strain on the personality/ego structure to contain its apparent impossibility, the soul rejoices in its liberation as each strand of the Higher Self is realized and expressed in form.

My quest for inner peace leads me on this great journey of integration. There can be no rest until I sit with all aspects of myself from a place of gratitude and compassion. My ego feels that this is a never-ending task, sometimes experienced as a punishment for being banished by Source to the realm of the human condition. It feels that it can only stretch so far to include warring parts of Self into my personality, knowing full well there are great pieces of Self still waiting in line for recognition. The healing agent in my transformation is to dance on the stage of life, fully expressive and visible to Self. If I stop short of this, I fail. I fall behind trying to bring my spirit into a psychic structure that has many rooms sealed shut. The pressure to open these doors increases through the years, demanding, no longer patient to be invisible and unheard.

This book is about my journey to liberate Self. This book is my patchwork quilt, an attempt to fit all the odd pieces of cloth into a thing of overall beauty. I hereby invite the many voice of Self to come forward now. I welcome you with open arms!

Razor's Edge

It is strange to consider that as our awareness widens, our path narrows. Early on in our experience on the earth plane innocence is bliss. Our youthful soul perspective on the human condition allows us lots of room for experimentation and exploration. This is the time to explore the many spiritual pathways available to us, just as children play dress-up and fantasize about all the possibilities that life may offer. We have a broad range of experiencing to do in order to begin to attune to the true nature of the human condition. Although we are held in Lady Fate's container, there is still much room to employ our free will as we stumble in and out of lifetimes of challenges, lessons, illusion, and development.

As we evolve and begin to understand and master the human condition, we are required to begin to refine our soul's unique expression in form. Our pathway becomes a reflection of our individual soul's mandate. This is a very specific differentiation from the Oneness that is Source. Our awakening comes as our ego surrenders to our Higher Self. In this surrender, the ego accepts the function of focusing the unique quality of its Higher Self very specifically. At this point the path narrows as we embody the very special soul energy that belongs to us individually.

We find ourselves most comfortable, joyful and energetic when we are walking our own particular pathway. While earlier on in our evolution we delighted in trying on all kinds of earth forms as an expression of our Higher Selves, we now feel distinctly out-of-sorts if we attempt to play out a life path that is not uniquely ours. We move from participation in the collective fundamental pathway to an individual journey that is mystical and highly differentiated according to the light and sound uniquely expressed through our Higher Self. Initially this can be a lonely experience as we reluctantly leave our collective tribe to respond to the unique call of our own soul. However, the fulfillment that we experience as we feel that soul energetic "click" surpasses our memories of past homogenization with the mainstream of humanity. Ironically, as we align ourselves with our individual soul, we are able to deepen our acceptance of the state of oneness that we share with all beings.

The razor's edge illustrates the experience of narrowness that our pathway takes on as we totally surrender our personality/ego self to our Higher Self's purpose. The Higher Self is very specific in its needs and expression. There is little room for "fudging it" because of the discrepancy in vibratory rate that occurs if we are not impeccable in the representation of our soul. As our awareness increases, any inconsistency between personality expression and soul embodiment is experienced as painful, heavy, "off," confusing, unauthentic, depressing and limiting. This gives us the feeling that we cannot get away with anything anymore. As soon as we stray from our soul's mandate there is an instant, energetic ramification that we may have been blissfully unaware of in previous lives.

Although our pathway becomes a razor's edge in its specificity, it feels expansive. However, if we are out of alignment with our particular soul's expression, all the experiential freedom in the world would still feel terribly limiting. Because energy creates more energy, the more that we walk our soul's walk, the less we are able to walk any other path. The energy compounds upon itself, naturally purifying and refining itself to the point that it is indeed the razor's edge. If we fall from this very particular vibration, it feels like a fall from grace.

Our egos would love to tempt us into leaving our unique walkway in order to have the "freedom" to experience what other people get to experience, "The grass is always greener on the other side other the fence." This freedom rapidly becomes a prison of dissatisfaction as we feel cut off from our true purpose which is to embody our own unique soul and anchor it in our human condition. So, let us rejoice in the apparent limitation of the razor's edge as it ultimately gives us our Universal Self.

IN THE BEGINNING

The Beginning

As a little girl I had a vision of myself working with many people, propelled by a strong sense of destiny. My life purpose appeared large, important, light-filled and joyous. Most of my childhood was spent waiting to grow up and embark upon the pathway to this wondrous destiny.

Childhood felt like a prison in which I was only partially present. While part of me was fully in my youth, my deeper self secretly counted the days until I would be free of the restraints and vulnerabilities of being a child, knowing I was simply passing the time needed to grow my body into adulthood. To ease the burden of waiting I spent much time fantasizing, having a vivid imagination, easily activated and difficult to stop. My imaginary world was far more spacious, loving and freeing than the day-to-day reality within my family. I didn't realize at the time that this "imaginary" world was indeed real, perhaps more real than my daily outer life.

As children our psychic doors are wide open. We have clear access to the causal plane where the records of our karmic history as well as our probable future are kept. Many of us in youth are still digesting our previous incarnation as well as lingering traumas from several prior lifetimes. Children are more inclined to experience bleed-through memories from a different time. This could be a partial explanation of the vivid fantasy world, imaginary friends and intense dreams that most children experience.

IN THE BEGINNING

As a small child I remembered fleeting images of being a great teacher, a high priestess, a dedicated world server and a great scientist. Perhaps these images came from the archetypal level of the collective consciousness and I was simply dipping into all appealing possibilities trying them on just as a child plays "dress-up" with Mommy's clothes. At a visceral level what feels truer to me is that these images are real memories, not yet closed off from conscious awareness.

It takes several years for the ego to solidify itself. The more ego based we become as we mature into our early teens, the more disconnected we are from our previous selves. This is necessary and healthy if we are to have the opportunity to experience a fresh new approach to our current life's purpose.

During our early years while the ego is still undeveloped and permeable, we are capable of experiencing other dimensions and time periods as well as communication with non-physical beings. Once our ego has jelled we are very strongly committed to that particular persona as our growth vehicle through the remainder of the teenage years into our thirties. Arriving at mid-life we have the opportunity to begin the return journey back to the state of open awareness we enjoyed as children, especially from infancy until age five.

Our greatest challenge is the ego and its tight hold on our orientation to life. Often we struggle with the awareness of the greater Self as we begin to awaken. Our ego doesn't easily accept past-life identities, other realities beyond the earth plane, and guidance from sources other than human. In order to open to our larger Self, midlife brings the crisis of having to let go of the context in which we identified ourselves. This crisis involves levels of ego-death bringing us into profound experiences of not knowing who we are. If we can stand it, this is a period of great opportunity.

As a result of the intensified energies currently impacting the earth plane, everyone, regardless of their age, is subjected to this "mid-life" crisis. The process of moving beyond the ego's narrow reality and opening to larger impressions and memories of the greater Self is catching like wild fire in the collective consciousness. For those of us who are in mid-life, this process may feel doubly intensified.

Reflecting on my own early childhood, perhaps it was fortunate that I experienced crisis when I was very young. Eventually, we all experience the "expulsion from the Garden of Eden"—the fall from innocence. Trauma often shatters the idyllic bliss infusing the utter trust and naiveté of the child.

I have vague memories of being in a state of pure delight, pleasure and play in the first two years of my life. My father often took me crabbing on the Long Island sound. I delighted in the songs that I heard from the stones being washed up on the beach. I tried to get him to listen to them, insisting that he put the stones to his ears. Perhaps he humored me, telling me that he too heard the songs emanating from the stones. My young ears sensed the stones as an orchestra playing exquisite music.

The sound current is a powerful vehicle. I have ridden it like a wave, allowing it to move me far beyond my immediate reality. Many past lives spent toning, chanting, drumming, playing unusual instruments and singing have provided me with a great love of the countless ways in which Source expresses Itself through sound. Even the few lifetimes I spent handicapped through deafness did not deter my quest to ride the sound current. The truest sound is internal, each level and dimension of reality bringing with it a particular musical quality. I love the bells and flute sounds of the etheric plane as well as the dramatically profound thundering rolls of the causal plane. All dimensions and levels of experience are pulsing with celestial music.

My cosmic bliss-filled Garden of Eden was shattered when my mother took her life in my third year on this planet. This trauma left me fragmented and profoundly disturbed. Essential trust was annihilated. I felt utterly alone. My father, distraught and disoriented, anesthetized his pain with alcohol. To escape the torment of his memories he often stayed an hour away in New York City. This intensified my experience of betrayal, abandonment and isolation.

This crisis was an opportunity to compress lifetimes of issues with unworthiness and lack of self-love into a vivid current experience compelling me to either resolve my karmic condition or perish into the vortex of despair that captured my mother. Without the benefit of this larger perspective at age three, I was simply a lost child.

The timing of this traumatic event was fortunate. I was still young enough to be highly sensitive and responsive to other worldly assistance. The chord between my mother and myself was strong. As she left the earth plane, a large part of myself left with her. I spent most of my childhood psychically traveling back and forth between my earthly and spirit self. On the spirit plane I was held and nurtured by my mother.

However, this astral dimension was difficult to translate into human experience. The constant adjustment from physical to non-physical experiencing (being psychically in and out of my body) was particularly stressful. Each time I returned to my earthly self I felt the excruciating pain of separation from mother, as if her death had just happened. Yet, at a deep level I wanted to be on the earth plane, certainly more than my mother did. Torn by my loyalty to her I often felt guilty for finding fulfillment and joy in being physically alive.

My strong life force ultimately saved me from the magnetic draw of my mother's wish to have me permanently with her in spirit. As I lay awake in my bed at night I could sense my mother in her light body sitting behind me holding my head in her lap and singing lullabies as I fell asleep. What a safe feeling that was. Ironically, after her suicide, psychically she never left me again. However, I longed for her physical warmth and touch.

Later in life I struggled with the natural process of "cutting the umbilical chord." Psychically she had a very tight hold on my soul, as if that would assuage her guilt, loss and grief. At some tormented level of her being she wanted me to make the same choice, releasing the hold on my physical body. Then we would both be on the spirit plane together. She would be vindicated of her crime of abandonment. My spunky determination and curiosity enabled me to stick around to see what might develop in earthly life.

Perhaps it was "the calling" I experienced as a young child that motivated my stay on earth. Images of compelling service to others fueled my existence. Even the attachment to my mother could not compete with the force of my own destiny.

Tremendously difficult and challenging was the trauma of finding my mother dead. My psyche could not break down and integrate the shock. Like poison, it was simply indigestible, unacceptable to my entire being. In carrying this unresolved trauma, I moved through life with a great psychic burden unable to be released until I approached the age of forty. At that time I had a vivid dream revealing an early memory of running happily into my mother's bedroom only to find her lifeless. This dream indicated my readiness to go beyond the internal imprisonment I had experienced since the day of my mother's death. How does one break down a traumatic experience deeply enough to be truly released from its grasp? Is it possible to go beyond the haunting nature and nightmarish quality of life when self has been terribly violated?

Complete healing and transformation is available to all of us. Healing is inevitable if we are to move into enlightenment. However, this process of reorganizing the energy of trauma into a growth experience requires guidance and support. The assistance arrived exactly at the moment of discovering my mother's suicide. That was the first time in this lifetime that I connected with the Tibetan.

Opening the door to my mother's bedroom and seeing her dead on the bed, reality was instantly distorted—shattered and fragmented. I may have been permanently caught in horror if it was not for a great and loving spiritual being who entered the room at that moment. The Tibetan, not manifest in physical form, was substantial enough in his light body to allow me to fully perceive him.

Feeling very familiar, he was beautiful and kind. He swept me into his arms. Although etheric in nature, I could feel the coarseness of the natural fiber of his robes. His eyes twinkled as he looked at me, saying, "It is all right. You are safe."

Psychically I was spared the ordeal of witnessing my mother's difficult transition onto the astral plane. Suicide leaves a terrible imprint on the soul making what would normally be a beautiful and ecstatic experience through the death tunnel into the light become a torturous one of severe regret, disturbance and remorse. This may not be true of people who take their lives when either old age or sickness is already bringing death to their door.

Within moments the Tibetan and I psychically traveled to the Himalayas. We had slipped out of time and space, reentering it at Djwhal Khul's hut nestled into the base of one of the great mountains. The hut, lovingly built by Djwhal Khul with his own hands, was humble, warm, and cozy. I can still smell the sweet pungent earth walls and floor. The Tibetan sat down on his small, single bed and swept me onto his lap. He then told me of my destiny, my future, describing the complete story of my soul's work in this lifetime. He explained why my mother had ended her life, describing it in a way that my child's mind could understand.

Dream of Window with Curtains Blowing

The mystery within my being continues to unfold. Whenever I dare to presume that the process of self-discovery is complete, psyche offers me yet another nugget of potential gold from deep within my soul's core. These offerings often come in the form of dreams working to provide messages reflecting unfinished business in the unconscious.

Thursday nights with my dear friend Nancy Howe are set aside for the sacred work of dream exploration. Week after week, year after year, we patiently pick apart our dreams searching for insight, release, guidance, healing and inner peace. I can't imagine hanging on to my "sanity" without our Thursday night dream fix.

July 24, 2000 brought me a dream gift holding a key to the remaining pockets of inner torment so hard to reach with my conscious awareness. The dream:

"I decide to see a psychologist. When he returns my call a friend picks up the phone when I do. She starts telling the therapist about her childhood in detail. I am uncomfortable that she (and I) are taking up too much of his time on the phone. She is saying that as a little girl she had to be hyper aware of every little sound in the house, noticing if anything was different because of the threat of secrets, things going wrong. She is speaking and looking into her dining room from the living room as a child. The room is well lit and curtains are blowing. But she still has a feeling that something might be going on. She has to be super vigilant. As she is talking I am thinking that this is so similar to my childhood."

Looking at this dream instantly sent me tumbling into a startlingly deep place. As I moved my consciousness into the awareness of the little girl in the dream I was three years old looking into my mother's bedroom. All that I could see was intense light, the quality of light that reflects the spirit plane. I knew it was my mother's room because I recognized the window with the curtains blowing.

This image of the window with curtains blowing was shown to me in a dream I had in 1989. In that dream I was given the key (a skeleton key) to the four basic food groups. The key opens a door in my childhood home in Bayshore, Long Island. I am very little, about three years old, trying to reach the doorknob. As I turn the key the door opens. Looking inside the room I see my mother dead on the bed, pillows, sheets and blankets strewn about. The room is drenched in light with the window open and curtains blowing. There is an awful feeling of chaos in the air, like a great psychic struggle had just occurred.

Fortunately when I had this dream at age forty, I was in Jungian analysis. We repeatedly worked on this dream, able to touch it only in small amounts. My super sensitivity to the moment of finding my mother's dead body made it unbearable to connect with the experience in this dream. I was able to sustain contact for only a few minutes at a time. Eventually I was desensitized enough to psychically "enter" this room without completely falling apart.

This dream suggested that perhaps I had been the one to find my mother the morning after her suicide from an overdose of sleeping pills. The lack of conclusive evidence (no family members still living or available to discuss it) left me wondering whether this dream was simply providing images for me to work through the shock and grief of my mother's suicide, or whether the dream was really a hidden memory of the actual event of discovering her dead. Accepting that I would never know the truth, I continued to mull over this dream throughout my forties. The potency of its charge never diminished.

Eleven years later my blessed psyche offered a dream gift returning me to that exact moment of finding my mother dead. This time the room is not physical except for the open window with curtains blowing. That image is forever etched in my being. Psyche gave me that as a reference point to know where I was.

In my dream work with Nancy, I consciously enter the room as a three-year-old. I know instantly that it is taking place on the spirit plane. I see Mama at the end of the room and run up to her. She is crying, in terrible grief and remorse, desperate to hold me. At the moment of embrace a huge angel strides into the room. It is a stern angel; very muscular, powerful and determined (not at all like sweet cherubic angels with harps). This one is about twelve feet tall with massively strong wings. The angel steps between us, forbidding our connection. I am sobbing, calling "Mama, Mama," trying to reach out to her with my little arms. My mother is hysterical, struggling in vain to hold me. The angel carries the "law" with him. This law prohibits me to stay on the spirit plane with my mother. My great need to be with my mother left me highly susceptible to leaving my physical body. I was not able to resist the seduction of our bond. But, it was not *my* time to die.

So I had to turn away from her and walk back into the adjoining rooms, well-furnished and very physical. It was agony to turn away from her, this woman who was my world. Only the overwhelming presence of this great angel could persuade my little legs to keep moving out of the room as I kept looking back over my shoulder to see her for one last time. Returning to the physical plane was the loneliest moment of my life.

This dream allowed me to re-experience my first psychic event in this lifetime. I am deeply convinced that I did find my mother the morning after her death. At that time my three-year-old psychic doors were wide open. The shock catapulted me to the astral plane (the next level of existence beyond the physical plane). There was my mother's spirit clinging to the site of the crime—her suicide.

Sudden or tragic deaths often leave the departed and disoriented soul caught in the astral level of the physical place where death occurred. Gladly, I would have given up my life to be with her in spirit. The Angel of the Law had to stand between us to insure that I fulfill my destiny in this lifetime. I was literally booted off the astral plane to face my karma back in the house in Bayshore.

However, all throughout my early childhood until about age five I felt my mother's spirit cuddle up enveloping me from behind at night, holding me until I fell asleep. I had found the psychic door that allows travel between the dimensions. I would never forget it. That awareness could not be sealed shut like it normally does in children as they mature. The great ache for my mother kept that door open allowing us to "sneak" visits. However, most of these visits occurred on the physical plane. She was able to make her presence felt in my physical dimension more than I was able to travel onto the spirit plane to connect with her.

As a result of this openness to receiving from the spirit plane it has been a great challenge to stay in my body. My struggle with grounding has been lifelong. It is all too easy to lift up and out, making contact with greater dimensions. My quest is to stay physical, rejoicing in and taking care of my body. The three-year-old inside believes it is her physical body that kept her Mama away. I still lovingly remind her that to be incarnate is a great gift and opportunity, not a punishment of emotional isolation.

Coming to terms with the pain that led my mother to destroy her physical body seems to be an endless process. After years of taking responsibility for her pain—believing I was the one who drove her away—finally I can fully accept that I had nothing to do with her suicide.

My ability to nurture and heal my physical body is a way to honor my mother. She is pleased that I have remained on earth to fulfill my soul's work and wants only the best for me. Our connection is eternal, regardless of physical touch.

The gift inside of this enormous wound is my open door, never able to fully seal shut, to the spirit plane providing me conscious access to the Tibetan. It is the three-year-old inside that readily aligns her awareness with him as I go into channel. She knows how to find his world and understands that it is filled with love. She plays an outstanding role in my destiny, the fulfillment of my mission. I am deeply grateful to her for her precious innocence, strength, endurance and ancient knowing that allows me access to all portals of perception and all beings of light.

Madness

To be caught in the web of madness has been a persistent fear. Although I have feared physical disintegration, it has been the loss of my mind that I have obsessed over. As a teenager when I first considered the concept of madness, I was caught in a feeling of horror and fascination. What would it be like to lose my mind? Even then I knew that thought creates reality. There is no external objective reality available that is not subject to the mind's influence. If the mind breaks down everything goes.

I have vague memories of past lives spent institutionalized, incarcerated, punished and murdered for the "crime" of losing the grip on my mind. The numerous internal hells available in the creative flow of a distorted mind are endless. They externalize themselves in the nightmarish ways in which others fear and wish to extinguish someone who has crossed over "the edge." I was particularly fearful of the realm of "eternal wastelands," the black holes, when I considered letting go into the vacuousness of "no-mind." Little did I realize that beyond the mind was exactly where I needed to go.

Inherently mentally oriented, living 90% of reality in my mind, my fear of mental disintegration was heightened. Without my thoughts I would be nothing. Yet, I knew if I continued to experience life solely through a mental focus indeed my mind would betray me someday, leading me on the path of delusion, confusion, incoherence and fragmentation. When we apply too much pressure on any one aspect of our being to bring forth our entire reality, that aspect eventually weakens and falls apart, probably as a signal to the soul to break its excessive attachment to a singular expression of Self.

Paradoxically, there is a part of me that would love to go mad, thereby offering relief from the responsibility of dealing with life. How pleasant it would be to simply meander through the inner recesses of the psyche caught in a maze of fantasy, inner chatter amidst a sea of images. If I could let go of the need for order perhaps this inner world of perpetual chaos would bring respite from my unceasing determination to control life.

I often wonder how others forget to think and process. Where do their minds go? What is the experience of being on the other side of one's understanding? Would I go through endless internal hells reflecting the breakdown of the ego's grip on my head in order to get to "no-mind"?

Did my mother lose her mind? When someone commits suicide, are they insane? What is insanity? Do we all have to risk insanity in order to enter the rarefied realm of enlightenment? I have often fearfully wondered whether my mother's madness was catching, perhaps hereditary. Was an impending experience of screaming confusion awaiting me in my genetic code? If so, when would this time bomb be activated? What emotional shock would trigger it? Would I be spiritually strong enough to ride through this explosion without losing my grip? Does one go insane slowly, gradually progressing through stranger and stranger levels of distortion? Or do we suddenly wake up one day looking at life as a broken mirror, jagged edges, one dimensional, as if something shattered in our dream state? In that rupture pieces are irrevocably lost, rendering wholeness impossible. Is that Source's idea of a cosmic joke? How many lifetimes does it take to recover a healthy mental and psychic body?

As a child I sensed the climate of madness in my home. It was subtle; everyone seemed to function. However, the silent concealment of truth created a vacuous madness.

On what do we base the coherence of our sanity? Is it not often reflected back to us through our relationships? If we never really express our truth to those close to us, how sane can we be?

We energize a false persona, making it as convincing to ourselves as to others. Behind that persona is the vacuum, the space of non-reality that is created by living a lie. If we can bear to consciously move through that dark space, eventually we reach the buried self, energy turned in on itself, distorted, constricted, fearful and dying. Is our obliviousness to the trapped self not madness?

How do we start to unravel all of our lies? Where do we find the courage to unconditionally commit to uncovering our truth? How did I find the courage to resist following my mother's footsteps into total self-destruction? What did I know that she didn't? Perhaps it was the deep sense of love in my soul, fed intravenously through the silver chord, nurturing faith and providing a perspective of love far beyond fear and loneliness.

It is impossible for me to go mad with my beloved teacher, Djwhal Khul, walking by my side reminding me of the absurdity of it all,

Source's humor within Its own creation. Madness is only possible if you take life too seriously, believing in the flight of fancy that takes you to the lower hells of the mind. Perhaps only in letting go of the mind can one see the great tapestry of Life, and the improbable adventure of awakening.

The Quest for the Divine Mother

My emotional life's journey has involved an ongoing quest for the Divine Mother. If I keep it on spiritual, archetypal terms, the quest for Mother can be cleanly directed toward my favorite icons of female divinity—Quan Yin, Tara, Mother Mary, and the Mother of the World. Then I can allow myself to be bathed in spiritual nurturance, safety, and warmth.

However, when I attempt to play out my need for a loving mother in relationships I invariably fall into painful, abusive dynamics that turn me into the victim. I truly become the "motherless child"—overly sensitive, abandoned, afraid, unloved, and unseen. My soul's inner child from many lifetimes has been waiting at the gateway to the Great Mother for nurturance. But the monadic wound makes it difficult to freely receive Her love. I know that it is only the pure love from the Great Mother that can heal the magical child within. If I try to get it from others I will be disappointed and disempowered.

In spite of years of therapy and training/experience as a therapist I still wrestle with these demons of abandonment. This is daunting, sometimes convincing me that my wound will never be healed. Djwhal Khul reminds me that this never-ending feeling expresses the Core aspect of my soul's pain, reflecting all the way back to its origination, the monadic level. He encourages me to believe that we can really transform and be enlightened. However, at times when I have been overwhelmed by the pain of self-imprisonment and repetition of self-destructive patterns, I wonder if any progress has been made at all.

Djwhal Khul smiles at this, reminding me that true spiritual progress is immeasurable because the path to the soul is obscured by veils and illusions. It is impossible to linearly go from point A to point B. He says that the wiring in our energetic body is tangled up in the matrix of the core wound within the soul. Each wire must be worked individually. Then the challenge is to integrate them all into a system that fires itself alchemically into a new level of awareness. That is why enlightenment occurs in a flash, appearing to happen in a moment, and yet is the result of an extensive process.

I have diligently untangled the wires, individually examining the false beliefs within each one. Often, after assuming I have straightened most of them out, an experience will occur to charge them in the old way, instantly re-entangling them into the original karmic knot. Frustration and helplessness abound at that point. I wonder if Source really is having a cruel joke at my expense.

Djwhal Khul reminds me:

The process of mastering the human condition requires the patience, determination and willingness to lovingly untangle the web of illusion over and over again until the old magnetic field that re-entangles them has been fully discharged. At that point the student is free to experiment with integrating all the pieces of the soul into a patchwork quilt—allowing all the wires to combust through their connection with each other—alchemizing the overall Self into liberation.

Reassuringly, the Tibetan stresses that this process is not an eternal hell designed for punishment, reminding me that we all have what is needed to master our human condition. I must purge all disappointments, betrayals, and illusions to experience my fullness. If fear takes over, my light is hidden and I betray myself, negating my enlightenment. The wires get crossed, tangled, and the fires of alchemy go dead within.

I tell Djwhal Khul it is my intention to straighten out the wires and immerse self in the creative possibilities of true integration and connection. He responds: *At any moment the student can completely let go of the "hairball" of karmic patterning. That moment is closer than one would think.* Heartened by this encouragement, I say goodbye to all false mothers, and goodbye to my earthly mother's sickness and limitation. I open up to the divine nectar that pours from the breast of the Sacred Mother. The torment in my soul is released.

After Mama Left

After Mama left this world my life of isolation began. My father, distraught with grief and guilt over my mother's suicide, took refuge in alcohol. Spending the majority of his time in New York City either lawyering or drinking in clubs, he left my brother and myself alone in the hands of a butler and maid. Our twenty-eight room, one hundred year old house was in Bayshore, Long Island, an hour train ride from New York City.

With both parents suddenly gone at the tender age of three I was cast into a bottomless abyss. The maid and butler were distant, unloving presences who cared little for my cries and loneliness. I ran many "fevers" that year, feeling as if I were burning up, unable to find a voice that could carry my cry for help through the many high-ceiling rooms and corridors separating me from the maid and butler's quarters downstairs in the farthest corner of the house off our huge "family" kitchen. I could faintly hear their voices talking when they were visiting over coffee at the kitchen counter. However, my own small frightened voice evaporated in the spaces between the labyrinthine rooms in this elegant old house that my father bragged was built by the Johnson (Band-Aid) Brothers before half of it was demolished to leave our vast half to be called "home sweet home."

My mother's death was plastered all over the walls and ceilings. Her spirit clung to the despair splashed everywhere. I could only wait and hope that the maid and butler would eventually remember me, upstairs, alone and sick. There was no comfort to be had anywhere in this cold, vacuous world of abandonment. Eventually my father fired these hired "keepers" when he found out they were stealing the food money and feeding us a steady diet of canned spaghetti.

After a year of this "solitary confinement" my father met my stepmother, Beverly. As a singer and actress determined to make it big in the theater world, she achieved secondary and chorus line parts in Broadway and off Broadway productions. At the youthful age of twenty-six, twenty years younger than my father, the farthest thing from her mind was raising a family and settling down. Multi-talented with a rich, powerful singing voice, Beverly had the persistence and grit to climb to the top in New York City's highly competitive cultural circles. Her pervasive narcissism allowed her to unilaterally push forward, keeping her blinders on to the feelings and needs of others. Passionately in love with my father, she persuaded him to move to the city with her and to send my brother and me away for a year.

To be sent away from home at the fragile age of four years old was almost the final straw that could break my spirit. Even though home was barren and cold, it was still home, the place where Mama had lived and held me. There I had a chance to see my father on the days when he made it home before my bedtime. Now, all hope was lost as my brother and I were packed up and shipped away to a boarding school in upstate New York called Green Chimneys.

Green Chimneys was a large working farm. I have few memories of that bewildering world. Good memories include having toast and hot chocolate on Sunday mornings in the cafeteria, swinging on a wooden swing hung with thick ropes from a magnificent, huge oak tree as I looked out into the open vista created by the New York whale back hills, and my father and Beverly coming to visit on Sundays for the entire afternoon. Bad memories, still haunting me when I least expect it, include: watching my five-year old brother being spanked in front of the entire school for wetting his bed; the nurse cutting my toenails so short they bled; watching the pigs go to slaughter and seeing the blood running down the ruts in the dirt road that ran along side the farm house. A few years later Green Chimneys boarding school was closed down.

It was a year spent in no-man's land, a world of abandonment, confusion and loneliness. My brother Michael, too young to offer support, seemed so far away in his dormitory for boys. In my psyche there was only emptiness—an endless stretch of emptiness—emotional isolation filling my soul with a particular kind of ache that never breaks down because the rage at my father encapsulated it, preserving it within my heart for years.

The Tibetan reassures me that I can digest and transform that ache, but the four year old child still wonders how she got there. Why was she sent to prison for a year? Was it a punishment for driving her mother to suicide? It is no wonder that I have worried so much about being too demanding of those that I love. To have emotional needs is to cause people to leave the planet. It's just too much. I am just too much. It's better to hide myself, my needs, give people plenty of space, don't crowd them, don't let them know how hungry I am for contact—and most of all, *don't trust anyone.*

Parole arrived exactly one year later. Suddenly there was my father and new stepmother telling me to grab my things and throw them into our Cadillac. We were going home. Michael and I jumped in the back seat of the car, holding our breath as we drove out the long dirt road, leaving the farm in the distant horizon of our memory, not daring to look back in case my father might change his mind. I was five years old, carrying the grief of a seventy-year old.

How much loss can a child endure? What is the extent of the damage? Would I be able to recover? Deep in my soul I tucked those two years since my mother's departure into a room bolted shut, hoping to seal away the grief, rage and unbearable loneliness to keep them from contaminating my expectations for a bright and sunny future. After all, I was finally going home.

Monadic Imprint

In 1988 I attended a series of three workshops given by an extraordinary medium, Kathlyn Kingdon, who channeled an entity named Vywamus, the "Earth Logos." In esoteric circles Vywamus is known to be the teacher of Djwhal Khul. In this workshop Vywamus gave the participants individual overviews of their monadic imprint.

The monad is the first level that is created as Source splits off from Itself. The impact of this split in creation is registered by the monad as a matrix of false beliefs emerging in reaction to this original separation. These false beliefs become the filter through which the monad extends itself forth into clusters of souls, Higher Selves, who individually experience themselves in various parts of the universe.

The Higher Selves work diligently gathering awareness of their divine essence in an attempt to dispel the illusion within the monadic false beliefs. The Higher Selves also extend forth aspects of themselves. That is how we arrive on the earth plane. We too are working very hard to undo the negative affect of the monadic imprint. This imprint is an extremely powerful filter coloring our entire approach to ourselves, others, life and Source. In our earthly condition, through our duality and human pathos, we create experiences that give us information, wisdom and liberation from the prison of false beliefs that would ultimately lead us to believe that Source does not really love us.

My monadic material constellates around believing that Source abandoned me as a parent abandons their child. Consequently, as a young monad I searched for other monads to parent me, compulsively seeking the ultimate loving and loyal nurturance. This search trickled down to my Higher Self, playing itself out in all of my past lives. Many incarnations were spent looking for parenting, experiencing abandonment and betrayal resulting in the feeling of being a lost child in the universe. Not only did I look to past life mates and friends for parenting, but also to the Masters.

I now realize that whenever I look to anyone, whether human or spirit, for parenting I am probably going to set up a situation to be betrayed or abandoned. I have a strong, unconscious impulse within to satisfy the hunger and craving for a constant, eternal, unconditional love that allows me to fall into the arms of the beloved with complete trust and letting go. In past lives if I had been able to receive some measure of this quality of love it was cut off by premature physical death.

This abandonment/betrayal karma was re-energized in this lifetime by my mother's death. Intellectually I understand that death is an illusion, love is eternal. My mental body tries to override my emotional body with its metaphysical logic concluding that ultimately there really is no loss.

However, my emotional body is deeply entrenched in the fallout from my monadic conclusion eons ago. From its perspective: death cuts off all support, love is impermanent, Source takes away Its love in a moment's flash and appears to turn Its back on Its own children. When I experience betrayal and abandonment my vulnerability feels excruciating, like a dark curse upon my soul. Despite my passionate faith, this false belief system left me devastated by a paradigm of extreme existential loneliness and invisibility, convinced there is no one who could give me the kind of care that I desperately need.

Djwhal Khul encourages me to release this painful filter in order to see the vast amount of love and support fulfilling all of my emotional needs that I do indeed receive. He reminds me that karmic pain contracts my creative channel, especially in the heart chakra, thereby greatly limiting the bounty of love and nurturance available.

As the Tibetan speaks I am filled with a mixture of grief and gratitude. My heart softens to his words. For a moment I see the light! In that moment my awareness of the truth of Source's love for me arcs back to my Higher Self which then telegraphs up to my monadic core. I am momentarily soothed and healed from the monadic illusion.

However, the inertia of many lifetimes, both on the earth plane and on planets in other dimensions, exerts its negative pull to the familiar. Djwhal Khul reminds me that this is the time to be vigilant, to stay fully focused on my enlightenment, gathering the energy to go beyond the illusions of betrayal and abandonment. He suggests that I rely on my higher mind to provide the big picture, the true knowing of Source's constant love for me, in order to release the turmoil in my emotional body. He teases me that he has certainly tried to be a good role model for Source's love, reminding me of his constant loyalty, bottomless love and nurturing of my soul.

When things have gone wrong for me in the past I often concluded that the Tibetan was betraying me. In retrospect there was never betrayal or abandonment. The commitment between us always endured. An example of this was immediately after the shock of my mother's suicide when Djwhal Khul swept me up on the inner planes, bringing me to his hut in the Himalayas. There my soul registered the constancy of Source's safety net for Its children.

As the accelerating energies currently impacting the earth plane dredge up levels of karmic debris our monadic imprint is revealed at a raw level. There is no time to soft pedal around the "original wound." The heightened vibratory rate is speeding us headlong into our soul pain, pulling out all the stops.

These energies insist that I confront the illusion of loss and abandonment. I can no longer afford to energize chronic patterns of being a "motherless" child. The karmic ball stops here and NOW. The potent opportunity for complete purification of all false beliefs is now available. Ironically, as I let go of needing to be parented by others, a space is created where the Divine Flow can pour forth, flooding my soul with such profound love that my eternal ache is eased. This healing externalizes through friends and loved ones who truly support my deepest being in all ways possible.

FROM THE EYES OF A CHILD

Truth

In this lifetime I am learning about my relationship to truth. My past lives were focused on a quest for the highest and most absolute, enduring truth. I believed that once found, this ultimate truth would lead me to God. I perceived God as a great being that was fixed in Its expression of Itself. Its truth would always be the same.

It wasn't until I was thirty-eight years old, hard at work on opening my channel, that I realized Source (God) was an *evolving* Being, not a static one. Therefore, Its great truth must also be an evolving one, nothing that could ultimately be pinned down. This awareness liberated me from my obsession with finding an absolute one-pointed truth. Suddenly I had the breathing room to play with paradox, ambiguity and a flowing evolving awareness.

The joy this freedom currently provides me explains my aversion to the fundamental religious pathways expounding fixed laws and interpretations of God. These pathways endorse strong statements of right vs. wrong. Their rigidity threatens my mystical nature, although I deeply appreciate the greatness within these religions. Djwhal Khul teaches:

> *The great religious pathways were established for the collective consciousness at an early stage in humankind's evolution. Due to its immaturity at that time, humanity needed very clear and definite guidelines for its spiritual*

direction. As a result, the early religious teachings include specific directions for ethics and spiritual growth. All of these teachings clearly point humanity away from its attachment to the ego and earthly desires in an effort to remind them that the earth plane is only an illusion compared to the great reality that awaits the fully awakened student.

There comes a time in everyone's process when they must break from the tried and true dictates of the great religions and bushwhack into their own unique mystical interpretations of these teachings. One's mystical response to metaphysics allows one to experience his/her own highest, evolving truth as it emanates from an internal place of true union with the divine. Because the mystical path is unchartered for the masses, it takes great courage and attunement to allow self to evolve into the experience of Oneness without any generic maps for guidance. At this point truth ceases to be an absolute statement of God but rather an evolving perspective on the Greater Mysteries within Source.

My personal relationship with truth has been fraught with levels of betrayal, confusion, frustration and deep yearning. Due to many past lives spent in ashrams, monasteries, and mountain-top meditations, I arrived into this current life highly sensitive to a strong code of ethics. I thought that surely everyone would tell the truth and strive for the highest possible code of conduct. My belief system indicated that there was a definite right or wrong in every situation. I had little tolerance for the ambiguity of our human condition as we struggle to accept and integrate, without judgment, earth-plane duality into our spiritual perspective.

Childhood blew apart my lofty expectations about truth. Secrets and lies were used manipulatively in our family as a way to repress the pain connected to skeletons in the closet. Our family's greatest secret constellated around my mother's suicide. I can only surmise how ashamed and guilty my father may have felt about her death. Consequently, he never spoke her name to me for the rest of his life. It was as if she never existed. There were no pictures of her anywhere. To this day I have no idea what she looked like. Even distant relatives now gone, carry with them the secrets of her life story.

I am amazed how fear can allow us to obliterate the memory of someone we have dearly loved. My father had an opportunity to keep my mother's memory alive through story, pictures and an openness to questions about her. However, his own inner turmoil eclipsed any willingness to bring her life, as well as her death, out into the open. He stole her memory from me and took it to his own grave. My inner three-year-old memory could not sustain images of her under the increasing family pressure to forget this woman who was my mother.

When I was five years old my stepmother's arrival sealed the coffin. My longing for and attachment to my real mother was forbidden. My father insisted that now my stepmother was my real mother—always to make sure to call her "Mom." I wonder if he thought that somehow my real mother could be replaced. Did he think that miraculously I would forget that my mother had lived and died? Ironically, his great secrecy almost worked.

Throughout childhood, although I had a faint notion that my mother somehow passed away, I felt no interest in knowing the truth of her death. I was so possessed by my overbearing stepmother and unnerved by my father's silence that I dared not inquire about my life before everything changed. I can only imagine what it must have felt like to my father to raise a daughter, who apparently looked a lot like her mother (according to his law partner), while trying to sever any connection to his past relationship with his thirty-six year old wife. Perhaps that explains his emotional distance from me. Hiding all the pictures and memories in the world could not erase the constant reminder of her existence. There I was, embodying her more and more as I grew into womanhood.

I often wondered if he hated me for that. I now understand that his coldness was more an issue of fear than hatred. I recognize the torment that suicide causes in those left behind. It creates a hotbed of guilt, rage, confusion and betrayal. Taking one's life breaks our fundamental collective agreement to "hang in there" on this crazy earth plane no matter how difficult things become.

I have carried a profound sense of responsibility for my mother's death which has translated into thousands of hours of service work for others, hoping to ease their pain sufficiently to keep them motivated to stay alive and flourish. Ironically, even that level of service has not nullified the fundamental wound that says: "I wasn't good enough for her to stay around. Somehow I should have been able to save her." My father's disconnect from his deeper feelings buffered him from the inevitable guilt we carry in the wake of a loved one's suicide.

It came as quite a shock at age 16 when my stepmother barged into my room one afternoon while I was doing my homework and said, "I suppose you want to know how your mother died." I couldn't imagine what she was talking about, so brainwashed was I that she was my only mother. "Well, she killed herself—took too many sleeping pills." she blurted out. As she abruptly left my room, apparently satisfied with her announcement, I sat on my bed, stunned.

It would take me another sixteen years to be able to tell anyone about my mother's suicide. The early years of anesthetization wore off very slowly. While my stepmother's words burned inside of me, presenting themselves when I least expected it, I still could not connect them to a sense of reality about this distant woman that was my *real* mother. Finally at age thirty-two, in therapy; I dared to begin to let in the truth of my early childhood.

Sometimes lies and secrets are so entwined with our reality that it feels impossible to extract the truth from the web of deception. Even when we are told the facts it simply doesn't register. In order to make it believable, I had to hear myself tell the story of my mother's death over and over again.

The first time I told my mother's story I was thirty-three years old, attending a death and dying workshop with Oh Shinnah, an American Indian teacher and priestess. Thirty people participated. We circled around the group telling stories of important death experiences in our lives. I mustered up all my courage to tell the group of my mother's suicide. As I listened to my words out loud I wondered if someone would tell me I was lying, so inverted was the family wound around the repression of truth. I was surprised when they all looked at me with compassion and concern. Suddenly I realized that it was all real. At that point the lies and secrets, like a dark cloak around my soul, fell away. It was the beginning of my journey back to the truth.

I now deeply comprehend the power of the truth and how it can free us from our demons. Any truth made conscious can be healed and integrated while no lie or dark secret can possibly serve us. The lies become wounds that we must excavate in order to unearth our soul.

Although I raged internally for years at my father's deception, I now accept and forgive him for his cowardice. It takes courage to face and share the truth with those you love. The process of accepting my father's limitations has taught me a greater tolerance for that aspect of the human condition that struggles with an inability to confront lies and secrets. If I can forgive my father then I can forgive myself for all the past lives of failing to live up to the highest standards of truth, especially spiritual truth, to which I aspired.

Djwhal Khul smiles in appreciation as I explore this process. He recalls what it was like to be human—filled with the rich complexity of duality, emotions, attachments, fears and illusions. He embraces me like a mother, soothing my heart's longing to go beyond the residues of torment still active in my soul as he teaches me acceptance and compassion for the vulnerabilities and shortcomings of the human condition.

Djwhal Khul reassures me that as a result of my early experience I will hold the truth as a great treasure and work very hard to find the courage to be the "Truth sayer" no matter how threatening the consequences may be. He reminds me that this honesty must be tempered with love and sensitivity to the power truth holds, sharing it carefully and gently, always within the light of kindness. So, I thank my father and stepmother for creating an experience that tempered my past life rigidity and judgment regarding truth. I am now learning new levels of integrity, ones that spring from the *heart's* truth and wisdom, embracing our illusions with deep acceptance and loving understanding.

Selling Our Souls

I spent most of my childhood waiting for it to be over, waiting to grow up. Keenly aware of each day passing, I was obsessed with the future, to finally be free to be myself. This was like "doing time." The prison sentence was not overly harsh. I had all my physical and some emotional needs met. However, my true expression was squelched. Never drawn out by my parents, I spent my time learning to tune in to their reality, trying to be as unobtrusive as possible. Well into adulthood I have had to dig through layers of their reality to find my own.

Djwhal Khul reassures me that it is safe to shine my light. It is my birthright. In moments of pure free-flowing energy and total self-love, I don't hold back. The world seems to be a beautiful and safe place. In recognition of self there is instant harmonization with my environment.

When the past threatens to bury me, I project disconnection onto the world. This stimulates the familiar feeling of being haunted by severe alienation. This alienation is so easily projected onto humanity. Often I have truly believed that Source created a monster when It established the human condition.

Having grown up just outside of New York City I witnessed humanity at all levels. Sitting on the midtown rush hour subway offered me the painful experience of observing unrealized souls. Most of the people seemed to be just flesh, not spirit. I searched their faces for traces of divinity, somehow buried behind empty masks.

I knew Master Jesus would be able to "see" their divinity. Why couldn't I? What happened? Who started all this burying? At what point did the collective agree to become victims? According to Djwhal Khul, we can't create unless we are empowered. Otherwise, we simply create disempowerment.

Riding the subway I was overwhelmed by the collective level of disempowerment, even in the faces of those who appeared somewhat "together." The air was filled with disappointment and resignation springing from common beliefs: "This is as good as it gets. Why bother to be more? We're doing the best that we can. I'm afraid. I don't know how. Life is hard." The collective pain and confusion cried out, seemingly into a vacuum.

I wondered what makes someone special. Isn't everyone special? Why do only a small percentage of humanity discover their significance? Do people realize when they have drawn a cloudy film over their faces dimming their natural brilliance? Or, does it happen gradually and subtly as resignation creeps deeper and deeper in their soul? At what point do we give our power away? Is there a way to recognize the moment when we lose faith in ourselves?

When I was twenty-one, reeling from the death of my father, I told my stepmother I would be moving back to Ithaca to live with my boyfriend who was finishing up his senior year in college. She looked at me and said, "You know, you and your brother are losers." In that instant I felt branded. My fate was sealed, never to rise above that judgment. I smiled back at her, trying to hide my pain. If I pretended she never said it then perhaps it would not cut so deeply into my soul. That seemed a fair exchange.

When I lost my mother a desperation set in that devoured my integrity. My mother's suicide took chunks of my soul with her. So, why not give over the rest to my stepmother? At least she was willing to keep living. I owed her my life. So, why not take on the persona of the "loser."

Chronically her words circulated in my mind for the next twenty-six years. They surfaced during lulls in creativity. I expected to be a failure, seizing any moment to validate that identity. I now appreciate the tremendous energy stolen in continual self-undermining. Sustaining self as failure, or light as dark, requires a determination to block out truth.

Where did we get the idea that love was so costly? Source never told us to sell our souls for love. But somehow, collectively we have decided selling our souls was a bottom line requirement. Even now I still occasionally muse over those words, "you are a loser." They feel like a Zen koan I am trying to solve. I am struck by the power of that pronouncement aimed directly at my heart. But mostly, I am amazed at the amount of power I have given those few words. I realize now that they were told to me by my stepmother, not by God.

Cruelty

One of my karmic patterns has been to be a victim of psychic cruelty from others. It is the inevitable result of playing the disempowered role, like transmitting an open invitation to be attacked by dominating people. Mistakenly all of us who would be victims believe that if we hide our power we are safe. Ironically, when we hide our power we are caught in the persona of someone weak, invisible, frightened and ineffective.

Energetically we attract our opposite. Those who cope with their insecurity through overpowering others are magnetized to us. From this perspective the world does seem to be an unsafe place.

With maturation and the benefit of years of therapy and other forms of soul-searching my victim self has gone underground. I no longer consciously identify with it. When I meet a character in one of my dreams that is mean to me I am reminded that the victim self is still there. These dreams reveal that deep inside I am still expecting to be attacked, overwhelmed and hurt by other's cruelty.

It becomes increasingly difficult to accept that these fears are still a part of me as I evolve into greater levels of personal strength, wisdom and empowerment. My heart still wonders whether it is safe to speak up when someone has wronged me, especially if the abuse happens on a subtle level. The victim ego tells me that I imagined it, that I'm oversensitive. It says that I should go with the flow, be compassionately yielding to the hurtful ways of others. My defeated ego insists that if I wait long enough it will all go away—it's not such a big deal. At that point I feel like a hardened boxer who is used to taking punches, who expects it. I have often prided myself on being able to "bounce back" quickly after being hurt by someone I love.

Collectively we all cry out about physical abuse. However there is so little recognition about verbal psychic abuse. Because we don't see the emotional wounds we can tell ourselves they don't exist. We learn to quietly go off and lick these wounds in private, pretending that whatever was said didn't bother us. We think our process is invisible to others. It is not.

As long as we are victims we invite more wounding. Over the years our emotional body begins to look like it has been imprisoned in a torture chamber, old wounds continually reopened alongside newer wounds that don't heal. In spite of expressing success through our outer personality, our inner psychic life is riddled with the imprint of defeat.

At any point in our lives there is usually at least one person we are giving our power to. That person then has an open invitation to be cruel. We magnetize cruelty to us through our inner victim's expectation, assuming that the emotional body is an endless receptacle of psychic abuse. We don't realize that our preciously sensitive emotional body has its limits. Eventually the emotional body asks the physical body to carry the abuse. Then illnesses and accidents begin to occur. The saturated emotional body finally makes itself felt in the physical.

The Wound Becomes the Gift

Psychic energy denied returns doubled in force. This is a well-proven psychological law. Energy has a natural impulse to move toward its innate fulfillment. If it is repressed or denied it continues to gather force even if it appears buried and/or dormant. People often believe that they can cut off a part of their psyche, pushing it deeply underground. They assume that when they "cut off" this part of self, it actually goes away. Perhaps they don't understand that all aspects of self are eternal and cannot be destroyed.

The disowned parts of self are stored in the "basement" of the unconscious, waiting for the time when permission is given to come out into the light of day (conscious awareness) and flourish. However, most of the buried pieces of self were "cast off" *unconsciously* due to childhood family dynamics, trauma and/or limiting karmic belief systems. They are like freshly sprouted seedlings uprooted and dumped into a heap of dirt that gets moved to an isolated landfill far from civilization. No one really knows that they exist much less how to find them.

How many of us feel that something is missing within us, even when our outer life appears full and successful? Perhaps it is a hollow sensation, like an inner ache, distant and undistinguishable. With patience, love and commitment we can hone our focus to track this remote pain as we play detective with our own psyche. If we are willing to be open to whatever we discover, there's a good chance we will encounter a part of ourselves, long ago discarded or buried for survival sake, hiding. While this part of self may be starved for love and attention, thirsty for nourishment and light, it is not dead.

The psyche has an indomitable endurance, no matter how great the odds are against its survival. While it does a great job at "playing dead" when the emotional climate is too dangerous for it to display itself, it is really just suspending its outward expression until a safer day dawns in the future. So it curls up within, nestled in a safe cove on the lower floors of the unconscious, waiting for the appropriate time to show itself. Its energy continues to move.

The true nature of energy is movement. Since the psyche cannot be totally destroyed, its energy gathers force within itself, like a volcano building its internal fires to a pitch while appearing docile on the outside. Due to the deeply buried nature of these unclaimed parts of self, consciously we may have no idea whatsoever that we are even missing pieces of self. As the energy gathers within this bundle of rejected self it reaches a peak of heat just like the volcano that finally needs to bubble over. At that point we start to feel a distinct discomfort like a deep splinter beginning to move to the surface. While we may not be able to identify this energy, we realize that it exists and that something is demanding our attention.

When the splinter begins to surface, it is a critical time of surrendering to an innate healing process that will temporarily take over our lives as it finally emerges. After all, psychic energy returns *doubled* in force. The extent to which it has been repressed is the extent to which it surfaces. Sometimes this can carry a great shock for people who have counted on the numbing abilities of their psyche to convince them that "everything is absolutely fine. I have no inner work to do—no problems or complexes to work out from childhood, past lives, whatever." It is a rare individual who has no work to do on themselves, especially now in times when our karma is concentrated, demanding healing and resolution. Few of us are experiencing a carefree lifetime with a perfect childhood, trauma free, and no illusions or veils to be dissolved.

If any part of us is "cut off," it leaves a gaping wound. Just as if an arm or a leg were severed, there would be a painful injury, a gash to our wholeness. Many of us are riddled with these wounds. If we were to bandage the wounds in our emotional body like we do our physical body we would be covered with bloody strips of cotton trying hold our sense of self together without bleeding to death. While this may sound dramatic, it is as real as the pure streams of emotions that flow throughout our being making their presence felt at all times.

The good news is that our wounds ironically become the gateway to our wholeness. So much energy moves within the repressed parts of us in reaction to the violation against our being that this energy becomes a powerful vehicle for healing and transformation. It is potent! Anything that would deny our natural wholeness sets up an intense reaction, a gathering of the forces for enlightenment. These forces imbue the wound with a power that gives it the potential to resurface victorious and with great wisdom. The wisdom is the result of a hard-earned recovery because one has to descend into the underworld to find the "splinter" (the denied part of self), fight the battle of resistance and fear, feel the pain as the wound is touched and treated, and reemerge with a deep commitment to that part of self as it is integrated into one's overall identity.

This process leaves us with a deep knowing about life, the transformation process, and ourselves. We realize that truly nothing can destroy us or overpower our individuation process. With such heightened energy surrounding and containing our wounds, we can break through all false beliefs that tell us to betray ourselves, to settle for less than who we are. When we truly realize our ability to reclaim our lost "limbs" on the psychic plane we feel a sense of discovery, limitless potential and deep relief that "all is not lost."

A core area of wounding in my own childhood emerged from being silenced. Growing up with an extremely narcissistic stepmother and a silently distant father who rarely directed a sentence to me left me with no place to bring my voice, no place of true self-expression. Every time my inner self attempted to emerge she was blocked by my stepmother's torrent of self-absorbed words reflecting only her reality. She simply could not hear my words, ideas, hopes, fears, dreams and feelings. If I attempted to communicate my inner world my timid words bounced off her narcissistic walls like hale hitting concrete. As my words ricocheted back to me the pain of my stepmother's indifference to my truth created a big hole in my belly as my throat chakra closed up to protect itself from the "crime" of too much self-expression. The veil of invisibility descended upon me, settling in for the long haul of my childhood. The part of Moriah that had oh so much to say about life scurried away. It burrowed itself deep within my unconscious, leaving me free to convince myself that listening to my stepmother was the most exciting thing in the world, that I had nothing to say about anything, and if I had anything to say it would be too much and too demanding.

I can now finally say that I have healed this deep wound of muteness. Recovering my voice through countless hours of self-examination in therapy, self-reflection, relationships, writing, being a therapist and a channel has been one of the greatest gifts I have given myself. It has involved deep exploration into the family taboos that made it illegal for me to speak spontaneously, expressively, dramatically and intensely, if at all. This road to finding Moriah's true expression brought me three pivotal challenges. First I had to become conscious of the pain of the isolation caused by withdrawing my true self. Secondly, I had to battle the demons (in this lifetime my stepmother and father) that would slay me if I dared to unleash the power in my throat chakra. And, finally I had to find the courage to dig out my true voice as I worked to convince my frightened, mute self that I had a right to have a self and EXPRESS it.

The psychic energy denied was enormous and came back with a tremendous potency. Once I found my voice I couldn't stop talking, processing, confronting when necessary, singing, writing, channeling. It still feels as if there is no end to the energy up rushing from the finally opened prison door deep within my unconscious. The gift of this transformation from muteness to bold self-expression is a high sensitivity to other people's muteness and invisibility, a throat chakra that opens full throttle to project the Tibetan's power (allowing his words to pour forth uninhibitedly as compared to the carefully measured and cautiously offered infrequent statements of my childhood mute self), a freedom to speak my truth at all times, and a passion for assisting other's in discovering that it is possible to come out from hiding and take center stage when it is their time to shine. Yes indeed, psychic energy does returned doubled and redoubled in force!!!!

Djwhal Khul chimes in:

> *When humankind truly knows that there is no aspect of self that can be destroyed, it will release its fear of loss and death and begin to explore its own eternal nature. Wounds are the activation of karmic contracts designed to focalize the soul's energy through a porthole of disturbance. This process of moving through the disturbance turns the heat up on that area of the being, allowing self's awareness to be heightened in that arena. This heightened awareness then expands the porthole, alchemizes the disturbance, and allows a greater Force to preside within this region that then becomes the place of service to the Divine Plan. This greater Force allows the dismembered aspect of self to be remembered and offered up and out in gratitude for the innate healing process within all beings.*
>
> *Therefore, look to the places of pain, imbalance and uneasiness to find the process of transformation. It is precisely in these deep soul wounds that the potential of the being is carried. The challenge of giving one's gift is to find the courage to confront the disturbance within one's being, knowing that priceless treasures exist within the maelstrom of energies encircling the wound. <u>Trust that the Force is greatest where it is most needed</u>. This is what is required for healing as well as providing the thrust needed to launch one's soul mission.*
>
> *To heal self is to heal the collective. To uncover lost parts of self is to pave the way for countless others to attune to their greater Self. To know the process of self-discovery, self -*

reclamation, self-healing and transmutation is to demonstrate to humankind that one's wounds are doorways into extraordinary new vistas within the Self. Let these wounds become altars to the great Love that makes all healing possible and complete. Bathing within this Love transmutes the pain within the wound, extracts its poison, and transforms it into a powerful conduit for the White Light showering the earth plane and washing away all distortions of the divine plan. Cleansed and whole, humankind can truly realize the new Cosmic Day where the wounds of the past are finally discharged into the Ocean of Love and Compassion that is Source.

Music

I grew up in a house filled with music. My father was an excellent piano player who surrendered the dream of playing professionally in the big band music world, opting for the financial security of having a career as a lawyer. Although he established a successful law firm in Manhattan I often wondered if he ever regretted his decision. My father wistfully reminisced about his big band days, reliving the joy of his creativity. He partially explained his abandonment of music due to having broken his ring finger in a boxing match at Cornell University. Although his boxer days left him with eight broken noses and a "cauliflower ear," his drooping ring finger took the greatest toll on him—the last straw that steered his life away from music into law.

Although my father stopped seriously practicing, he often played the piano while he waited for my stepmother, a professional actress and singer, to glamorize herself for their evenings out on the town in Manhattan. While he played I sat under our Steinway grand piano, enthralled with the power and magic of the sounds sweeping over and through me. I was in love—with my father—with God—with music—with life. He and my stepmother made incredible music together. Her powerful voice blended with his piano, as they dramatically belted out

Broadway tunes. Riveted to the music, I was spellbound. The music filled my soul.

I yearned to be a great musician, an artist. However, a harsh voice squelched my yearnings with, "Don't you dare be as great as they are. After all, you are better off dimming your expression or it will rock the boat. Your parents will get angry with you if you dare to be more than a pretty, smiling face." My father never suggested, much less encouraged me to become a musician. I assumed that playing the piano was his world. I had no right to that realm.

To my stepmother's credit she taught me how to read music, play scales and tunes. For two years she was very diligent with her instruction. After that I played the piano on my own, often sneaking downstairs to the music room at night while the rest of the family watched TV in my parent's bedroom. Playing show tune after show tune to my heart's content, I bowed to the standing ovation of my imaginary audience after each rendition of songs like "Climb Every Mountain," "Embraceable You," "My Funny Valentine," "Oklahoma," and "Shall We Dance." Those songs are forever etched in my mind and body.

I felt that I had to hide my musical efforts, fearful to reveal talent or creative desires. I never once played for my parents, not daring to perform and receive their undivided attention. They showed no interest. I assumed, once again, that performing was their domain—not mine. My soul's false belief, "Stay in your place." resounded, cautioning me to not be too smart, too expressive, too creative, or too anything. "Do not outshine your parents or they will abandon you."

At the time self-inhibition seemed like a small price to pay for safety and security. It took thirty years to begin to realize the full extent of what that hiding cost me—the loss of deep communion with my soul and the freedom to express myself creatively, openly, and joyfully.

I wonder how many people are taught to hide their soul, cutting off their magic for fear it will be judged. Djwhal Khul teaches that the soul needs to be fed through our creativity which allows the chi, life force, to activate the higher self. If we block our creative flow, our soul withers from malnutrition. Contemplating the Tibetan's teachings I realize that expressing our creativity is not a luxury. It is a necessity.

My stepmother stopped teaching me music when I was eight years old. I asked her if I could take piano lessons with a professional teacher. She agreed but required that I prove my motivation by playing forty-five minutes of scales daily until she was *convinced* I would be a good student. Her response completely shut me down. I interpreted her words to mean, "No, you have gone far enough with this. Don't even consider taking yourself seriously as a musician." I knew I was too young to have the discipline to sit at the keyboard tediously playing endless scales, especially as a proving exercise and not a real learning. Defeat set in. I quietly resolved to be at the keyboard only at night, behind the scenes, spending the rest of my childhood playing and replaying old show tunes. When I went to college the music stopped.

The only musical encouragement my father ever offered happened three days after he died. He came to me in a dream and displayed reams of sheet music, heavenly music. I could see the notes clearly in the dream, knowing that this was something very special. However, the sharp clarity of waking consciousness obliterated my dream vision making it impossible to remember the sheet music. At long last, receiving his interest after all these years was deeply healing. Perhaps in spirit my father was making up for his neglect.

Finally at twenty-eight years old I gave myself the lessons I so dearly wanted and deserved. I studied with a wonderful classical teacher. Rejoicing in my "collaboration" with Bach, Mozart, and especially Beethoven, my soul soared. A move from Ithaca, New York to Cambridge, Massachusetts terminated this five and a half year tutelage.

Settled into city life in Cambridge, I was given the name of an eccentric jazz piano teacher. This was my opportunity to break free of the traditional structure of classical music, hoping to recapture my father's musical flow through jazz and improvisation. His music, deeply etched in my soul, drove me to study for seven years, to try to capture his free-flowing style. My jazz teacher, the opposite of my classical teacher, was cool, unstructured, into *feeling* the music, encouraging me to break into "free stretches" whenever the musical muse inspired. I learned to relax, feel the music, and sing with Billie Holiday songs. The singing contributed as much to the opening of my channel as did the practice of tai chi.

However, in spite of opening up creatively, I could never "capture" my father's sound. His music existed in the realm of perfection, established through the ears of a five year old deeply intoxicated with her Daddy's creative gift. I eventually realized that classical music was closer to my soul, free at last from my father's spell to pursue my own music. I now experience all forms of music as divine, serving as a true vehicle for mystical union with my soul.

The Sound Current

The Tibetan emphasizes the power of the sound current. When I am really open, often during or after channeling, the sound current is felt surging through me like wind in the trees. Perpetually buzzing with strange sounds, my ears react to the accelerated energies.

As my vibratory rate heightens I am more aware of referencing energy through sound. Many levels of ringing, static, humming, high electrical buzzing, and other indescribable sounds continually run through my head. This inner orchestra is accompanied by varying levels of inner pressure. The intensified vibrations push against my inner ear demanding that I stretch, unblock and expand my true "inner listening."

Sensitive to airplane take-offs and landings, I tightly cover my ears to compensate for the painful pressure. Collectively we are all "gaining altitude" as we leave our familiar third dimensional level of density and move into the rarefied atmosphere of our Higher Self. As we accommodate the dimensional shift we seem to ascend and descend in cycles. Just like passengers in an airplane, we are constantly adjusting to take-off and landing. Djwhal Khul teases how eventually we will only be adjusting to take-off! That comment sends currents of apprehension through me. The Tibetan reassures me that this is a process involving gradual adjustment, no shocks necessary.

We are taught that the spiritual plane is made of light and love. The component of sound is not taught nearly enough. In the bible there is reference to "The Word" which I understand to be the sound current. Sarah Benson, a wonderful sound healer and teacher, describes the sound current as a hose for focusing light. During shamanic journeys I find myself riding the sound current as if it were an express train to the Divine. In past lives I have opened my inner ear and felt myself overwhelmed by the intensity of the inner sounds, also audible by my physical ears. When tuned in we can hear the voices emanating from trees, waters, winds, plants, animals and human thought patterns. And, if these earthly sounds are not enough we can attune our ears to the next level, the music of the heavenly realms, the angelic orchestra.

When the sound current literally moves us into greater awareness it is a challenge to stay grounded. Riding the sound current through our channel to the Higher Self eventually takes us to the exalted realm of original music. This rarefied etheric realm is composed of great waves of sound bestowing ecstatic levels of bliss and awe. Mozart, Beethoven, Bach and other great musical masters must have retrieved gifts from this realm.

To connect to this elevated sound current we do not need physical hearing, just an inner attunement. Djwhal Khul teaches that toning, chanting and singing move us into alignment faster than many other practices because sound concentrates the power of light and its ability to melt blockages.

Through sound we can recognize the heavenly realms perpetually emanating celestial music. Sound bridges us back to our original essence. Djwhal Khul encourages us to tone or chant, at least sing, as often as possible so that we can try on what it is like to be an angel. He suggests that our collective language may eventually be song, like living in one grand operatic celebration.

Toning is a requirement for me to open into channel. Six HU tones heighten my energy to a level where I can comfortably meet and interface with the Tibetan's higher vibration. These tones stimulate my energy with a bubbling action like champagne, filling my awareness with light and joy.

What a simple, profound gift Source granted us by extending Itself through the sound current. We are all musicians of the Divine, playing strands of light through our love allowing a great resounding YES from the Universe. Djwhal Khul adds:

> *Suspend the familiar physical orientation to sound and allow the imagination to pick up the subtle nature of the universal sound current emanating from all beings. Trust that inner sounds are divine vehicles of soul transport conducting the lower consciousness through the veil of illusion into the higher realm of pure spirit. Allow the sound current to move through the physical body and wash away karmic debris—energetic blockages, seemingly dense, but truly permeable by a force as potent as sound. Use the sound current to transmute a negative charge into a positive one as it establishes a field of resonance with light that uplifts the heaviness of the shadow material.*
>
> *Know that self is a dancer moving to the exquisite vibrations of sound emanating self's soul mantra—matrix—rhythm—chord. Play with sound. Sing—create songs—open the throat chakra and rejoice together. Enjoy the efficiency of the sound current, the speed with which it escalates self's process and alignment.*

Know that when self listens to the sound current and responds with toning, chants, and song that the angels are fed. Primary conduits of celestial song, angels bask in humankind's melodic response, and delight in experiencing the common ground that unites all beings in this universe. The sound current is the bridge that connects all forms and levels of consciousness, dissolves illusions of separation, and merges all multiplicity into the deep, unfathomable sound that existed before creation—the ONE.

The Mask

I was a lonely child, probably lonelier than I even realized. Childhood is bearable because there is no point of reference for any other reality. We accept our lot in life because we know no other. The real pain sets in when we first glimpse alternative possibilities.

At age twelve while visiting a new friend Beth who moved in next door, I first witnessed family warmth, affection and consideration. I also experienced Beth exercising her right to yell at her parents, defying them and expressing her rage and sense of injustice. This baffled me. How could this be so? Weren't all children scared to death to open their mouths? Didn't all children feel invisible? How I ached for the freedom to speak my truth and spontaneously blurt out all I was feeling inside, unconcerned about the consequences.

Why was I so terrified of upsetting my parents? When you live on crumbs, the thought of not having the meager amount of nourishment you are used to is unbearable. It is much harder to lose, or to risk, when you have little.

I laugh at the concept that I had little. My external physical reality was quite abundant. Home was a large mansion-type dwelling complete with a live-in maid named Annabel, and a brand new periwinkle winged 1950s Cadillac. My stepmother wore minks, chinchillas (oh the consumer indiscretion of pre-animal rights days) and diamonds galore. Shouldn't I have been happy surrounded by all this "wealth"?

It is hard to be happy when we are told to be. Happiness springs from the heart and soul. It cannot be manufactured no matter how strongly we plaster that smile on our faces. However, if we carry that smile consistently over time it has the anesthetizing affect of dulling the part of our brain that registers discontent. We actually believe we are happy, bubbly, and sunny.

There were so many rewards for the "happy mask." Parents found me easy to be around, no trouble at all, not like my black-sheep brother with his constant sulking and pouting. I told myself what a great child I was, how perfect, and how much they must love me for it. I began to believe that it is possible to be happy all the time. It became like a drug requiring that I always have the energy available to be happy, smiley, laughing at nothing.

Of course I had to be vigilant about my "happiness." The moment any rebellious thought, discordant idea, or disturbing emotion surfaced, I had to SLAY IT! I dared not jeopardize my standing in the family. I believed that without my happy face the sun would not shine. If the sun didn't shine, the real chaos, the pure isolation, the deep chill in my soul might surface. If my parents saw that pain they would find me unacceptable. I would be attacked, ridiculed, shamed and punished. That wasn't worth it. It was best to stay undercover and be the bubbly little girl, with her blonde curls and big beautiful smile. How skilled she became at dazzling away all the undercurrents, not daring to let the vortexes take her down. She was a true Persephone playing with the wild flowers in the meadow, but drew her innocence out for years (way beyond its time) unable to bear the danger of her wisdom.

What is the price of wisdom? Yes, we lose our innocence. Yes, we wrestle with the impossibility of the duality within our nature, our true ambivalence. Yes, we have to face the responsibility of applying this hard-earned knowing. However, the most difficult aspect of wisdom is the inevitability of revealing it. It is ultimately impossible to hide what we know. The wisdom factor shapes us, expanding our world view. Our old facades shatter under the force of the emergence of our truth.

The pain of trying to keep the old veneer sewn up tight becomes unbearable. If we don't have the courage to express our wisdom our body carries the torment—joint pain, headaches, stiffness, weakness, illness and eventually death. If we cut off the nourishment to our soul we begin to suffocate. The suffocation is deeply internal for years and years. Eventually it surfaces. The rest of us suffocate for there is no way to breathe our reality in and out. Our self-made facade becomes a plastic bag over our head. Without breath there is no life. We are eventually done in by our fear.

Pregnant women have no choice when the time of labor arrives. They face the arduous agony of birth or certain death. We all have birthing junctures. How many of us go forward into birth? How many of us commit suicide through our inaction, avoidance and shutting off from the Great Flow that sustains us? Suicide is so emotionally charged for all of us. How can people consciously take their own lives? What are they thinking? The great percentage of suicides are invisible, slow, the result of saying No to ourselves, saying No to our God.

Intelligence

Intelligence is for men. Beauty is for women. According to my father, men are the important ones. Why is it that the great religions have only male models of enlightenment and teaching? According to my father Jewish tradition mandates that when a man is forty only then can he study the Kaballah. A woman never enters the sacred realm of those who teach the mysteries. Does the mere fact of her sexuality make her unclean, unfit for the pursuit of wisdom? Was the powerful sexual force in my beautiful female body going to deny me entry to the knowledge of the Divine? I learned that the taboo against women cultivating spiritual authority includes a subtle mandate to be only "mildly intelligent" at best.

My father was quick to point out the foolish and silly statements blurted out by my childlike mind. However, at the same time he did not want me to be too smart either. This paradox dropped me in limbo with no place to experience and express my brilliance. I identified myself as the pretty one, the bubbly one, the one with the happy personality. This insured my survival in a household filled with narcissists. I posed no threat to anyone. I was invisible and empty-headed, so I thought! My creative drive went into maintaining my beauty and sweetness. This identity was so crystallized that I wholeheartedly believed it. Nurturing my intelligence wasn't a consideration, even to me.

First grade through high school was a blur. My report cards admonished me for working beneath my capacity. I wondered what the teachers were referring to. I had no sense of intellectual aptitude. The family intelligence was reserved for my brother, the brilliant one, my father, the shrewd and successful attorney, and my stepmother, who even my father had to admit was pretty smart for a "broad." I was secretly grateful that at least I had blonde hair and blue eyes, inevitably making a smart man very happy some day.

My time in school was spent daydreaming. I was so lost in reverie and fantasy that the shrill bell marking the end of class jolted through me shocking me back into my young body. Looking around, stunned, I wondered where I was. I was in an alien reality, untapped, unexpressed, and disconnected. Thank God my fantasy life was rich, colorful and compelling.

College academics came as a shock. I had no idea what to do. Freshman year started out as an academic fiasco. My father and stepmother were annoyed that I was too busy partying and not applying my mind enough to warrant the tuition bills. Suddenly I was expected to apply my mind? How confusing!

The first paper I wrote was for English Literature. We were reading the old classics. I poured my heart out into this new academic endeavor, filling it with insights, feelings and conclusions. Proudly I went to pick up the corrected paper, eagerly looking forward to the teacher's feedback. My stomach sank as the "F" cruelly jumped off the page. In large, impatient handwriting the teacher scrawled that she hadn't even bothered to read past the first page because she thought it was such garbage. It seemed that somehow I had insulted her intelligence with my lack of academic sophistication.

Initially I was convinced that she was right. After all, she was the teacher. After a few days of reeling through self-hatred I came to my senses. Furious, I dashed down to her office. I told her that no matter how "stupid" I may be, it simply wasn't right to treat another human being that way. At the very least she owed me the willingness to read all the way through my work. As I confronted her I felt a new sense of power flow through my veins, noticing a new strength in my body. I had discovered a potency and worthiness within that allowed me to challenge this "intellectual authority," the teacher. Although the road to realizing my brilliance would be long and convoluted, this was the beginning of trusting my truth and the right to my own mind.

The Negative Pole

Many students have asked the Tibetan how to strike a balance between allowing negative energies to surface within self in order to integrate the shadow and cultivate a positive attitude toward life. I have always been skeptical of the Pollyanna types who insist that thinking good thoughts and smiling your way through life can actually have a positive affect on one's experiences. I am my father's daughter. His cynical orientation toward others lies deep within me no matter how spiritual I try to be. It is ironic that my father and stepmother were hardened "realists" always cautioning me about the "dog-eat-dog," nature of this world. They scoffed at my humanitarian inclinations, my stepmother insisting that I keep the UNICEF money collected on Halloween of my ninth year.

Djwhal Khul talks frequently about duality, our beloved earth plane being a realm of opposites. He teaches that the poles are separating more dramatically than ever as the core vibratory rate within the earthly dimension accelerates. The Tibetan instructs that we must allow all aspects of our human condition to be integrated, including the negative.

My psychological training suggests that it is mandatory work to become conscious of all our buried pain, rage, hurt, and fear in order to heal and transmute karmic wounds. However, I have seen many clients caught in their negative vortexes, forever spellbound by the wails of their past. It is a delicate balance to know when we have appropriately paid homage to our soul's anguish and are ready to move on through a positive focus without shortchanging the insistent need for attention our unresolved wounds require.

A shadow aspect of therapy is the temptation to look for more and more pain. This re-energizes the very maladies we are attempting to heal. How many times does one need to lance the boils of affliction?

Perhaps this imbalance appropriately counteracts our collective tendency to be in denial about our negative experiences. Even if we know they exist, how many of us are courageous enough to touch those highly sensitive areas of *dis*-ease within our soul? Deeply appreciating Djwhal Khul's teachings about the power of the mind and one's attitude, I have witnessed clients caught on the negative trajectory, self-destructing with alarming effectiveness.

Yet, I also have observed the "happy" person who has insulated their negativity in a steel-lined container deep within the soul as if it were non-transmutable radioactive material. This eventually leads to disease in the area of the body where this soul pain is stored. It is quite an effort to convince the "happy" person to accept their not-so-happy self in order to integrate their duality.

Djwhal Khul reminds me that we must release all judgment about either side of the duality, "Good is not better than bad, happy is not better than sad," etc. Contradicting this teaching he encourages us to attune to a greater Light factor indicating that light is better than dark. This paradox is baffling to my ego, although it makes perfect sense when I am in channel bathing in the Tibetan's magnificent perspective.

When I was twenty-eight I swam a mile everyday. In the pool I experienced sensory deprivation due to goggles, ear plugs and nose plugs. In this state of sensory disconnect I endlessly repeated affirmations that I hoped would manifest my wildest dreams. Reviewing that time, I realize that those dreams did come true. Yet, while appreciating the power of affirmations I question their effectiveness if one hasn't cleared away the pockets of blockage springing from negative false beliefs.

At that time I had not done in-depth therapy and was riddled with veins of unresolved grief, guilt, fear and anger. Yet, in that swimming pool I managed to circumvent those shadows, relying on positive mind power to call to me all that I hoped for and more. Five years later I began an intensive journey of self-exploration. Shortly after starting therapy I looked inside my soul. It appeared to be eaten up with cancer, so great were the pockets of pain festering within the neatly insulated containers I had unconsciously created to prevent contamination of the rest of my being. This brought me face to face with the opposite side of my affirmation-oriented self.

I needed those early years of positive thinking to harness enough spiritual juice to cultivate the courage to meet my demons. It has been decades since I started that process and I am now at a point where I am well acquainted with my darkness. At times I am too aware of those internal, menacing, undermining voices, always ready to contradict my soul's message of light and transformation.

Djwhal Khul coaches me to hold both poles lightly, not attaching to either one, accepting the human condition and yet moving toward the Light. He says:

> *This Light is beyond the polarity-ridden earth plane, reflecting Source's glow within all. This glow cannot be*

undermined by a point of opposition. This is the Cosmic Glow that gave birth to the duality and therefore cannot be compromised by it. Continue to embrace the duality while looking toward another level of Light, of divine essence, which carries a dimension that truly stills the torment within the human soul and uplifts it to a true state of peace in the Garden of Eden.

JOINING THE HUMAN RACE

Dad's Death

I became a volunteer for Hospice shortly after turning thirty-three years old. I had hoped this service would resolve the guilt and pain I carried from not having been fully present for my father when he was dying of cancer. His illness occurred during my senior year in college. I saw him only for holidays and during the two months after graduation before he died.

I was twenty years old, home from Ithaca College on Thanksgiving vacation, when my stepmother told me Dad had bone cancer. The prognosis was not good. We were standing in the subway station waiting for the Lexington Ave express train to take us uptown to my parent's apartment on 57th St. Although I heard her voice, I could not fully register the impact of her words. How could my father be dying? I was too young. He was only sixty-two years old. She grabbed my hand telling me that somehow we would get through it. I thought she was indulging in her usual dramatic tendencies. My father's presence in my life was so distant and unreal. His death seemed equally untouchable. No more was said as we pushed our way onto the crowded subway. That was the only real intimate acknowledgement of Dad's dying process that would pass between my stepmother and me.

In the nine months leading to his death, letters and phone calls provided information on the medical treatment my father was receiving as well as my stepmother's valiant efforts to save his life through the use of raw juices and home care. However, I felt like an outsider, helpless and hopeless, witnessing his demise from a distance and unable to do anything about it. Although I often made him laugh with my usual playful manner we were unable to have a meaningful connection. The fact that he was bedridden and dying right before my very eyes was never acknowledged. The same secretive nature that prevented him from ever mentioning my real mother and her tragic death once again closed the doors between us. The gap of silence and secrecy irrevocably sealed in the disconnection inherent in our relationship.

While I knew that this man was my father, I had no idea who he really was. I could only feel guilt and confusion when sitting by his bedside. I concluded, "I must be doing something wrong. Perhaps I don't know how to love well enough." It never occurred to me that the problem in our relationship had something to do with him.

The night before he died I sensed death was at the door even though his physical body was still functioning fairly well. Searching the city for an open church or temple, I needed a sacred place to pray for his departure. The next day my stepmother, brother and I were by his side as he took his last breath. When my stepmother exploded into dramatic hysterics, sobbing and wailing, I shrank into myself.

Later, when my stepmother was downstairs calling the funeral service and the room was momentarily empty, I went to my father and kissed him goodbye. His face was peaceful in a way I had never seen when he was alive. He was bathed in light. This was my first tangible experience of the invisible realms. I sensed angelic presence and knew he was in good hands. Noting the contrast between the peace on his face in death, and the tension and bitterness in his personality when he was alive revealed the amount of psychic pain he had carried.

In that moment death was a great teacher. As my father transitioned into spirit, I was released from carrying his soul's pain. However, it would take years to fully let go of the visceral sense of responsibility for his suffering. It is sobering to realize how deeply children absorb and carry their parents' hurt, especially if they are karmically programmed to assume unnecessary levels of responsibility.

Perhaps when his spirit left his body the awareness of his true divinity graced his body, allowing his features to relax, smoothing out the tension, even bringing a slight sweet smile to his lips. My heart opened with joy as I kissed him goodbye on his forehead, grateful to carry this last beautiful memory of him with me as I set out on my life's journey.

In the subsequent weeks, months and years I felt the impact of the finality of never having received expressed love and attention from my father. Although I grieved and raged at the missed opportunity to mature in his presence and perhaps bridge this unfathomable gap, I also treasured our last exchange at his deathbed, imagining how that sweet smile of love and acceptance was his last and truest message to me. Perhaps he was trying to teach me that death carries the opportunity to take in the big picture. In this realm transformation is possible, even within a split second, when we accept our place in the divine plan and release all judgments. My father's peace-filled, loving face released me from the profound guilt I always felt in connection to him. I had carried his emotions and soul pain since my mother's death, strangely feeling terribly responsible for them. His death gave me my "ticket to fly"—permission to return to my own soul and follow its passion untethered at last from his intense, unfathomable silence. Yes, death is a teacher and a liberator.

Twelve years later I began the arduous task of working through unresolved feelings about my father. While walking through one of the beautiful parks alongside Cayuga Lake in upstate New York I called his spirit out loud to me. When I felt his presence I talked endlessly to him—expressing all the thoughts and feelings I had hidden from him when he was alive, hoping that he was beyond human judgment. I trusted that his spirit shared my commitment to slosh through the emotional muck together. I knew that he felt badly for his mistakes and wanted me to know how truly sorry he was for the pain he had caused.

Somehow, through the veil that separates our human experience from the spirit plane my father and I connected in a way that was never possible when he was alive. I still carry that connection even though residual layers of betrayal, neglect and abandonment still surface.

Djwhal Khul teaches that humankind so limits itself in its collective belief that relationships with loved ones end through death. My true relationship with my father began at the point of his death. Djwhal Khul encourages me to remember that the veil between the earth and astral plane is thinning, allowing the illusion of separation to dissolve. He states:

> *The awakening process in the collective consciousness brings an awareness that there is no separation. As humankind truly experiences this, it ceases to energize the veil between the dimensions in its collective thought patterns. As this veil dissolves, humankind will truly recognize its eternal essence.*

Entering the Real World

Finally the party was over. I was twenty-one years old, freshly graduated from Ithaca College and ready to face the "real" world as an adult. I had no idea how to be an adult or what I was supposed to be doing with my life. Everything in college was theoretical, big ideas and concepts floating around late night dorm rooms: "How we will save the world. Nothing can stop us. If only "they" would listen to us. We know a better way."

As I stepped out of the express subway onto the litter-strewn sidewalk with my suitcase in hand on that exceptionally muggy June afternoon, I dreaded the walk to my father and stepmother's apartment on 6th Avenue, between 56th and 57th street. New York City was a culture shock after the sweet rural mysticism of upstate New York. In that moment I knew I was unprepared for life.

College was wild, wonderful and liberating, but completely impractical when it came to the mundane. Suddenly, all of those late night philosophical vigils evaporated in the smoke of Manhattan's greasy hot dog and doughy salted pretzel stands. People pushed past me, everyone seeming to know exactly where they were going. I was dazed, immobilized by the sheer rush of humanity stampeding every which way into the horizon. I wasn't sure how I was going to fit into the "real" world. It seemed to be such a negative, unhappy place.

Leaving Ithaca College, I had to face what most BA graduates in sociology experienced—a college education useless in the job market. All employment opportunities in human services required experience or a graduate degree. I couldn't imagine how to gather this experience if no one would take a chance on giving me a job. I simply wanted to serve humanity in some small way. Yet entry to the human service arena seemed remote and inaccessible. In spite of having loved college, I wondered what it was all for.

I attended two courses at Fordham School of Social Work, beginning the task of earning a master's degree. However, I was overwhelmed by new adulthood, the time constraints of full-time employment as a secretary for the National Council on Alcoholism, grieving my father's recent death and having no money. When I asked my stepmother for an academic loan, she sharply refused. Her pronouncement, "You can't always do what you want to in life," resounded within me. I couldn't reconcile her insistence that I accept restriction when she was living in an expensive penthouse apartment near Central Park, traveling to Europe and funding daily singing lessons.

Double standards have always confused me. Past life metaphysical teaching did not explain people's justification of a double standard when the law of karma is the great equalizer for us all. The message that I should settle for less in life burrowed itself into my soul, leaving me destitute. After all, she was my stepmother, the not-so-kind woman who had raised me since age five. Her words cut into my psyche, battling my ambition and desire to do something with my life. It was a month later when she added salt to the wound with those damaging words, "You and your brother are losers." This was a Catch-22 situation, telling me to give up my dreams and settle for less, and then pronouncing me a loser.

I am grateful for my spunky, rebellious Aquarian nature. The more my stepmother attempted to undermine my sense of self, the more determined I was to reach for my star. However, I wasn't sure that the world as it appeared through my stepmother's eyes would make a place for me.

I decided to follow my passion, finding myself on an express bus uptown to attend an introductory astrology course given by what appeared to be some very strange and interesting people. The moment I saw the glyphs (beautiful magical images of signs and planets) I was in love with this ancient language of symbols. Studying my chart helped me to touch a sense of potential never previously mirrored to me. My chart spelled out in black and white that I was not a "nothing," but a person with exciting energetic patterns waiting to be tapped and channeled to others. Even the effects of parental repression ebbed as my chart came alive.

On Wednesday evenings I eagerly hopped on the Lexington Avenue express bus traveling uptown to learn what gifts the planets had in store. In that class I met a wonderful Gemini black woman, Rainee, who took me under her wing. She asked if I had ever heard of reincarnation. I had no idea what she was talking about. After class she visited my little second story studio apartment on 62nd Street where we drank tea, and she offered me my first metaphysical lesson in this lifetime. My eyes were as round as saucers, heart bursting with joy, solar plexus agitated and excited by this wonder-filled new world she was introducing. I knew I had found home. As I look back to that enchanted evening with Rainee I wonder if she wasn't a master in disguise. Immediately I loved her, and her knowing.

From that moment on I couldn't get enough of metaphysics and astrology. I found my way down to the Village, seeking out an obscure little metaphysical bookstore called Sam Weisers. Walking in the door, my breath caught in my throat as I felt the vibrations in the shop. Books from floor to ceiling, about God, Goddess, angels, the universe, the rays, the Masters, auras, chakras, astrology, psychic phenomenon, Edgar Cayce, and on and on. There were posters of energy fields in and around the body, glorious flowing chakras, kundalini snake images curling their way up the spine, and opened crown chakras with their thousand-petal lotuses exploding light into an ultimate cosmic shower. It was 1970. I had just entered a new and yet old and familiar world.

I finally felt safe as my soul settled in comfortably to the ensuing years of study and exploration in hot pursuit of the "ultimate truth." How I loved being a student of the universal teachings. As I uncovered more of the mysteries my cells tingled in recognition of a knowing carried over from previous lifetimes. This knowing had been contained in a time capsule waiting to be triggered at the right moment.

My father was dead, "off the plane," no longer a block to my emerging intelligence and wisdom. I owed him nothing. Finally liberated, I was free to pursue my soul's passion. Through releasing my father one door shut and another opened. I now had the freedom to become so much more than my father could allow. His death expelled me from my self-imposed prison. Perhaps it was his prison all along, and I felt I had to carry it for him. I didn't dare shine my light more brightly than his. That would have been disloyal.

Despite learning about energies, heavens, and metaphysics I could not imagine accessing past lives. My fears indicated I would be unable to break through the veil separating us from a greater reality. So, I waited and studied, wondering who I really was on a soul level. Little did I realize that Djwhal Khul sat with me in Weiser's book store, tutoring me on the inner planes, reinforcing my knowing with his ever-present approval, fathering and mentoring me in profound ways.

In retrospect I consciously could not have handled the Tibetan's presence at that time. My awareness of the spiritual dimension was so new, fresh and innocent. I needed time to heal and grow a healthy ego. The narcissism in my family hindered the healthy development of my ego structure. There would be future opportunities to ask this ego structure to stretch, allowing in the "unfathomable"—my relationship with a non-physical teacher, Djwhal Khul—as well as the contents of past lives needing loving attention in order to heal.

Astrology

Astrology is my ultimate road map. Just as the sailor guides his boat by the twinkling night reflections of starry patterns constellating ancient forms, so too am I guided by celestial manifestations as they create a unique blueprint, the natal birth chart, for my soul to follow. Magnificent planetary beings encircle us with their knowing. The Sun, Moon, Venus, Mercury, Mars, Jupiter, Saturn, Uranus, Neptune, and Pluto contain the playground upon which we toy with our human condition.

Each planet, including the Moon, represents a great Force having its way with us. Our only requirement is to accept this Force, understand it, work with it, create with it, and surrender to it. In our lifetime these planetary teachers each ask us a life question that is unique to our individual chart. Answering this question sometimes seems to have the impossibility of a Zen koan or an ancient riddle posed by a crafty old wizard. We shake our fists at the heavens and demand to know why these large, mysterious Forces are buffeting us around like ping-pong balls. However, once we crack the riddle, truly allowing ourselves to hear the messages astrologically relayed down to planet earth, we are freed from the experience of being puppeted about at the whims of these planetary archetypes.

Then we have the CHOICE to work with the Divine Plan as it is expressed astrologically. We can celebrate these energies showering upon us just like dancing in the rain. When we understand what each planet is trying to teach us, we can receive their influence from a place of gratitude, not resistance. This is the difference between swimming downstream vs. upstream. Life becomes easier as we cooperate with the planets because we are able to trust that these divine teachers want only the best for us as they evolve us along, pushing us into much-needed challenges and lessons.

We begin to understand that our birth chart reflects a karmic contract that we made on a soul level before we came into this lifetime. Just as our physical body is not something that we consciously choose or can trade in for another model, so too does our birth chart indicate a specified learning curriculum that we are "stuck" with, whether we like it or not.

The birth chart holds the matrix of required courses for graduation. It indicates which of the ten planetary influences will be the teacher we have to meet with the most often, and whether the remaining teachers will be strict or lenient with us in their demands. The birth chart also holds past life records, reminding us that this lifetime is but one in a long series of incarnations. During these past lives we have developed gifts and talents as well as negative attitudes. The higher self encodes this information into our birth charts reflecting the importance of just the right moment of birth.

I am always in awe of the intricacies of the Divine Plan. Just as the spider creates a beautiful complexity in its webbing patterns, so do all the delicate karmic strands weave together in the soul portrait contained within the birth chart. The exact time and location of our birth places us in a precise relationship to the ten planetary teachers. This relationship specifically generates our exact karma in this lifetime.

The natal chart is a blueprint for our soul's evolution. We can study it endlessly and still not reach the bottom of it. Within it are clear-cut designations for learning and exploring as well as mysterious patterns that yield only further questioning. Our birth charts hold the key to vast levels of self-knowledge.

JOINING THE HUMAN RACE

We can use this key any way we wish. What we do with our knowledge is our choice. We can either work with it optimistically or fear it and try to dismiss it. It doesn't matter how we approach it. The planets will still do what they do; they reflect the impersonal nature of Source. As we yield to our birth charts, so do we yield to the big picture. Just as the sailor doesn't argue with the configuration of the constellations, why would we want to waste our energy fighting the astrological energies particularly available to us in this lifetime? Djwhal Khul teaches:

> *Astrology is a metaphysical tool offered to students willing to embrace their soul's destiny. This tool is divine in nature as it implements Source's vast intelligence. It is offered to humankind as a mapping device for the path of evolution. The planets do not determine one's destiny. One's soul does that. Rather the planets evoke that destiny through the interface between the heavenly realms and the earth plane.*
>
> *Students often shout out that they have no idea of what to do or where to go with their lives. Ironically, the astrological map is available to all who wish to take charge of their self-exploration. Use this tool wisely; allowing self to remember that one's fate is not sealed within the stars. Rather master this art of seeing truth as it is so beautifully expressed in this divine science of metaphysics. Each planetary Force is designed to create an aspect of human nature. As these Forces intermingle, they represent the entire human condition at its lowest and highest level. Penetrate to the deepest level in the exploration of these heavenly messengers. Know that one's birth time and place are divinely orchestrated to respond to the soul's greatest need. Once students "know" their birth charts through and through, then they are free to toss them away as the sailor eventually throws away all navigating tools, allowing only the winds of life to take him where they will.*

Unfortunately, this glorious ancient metaphysical science of astrology has suffered a bad reputation in our culture. People read the daily astrological columns in their favorite newspaper and often laugh at its superficiality. At that level it can only be a generic Band-Aid tiding one over until the real guidance emerges. Any generalizations on a large scale inevitably carry oversights. They leave out the highly individual nature of each human being. Only the full astrological natal chart can carry the vast amount of information involved in explaining one's life's path on a soul level.

In 1970, when I first discovered my own natal chart at age twenty-one, I was both awed and relieved, truly amazed at how accurately I was described by the chart. I could see my potential as well as learn to accept the areas that needed work. Instead of judging myself as bad for having certain shortcomings, I was able to see them as unpolished planetary frequencies waiting for integration and mastery. Through my chart I could view myself as an art project in process as I eagerly dove into the multitude of mysterious symbols and patterns informing me of the many missing pieces of self.

The more I studied my chart, the more I filled with questions. Instead of waning, my curiosity grew and grew. I devoured books on astrology like food given to a starving mystic. Making my way down on the subway to Sam Weiser's book store in the Village was my greatest passion. Upon entering the store I felt "beamed" over to the astrology section as my heart raced at the volumes of unread books waiting for me. Having probably been an astrologer in past lives, this world felt like home sweet home.

Now, over thirty five later, my heart still races as I enter metaphysical bookstores in quest of the latest astrological research. These days astrological information abounds like never before as it gains credibility and acceptance. The metaphysical scientist within me can never have enough data.

JOINING THE HUMAN RACE

Although the Tibetan teases me not to become too attached to "knowing," I laugh in response just like a child that runs out to roll in the dew-covered grass while her parents call out to tell her to be sure not to get her clothes dirty. He smiles tolerantly knowing that my passion for the Greater Mysteries is activated through astrological symbols and archetypes. Djwhal Khul jokes that maybe he will throw a few more planets into our solar system just to keep me on my toes.

I know he is concerned that I will get too set in my thinking, perhaps referring to the astrological galactic atlas too frequently without keeping my mind open to the Unknowable. However, the Tibetan smiles in this moment. I am aware that he truly delights in my joyful dance through this world of planets, moons, symbols, glyphs, relationships and energies that capture and refine the human condition. Djwhal Khul encourages:

> *Take this divinely inspired metaphysical tool and master it as the wizard masters his/her magic wand. Allow this tool to teach you that knowing is available to all who wish it. Astrological maps of the soul reveal the very real guidance and instruction that is your birthright. Don't take it too seriously, for all concepts evolve into newer and greater understandings. Rather, let this realm be a jumping off point into the vast reservoir of knowledge that awaits humankind.*

Unleashed into the scientific meta-world called astrology allows me to be brilliant, creative, intuitive and compassionate. We are larger than the planets as we carry within us entire galaxies and solar systems waiting to be discovered. Through our charts we realize that there is no end to the possibilities of all that we can be as we touch the Infinite.

Fate vs. Free Will

As an astrologer I am often asked the question regarding the part that Fate plays in our lives. People often see their charts as a rigid map of their predetermined destiny. I view the natal chart as a blueprint describing our souls' learning patterns as well as our engagement with the archetypal realm. Our birth chart teaches us how to go with the cosmic flow rather than against it. There is no point in swimming upstream, especially at a time in human history when we are dealing with the intense challenge of a collective accelerated learning curve.

Djwhal Khul has made it abundantly clear that it is time for us to grow up. He says it more diplomatically, *Humankind is in an accelerated maturation cycle in order for it to consciously take its rightful place in the intergalactic community.* In order to collectively take a giant step in our evolution we need all the energy we can get to move through old illusions and false beliefs.

Our astrology charts specifically point out these illusions and guide us into the new possibilities for self-transformation. All of this soul searching is done in a unique context for each individual. This context is described by our chart, our soul's blueprint in this lifetime. Some people rebel against the notion that we have to do our soul's work within a particular format, such as the birth chart. They squirm under the presence of a specific mandate for their life's journey. They want to erase any notion that there is a Hand of Fate. They equate Fate with disempowerment, imprisonment, and cosmic tyranny.

People with this perception can spend tremendous energy fighting their destiny, assuming that if they negate it, it doesn't exist. They prefer to see themselves as free agents, completely self-initiating and invulnerable to the Greater Forces at play. This can lead to an existential feeling of separateness and unrelatedness in a totally random universe. Yes, it can be quite a heady feeling when we assume we are sailing our own boat, absolutely free to go in any direction that we desire, our whims becoming our maps. That presumes that there are no soul contracts signed previous to this incarnation.

Djwhal Khul makes it clear that we have definite karmic assignments for each lifetime that have to be completed, just like required courses for college graduation. If we don't comply with the higher plan for our soul's education, we can't progress. Our egos hate this notion. They want to believe that they are completely in charge of everything down here on planet earth.

Also, we live in a collective environment, each of us responsible not only to ourselves but to others. We don't always realize that our fate is intricately connected to the fate of those around us. If we don't surrender to the destiny that the Divine Plan has in store for us, we may be inadvertently blocking the opportunities and avenues needed for the evolution of those whom we love, and even those whom we hate. We are all in this cosmic stew together, alchemizing each other though our collective intention to burn away the dross preventing our true selves from being realized.

The Tibetan emphasizes that in order to work with the Divine Plan we have to be able to attune to it. This involves our acceptance that Lady Fate does exist and is here for our benefit. The Divine Plan is not some crazy construct authored by a cruel God to hurt and imprison us. Rather, it is a malleable, light-filled matrix for Source's evolution through Its human focus.

As we enter the human condition in each incarnation we have no choice but to participate in the Divine Plan for humankind and mother earth's evolution. We become instant agents for the collective awakening, whether we like it or not. So, we might as well surrender to it!

When we give up the notion that Lady Fate is against us, we can rejoice in this opportunity to be part of a great army of rainbow warriors marching its way into the heavenly realms. This is done collectively in groups, as a "we" consciousness. From this perspective we bow to the Hand of Fate as it irrevocably moves us toward our divine destiny. However, this does not negate our creative prerogative in this grand process.

Djwhal Khul teaches over and over again that true mystical union is a collaboration of our earthly selves with our higher selves. He emphasizes the creativity, improvisation, and unique energetic spin we are free to put on our destinies. We are not sheep, herded unthinkingly into a cosmic corral as Fate stamps out our life pattern on our backside. Through our free will we initiate our becoming process through interest, curiosity, innovation, creativity, questioning, and originality. It is up to us to energize the Divine Plan with our unique spark of consciousness. As our spark interfaces with the Hand of Fate, the Divine plan is alchemized and transmuted. At that moment we have altered the agenda of Lady Fate while still working within the cosmic construct of the Divine Plan.

As we intensify our learning curve, our karma burns away with great ferocity. This affects the Akashic records held on the causal plane. These records hold our karmic history and future. With each causal plane particle (holding our karma) that transmutes into light, we are left with a destiny that is somewhat altered by the affects of our transformation. There is no need to gather experiences if one has already mastered the karmic lesson.

It is then that our free will steps forward to challenge the existing pre-determined order of things. Our free will allows us to use the energy released through our healing to propel us to higher levels of our destiny. Although we still need to move through the matrix of our souls' puzzle pieces, we are working efficiently and highly creatively to release outmoded aspects of our fate.

While this appears to be a karmic dispensation, it is nothing more than a rearrangement of energetic patterns that allows for more individual say in our encounter with Lady Fate. Our free will bounces along interactively with Lady Fate's grand plan. Together we explore all the possibilities for our enlightenment while simultaneously serving the needs of the collective and mother earth. It becomes a true co-creation as our wildest dreams piggyback with Lady Fate's cosmic mandate. We rocket into the realm where all conflicts dissolve and we are truly one in our devotion to all that already is!

Moon's Nodes: The Soul's Cutting Edge

The karmic point in our astrological charts that describes our soul's cutting edge in this lifetime is the North Node of the moon. Moving toward it is not easy! The tug toward past lives, the South Node, is tremendous. We instinctively reenergize what we already know, keeping ourselves trapped in the "familiar zone." In addition, the unconscious hides deeper motivations/fears of why we don't move toward our cutting edge, our natural evolving self.

At times it feels like a losing battle. We struggle with intangible parts of ourselves tethering us in the dark to old distant, "irrelevant" versions of reality. Bringing light to the darkest regions of our unconscious requires tremendous determination.

The contact we wish to make with our deepest self often eludes us, slipping from our grasp. Trying to catch our unconscious fears is as illusive as trying to recall a dream. Yet we must persist if we are ever to liberate ourselves from our prison of limiting belief systems. This perseverance involves digging deep into our karmic banks—stored piles of illusion, trauma, and fears that are convincingly show stopping. The awareness of the obstacles that block liberation can be overwhelming.

Since early childhood I have craved freedom. My youthful definition of freedom was to be out from under the dominance of insensitive parents. I wanted the liberty to fully express myself in whatever way I wished, living free from apprehensions about being the recipient of my parents' negative moods.

After my father died, as I grew into my twenties, I felt free to do whatever I wanted. To be orphaned at age twenty-one has its benefits—no family obligations, parental judgments and criticisms. I felt a strange mixture of guilt, grief and release at my father's death. I knew I would miss him. However, life had just presented me with a wide-open blank canvas—no parents to answer to. There was no frame of reference in which to orient myself as I set my life's course. As bewildering and disorienting as that was, it carried within it a sense of expansive freedom never previously experienced.

Several years of free-fall under the guise of being a hippie led me to the realization that wide-open freedom was not so freeing after all! I was bored! My attachment to freedom prevented me from committing to anything. The formlessness, while appearing free, became another prison. Feeling trapped in my inability to engage in the human condition, I didn't know how to plug in to the rest of the world. My daily question, "What do normal people do?" haunted me. Floating through life, unable to tether to anything meaningful, evoked deep levels of despair.

It became clear that I had explored a nomadic, non-committal lifestyle for too many lifetimes. This lifestyle wasn't getting me anywhere. Looking out the window, I often wondered, "Is this all there is?" The plague of aimless emptiness revealed the necessity to break this karmic pattern. We receive very clear messages from our souls when we chronically energize old behaviors. Living in our karmic past leads to feelings of blahness, unfulfillment, restlessness, emptiness, boredom, stagnation, blindness, purposelessness and disconnectedness.

It is necessary to open our awareness of past lives to retrieve previously developed precious gifts contracted to be offered out into the world in this incarnation. However, the magnetization of the past is so great that in giving these gifts we may be lulled into thinking that we are breaking new ground in our souls' evolution. It is our souls' destiny to grow, evolve. That means bushwhacking new territory within our being. This unfamiliar terrain, no road maps, allows us to experience new levels and identities of self. We must be careful to offer karmic talents while discarding negative past life belief systems that may have been intertwined with the development of these gifts. At times this process may feel impossibly paradoxical. The challenge is to extract and apply the gifts we have cultivated in past lives without repeating old karmic patterns like a mouse on a treadmill.

The good news is that the law of inertia is working for us. If we rest in the past, the energy simply collects there entrenching us in the "old way" of knowing ourselves. However, if we can get the ball rolling in a new direction, the energy builds and builds. Suddenly the impossible has happened! We have touched our cutting edge, the North Node, and discovered ourselves in a new light. The more energy we bring to it, the easier it gets. We are filled with the wonderful feelings inherent in the north node: fulfillment, excitement, wonder, curiosity, newness, potentiality, and balance. We discover our capacity for accomplishments never dreamed possible in previous lifetimes and bask in the joy of our tangible becoming.

All that is required is a willingness to leap into the unknown, staying long enough to infuse it with ample energy to set our potential self into motion. Once this energy is moving, most of the work is done. We simply have to stick with our commitment as it gathers momentum.

However, it is important to remember where we have come from. Integrating past into the present allows our soul to truly balance. If we become overly attached to our cutting edge we unnecessarily obliterate the past, squandering our inheritance with all of its richness, however difficult it may have been. Ironically, at that moment we dishonor our ancient selves, giving the message that their lives have no value for our current self. This leads to the risk of an inflated current self. After all, this is just one more incarnation of many. Yes, we want to become enlightened in this one. But is this current readiness for enlightenment not the result of lifetimes of experimentation, release of illusion and preparation for this moment of breakthrough? Somehow we must honor the past, bring forth its gifts with gratitude, while cleansing ourselves of the stickiness of old karmic patterns. It is indeed a great balancing act—the place of true freedom.

It is quite difficult to let go of my Scorpio South Node intensity infusing many past lives. How will I reference my aliveness? How can I possibly be expected to mellow out when my Scorpio South Node reflects a karmic past of addiction to walking the dangerous edge, cliff-hanging from the walls of my soul, hanging on by my fingernails, feeling adrenaline flooding my body with the alertness of an animal smelling danger, sensing death at all times with never a moment for peace and quiet?

My karmic patterns consistently carry the relentlessness of South Node in Scorpio's urge for transformation, instilling my soul with an impatient restlessness, not to be satisfied until the transformation is complete. Yet the missing ingredient in this alchemical stew is trust, the trust that allows me to nap peacefully bathed in the afternoon sun as it warms my face, belly up, exposed, vulnerable, trusting that no animal or person will go for the jugular as my soul rests peacefully in the Land of Safety, reflecting my North Node in Taurus. How do I break my attachment to change, always preparing for death, the inevitable loss, the stab in the back by a loved one?

This karmic pattern was catalyzed by my mother's death and father's abandonment. I was conditioned at an early age to struggle for survival. Even my birth, one month premature and weighing in at a hefty three pounds, followed by two weeks in an incubator, enhanced this life struggle. Would I be able to hold a grip on this physical body? This is the on-going quest for grounding with a soul eager and ready to lift up and out, to merge with spirit.

Of course I'm a natural to be a medium between the dimensions. How strange it is in this lifetime to learn to trust my physical senses (North Node in Taurus). What does sensuality have to do with transformation?

Propelled by the call of my North Node in Taurus, I moved to western Massachusetts in August 1990 to study meadows, cows, peace, and changelessness, to dare to trust this physical dimension enough to enter into it. The Buddha, a Taurus, sat under the Bodhi tree for seven years, not complexifying the process. He just sat there! The Tibetan works hard to keep me on track, repeating the mantra, "*Your needs will be met.*" And yes they have.

But, I miss the South Node in Scorpio: the rush, the edge, the complex mystery of staring death in the eyes, the agony of loss. Cultivating inner peace might be too boring, too still, too silent. Does true contentment erase the need for turmoil? Is it like a salve that soothes the soul's torment, healing the scars of torture and revealing the soul's original beauty? It is time to sit under a great oak tree and rest, releasing the heaviness of so many battles fought, so much unfinished grief, daring to smell the sweetness in the air as a butterfly lands on my hand inviting me to witness and be grateful. Patience is the gateway to the eternal.

Ithaca

I eagerly returned to find peace and nature in Ithaca, the town in upstate New York where I attended college. It was five months after my father's death. During the following twelve years Ithaca bathed my soul in transformative water. Waterfalls melted my consciousness, dissolving my linear brain, soothing my soul, giving permission to sit and receive, teaching about the flow, opening up intuitive knowing, easing my walk on the physical plane, and allowing me to breathe in Love.

Even in my twenties, ignorant about "who's who" in the metaphysical world, the name Madame Helena Petrovia Blavatsky was introduced to me. She was a psychic Russian noblewoman who introduced the Masters to the west and started the Theosophical Society in the late 1800's which helped to launch the new consciousness of our age. Having heard that she lived in Ithaca, I tried to walk in her footsteps. I focused on placing my mind into hers to know the vastness of her awareness as I connected to her through our common physical Ithaca experience. I knew she was mystical, occult and connected to profound teachings and teachers, and that she shared the same magic that filled me as I walked Ithaca's gorges under dramatic, gray skies.

Laughing as I look back, I realize that through referencing Madame Blavatsky I was connecting to Djwhal Khul and the other Masters. Although I had to attend to the pressing matters of youth, complete with all its identity crises, my awareness that Madame Blavatsky walked alongside the waterfalls with me, where the past meets the present, offered a soul perspective on both my potential for magnitude and the power of the Divine Path. Ithaca still holds my soul in her boundless waters even though destiny has taken me away.

Freedom!

As an Aquarian I have had my moments of being obsessed with freedom. After moving back to Ithaca in my twenties, I primarily identified myself as a hippie. This identity appealed to me because the hippie movement based so many of its values on the ideal of freedom.

When I left home for college at age seventeen, I felt as if I were being released from prison. Perhaps many of us feel that way when we finally have an opportunity to get some distance on the childhood family dynamics that enclose and constrict our souls. Even if our family life outwardly appears permissive or expanded, there are often hidden expectations, beliefs, and subtle pressures and needs for approval that shape our actions and feelings.

To fling open the front door of our parents' home and embrace the blank canvas upon which we start to paint our life's journey is a thrill filled with great expectations peppered with fears of the unknown. At that moment we are supposedly "free" to do whatever we want, whenever we want, however we want! Ironically, we soon realize that the outer freedom we seek is greatly limited by the childhood conditioning that maintains and continually re-energizes our inner psychic prison.

No matter how much external freedom we give ourselves, our souls inevitably feel trapped, repressed, stifled and blocked until we can find the keys that release us from our karmic belief systems played out in this lifetime's childhood. I spent my entire twenties determined to live a life of freedom. Breaking the rules, moving frequently, doing marginal jobs that would support me with the least amount of responsibility, avoiding routines, sleeping at strange hours rebelling against disciplines, and frequently changing my eating patterns were my attempts to feel as free as I wanted to be. After many wild and crazy adventures, inside I felt as trapped as if I was still under the dominion of my father and stepmother. The more I "freed" up my external life, the more I felt the internal walls of my psyche closing in.

After several years of this freedom experiment I began to question the real nature of freedom. I finally understood that it had very little to do with external conditions. I could feel my soul caged, pacing around inside of me like a wild animal. Nothing that I did externally could release it. I had tried everything, spending ten years of my early adulthood reluctant to put form to anything, fearful that it would take away my freedom and entrap me. This reflected my false belief that the earth plane and all of its forms encapsulate and close in on the soul, dimming one's light and full expression.

Now I know that form actually enhances the soul's expression and vivifies it in a way that the etheric plane cannot. In my quest for deeper levels of freedom I began to release my foolish rebellion—the part of me that would waste energy destructively rebelling against any aspect of my life that would hold me accountable. This destructive rebellion dissipated my energy and alienated me from the fullness of being human. My anarchistic attitude prevented me from fully engaging in life because of the illusion that this engagement would rob me of my precious freedom so long awaited from the restrictive days of childhood.

I began to allow the "wise" rebellion within to spark off an internal revolution geared to overthrowing all karmic tyrants overpowering my soul through false beliefs. For every layer of conditioning that I burned away, my soul's energy came rushing forth, filling in that space with a deep feeling of freedom—free at last to be human, to be authentic, to be in involved in life. I began a quest for the "perfect" forms of my soul's expression. These forms are always evolving and changing. I surrendered to my piano teacher's motto: "Discipline is the KEY to freedom." Allowing myself to be disciplined gave me the commitment I needed to unleash my soul's passion.

To overthrow our internal karmic tyranny is quite a revolution. It can only begin when we look inside, not outside of ourselves, for the keys to our liberation. My current definition of freedom is that it is a state of consciousness, one that allows us to go beyond the conditioning of all of our lifetimes and embrace our true essence. This freedom is uncompromised by the external events or conditions of our life. It is complete permission to be all that we are at all times. It is available to everyone regardless of one's social, political, or spiritual orientation.

Djwhal Khul tells me that this internal revolution is key to true liberation:

> *One must stand in defiance of the collective, as well as the personal false belief structures that would teach turning against one's humanity, soul and divinity. It is possible to revolutionize awareness by overthrowing the old world order that cuts one off from the Higher Self. This connection to the Higher Self is one's birthright and can tolerate no oppression. Until humankind questions its false authorities encouraging it to shrink from its magnitude and responsibility to the Divine Plan, it will be imprisoned in a collective belief structure that tyrannizes the mind, blocking out original thought and new creation.*

The freedom humankind seeks is rooted deeply within itself at the cellular level. No one can rob another of his or her enlightenment. No one can talk another out of it or make rules that prohibit it. Freedom is encoded in the spiritual nature inherent in all beings. No one can take your freedom or give you freedom. Dare to touch it within, as the karmic veils fall from your eyes, ears and heart, and freedom is yours. As more of humankind realizes this liberation, the Great Revolution occurs. This revolution cannot be squashed. It is the revolution of the soul's dominion on the earth plane. Let this revolution begin and gather momentum. Dare to be self-realized. Dare to be FREE!

As I listen to my beloved teacher, I realize that we are going through a revolution, an upheaval in all of our agreed upon perspectives on the human condition. As we let our spiritual natures infuse our earthly ones, the old belief patterns melt down in the heat of our heightened light factor. The revolution in our minds and hearts externalizes itself in major changes in our social, educational, economic, political and family structures.

This is an organic revolution, not violent or confrontational, but rather a natural falling away of illusion. With no belief to sustain the old ways, they simply dissolve, giving way to new creations of a world order based on transformed values stemming from the knowledge that we are first and foremost spiritual beings. As we heighten our light factor through human form we practice our freedom to create universes within ourselves and without. All is possible—and such is the path of true liberation.

Spiritual Awakening

I never imagined I would become a channel. It is rather strange to allow some "dead" person to speak through you. To be a medium was the farthest thing from my mind. Tracing back to my beginning awareness of Djwhal Khul returns me to age twenty-three when I became involved in a spiritual practice called Eckankar, The Ancient Science of Soul Travel.

For several weeks I had been struggling with an undiagnosable sickness exhibiting flu-like symptoms, fever and fatigue. The tenacity of this "illness" caused me great concern. What was wrong with me? Feeling sick and disconnected from life, I managed to get out of bed to take my dog for a walk on the Cornell campus a few blocks from my apartment. As we strolled along I noticed an outside table filled with books and flyers describing the path of Eckankar. I was immediately attracted to this material. So began a two-year involvement with the Ancient Science of Soul Travel. This was a spiritual initiation. Practicing the meditation and toning, central to the Eckankar path, stimulated the beginning of my outer spiritual life.

Prior to Eckankar there was no form for my spirituality. My Jewish father and Protestant stepmother were not interested in formal religious services. Throughout my childhood I was never inside a church or temple. Ironically, this was the best thing that could have happened. I was untouched by any kind of religious dogma. My spirituality was fresh, flowing and unformed by outside structures. My relationship to Source was spontaneous, loving, constant and free.

Many Eckankar books describe different levels or planes of existence. Reading these books provided a foundation of understanding about the different dimensions, heavenly realms, and stages of spiritual evolution. For two years I worked diligently to open to an experience of "soul travel." I had no idea what soul travel would feel like but everyone in Eckankar had been successful in their efforts. Nothing seemed to be happening in my meditation. I assumed I was a spiritual failure.

On the contrary, significant things did happen. Eckankar introduced me to the profound affects of toning the word "HU." This is an ancient sound. Eckists emphasized the sound current as a potent vehicle for soul travel. Something ancient within me remembered the importance of the sound current when I was reintroduced to it in this lifetime. It was as if I had remembered one of the "keys" to the universe, a key that I was given many lifetimes ago when actively working with the Greater Mysteries. The sound current is the most expedient way to override my ego, neutralizing the constant mental buzz of internal dialogue.

I did have one experience when I thought I might indeed be connecting to the "Eck master" (Eckankar's chosen human leader who also works with the Eck students on the inner planes). The Eck master was described as making internal contact in the form of blue light. I was spending the night at a friend's house, in a light sleep due to the unfamiliar bed. I woke up in the middle of the night to see a large, round illuminescent blue ball hovering in front of my face. Realizing my eyes were closed, I opened them. The ball was still there. I panicked! My heart raced as I grasped that I was *really* seeing this, not just dreaming. I was petrified to relate to this visitation. All I could say was, "Please, not now, I'm not ready". At that moment the blue ball disappeared. Both sad and relieved, I felt that I had missed a great opportunity to open spiritually. However, I accepted my unreadiness, having no grounding or confidence to handle other-worldly phenomena. I've often reflected on that experience, wondering what would have happened if I had allowed myself to simply let go and be taken by that beautiful blue ball of light.

After two years of trying in vain to experience soul travel I gave up in frustration and defeat, not realizing how much I had indeed opened up. It was hard for me to appreciate the subtly of the path. My ego wanted things to happen in a very tangible way. I needed more time to mature. Determined to back off from my spirituality, the next year was spent drinking every night in the local bars and leading the promiscuous life of most hippies back in the early 70's.

I realize now that the "blue light" had been the Tibetan making contact with me when my ego was asleep. He comes to me as a blue light when I channel. In spite of sensing a strong pull, I was not ready to honor the agreement we had made previous to my present incarnation. Ten years passed before I had the opportunity to reconnect externally with Djwhal Khul again.

THE PRESENCE OF PAST LIVES

Having It All

I want to reclaim the girl who I was in my early twenties when life was uncomplicated, slow and "unreal." I don't wish to reclaim her because I want to go back to the good old days but rather to bring her forward with me as I enter the new world. This new world is a place that holds the wonder of Self. I am awed at the fullness of self that is emerging. Can this really be my destiny? Do I dare to have it all?

We are often taught that we can't have it all. Does that mean we should compromise our dreams, restrict our imagination, settle for less, let "reality" form our limitations? It is only through believing that we can have it all that we begin to envision our enlightenment. Having it all reflects deep fulfillment, satiety, fullness, no hunger for anything more, a cup that truly runneth over. It is only at that point that we can let go of wanting or desiring. The cravings have run their course. The awareness of all possible needs met brings us our return to the Garden of Eden. We are liberated from attachment. But this liberation only comes from having it all, not forcing ourselves to do without. To do without makes us hungry, cranky, resentful, deprived, frustrated. Surely this is not a useful launching pad for enlightenment.

As a young woman, my perspective on life was wide open, horizontally expanded. Anything and everything was possible. I wanted it all and was determined to have it all. I was wild with desire for life and rebellious toward anyone who would leash me, corralling my free spirit. My supposed "close friend" at the time tried to ground me, encouraging me to remember that I can't have it all. She said it with great definitiveness as if it were gospel: "Moriah, you must remember that you can't have it all." The love in her eyes belied the strange undercurrent of jealousy emanating from her.

I tried to believe her at the time, so eager was I to get it right. Getting it right meant accepting other people's definition of reality. After all, they should know, especially since I felt so inexperienced at this game called the human condition. The world seemed so foreign, strange and confusing. Everyone else appeared savvy, on top of things, with all the answers, having read the guidebook to success on the earth plane.

Feeling like an alien being, I hunted high and low for guidebooks to this strange world. All through my early twenties I muttered to myself: "How do you do this life"? Everything from providing myself with proper clothes and shelter, good food and healthy relationships seemed absolutely baffling.

It's not as if I was raised as a feral child in this lifetime. Our material world was abundant. My cultural life was stimulated by only the best that Manhattan had to offer. I experienced dinners at the Plaza Hotel, clothes from Lord and Taylor, maid service, elegance, sophistication, ambitious and accomplished parents. Yet, I still felt like a visitor to the earth plane.

Past life memories pushed up inside of me at a non-verbal level reminding me that I didn't belong. I was infinitely more comfortable with animals and nature. I felt like myself when my hair was wild and tangled, clothes old, crumpled and mismatched, laughing out loud at inappropriate moments and supremely distrustful, like a wolf hiding behind the trees sniffing the air for danger at any moment.

I remember at least one lifetime as a feral child brought up by wolves in the wilds of Russia. I was abandoned by impoverished parents who could barely feed themselves and the other hapless children they had brought into this cold, unforgiving world. They meant no harm, hoping merely to return me to the earth before I would be conscious of death—extinguishing my light before it began to blaze.

As Lady Fate would have it, it was not my time to leave the earth. My soul was eager to meet the challenge of the human condition one more time. A female wolf gathering food for her cubs uncovered the leaves and torn blanket cocooning me, a final futile protective gesture from my tearful mother as she turned away from her newborn. Even today, several lifetimes later, in the cells of my current physical body I can feel the warm, moist breath of the wolf on my cold partially frozen cheek. Although food was scarce for the wolf community at that deep, frigid time of the year, I was not immediately devoured. Something in my soul called out to her for help: "Let me live!" She grabbed the blanket I was cradled in between her teeth and took me home to her pups, deciding that one more mouth to feed wouldn't be the end of the world. The pups instantly sniffed, pushed, licked and rolled all over me, imprinting family—clan—claiming me as one of them.

I lived into my late twenties in that lifetime, always in the wild, non-verbal and yet filled with sounds expressing the moans, groans, yelps, growls and whimpers of the howling language. I lived by instinct, loyalty and love for my fur family.

The wolf wisdom still fills my soul. Often I trust it far more than my human knowing. I am grateful to that distant mother for abandoning me to the wild. She gave me the opportunity to be both pure wolf and pure human.

My wolf mother adored me, as she did all her pups. While I was disciplined with nips and nudges, often leaving black and blue marks on my unprotected fur-less skin, I was deeply loved and respected as a valued member of the pack. I never learned how to stand up straight on my two legs, so identified was I as a four-legged. However, I knew a physical strength no human could imagine. The power of the mind sets the parameters for the physical experience. My mind was the mind of a wolf. So, too, did I have the strength of a wolf. My body simply responded to my assumption that I could do everything that my fellow pack members were capable of.

The interface between human and animal is a place of rare beauty—a wild terrain blazing with an exquisite light. Ironically, perhaps that was one of my happiest lifetimes as I learned about Source's love for me even in the most precarious of times. Source's love goes beyond the boundaries that separate animals from humans. Its great love binds us all as One. My feral lifetime brought the wild into my soul, nourishing it with boundless love, uncomplicated and unconditional. I learned the freedom within instinct, uncensored by civilized codes of behavior.

As I reach back into this lifetime's youth, recollecting myself as a young twenty-two- year old woman, I can still feel the warm, moist breath of Momma wolf on my cheek. In that moment I know that I can have it all. Wolves don't question bounty when it is offered. They simply romp within it, knowing that there is no end to the wonder and magic within creation. Looking into wolf eyes we see the mystery within the wilderness. In that mystery all is possible.

Past Life Selves

Our past lives "selves" are quite present in the unconscious. Djwhal Khul teaches that the matrix of our Higher Self's core issues is stored within each of our cells. These issues are played out lifetime after lifetime giving us the opportunity to explore and experiment with new experiences that would ultimately allow us to break through the illusions the Higher Self is working to release.

The unconscious is loaded with past life memories. Our karmic selves are expressed through dreams, fantasy, imagination and unconscious actions. The less we explore our unconscious, the greater the impact our past life selves may have on our current lifetime. These karmic energies seem to jump out of the causal level (the plane of existence holding our karmic records) into our current physical body in order to replay and resolve old trauma/ confusions/ illusions. Reminding ourselves that our current ego has dominion in our body allows us to comfortably invite our karmic selves out into the open. We then become conscious of the karmic patterns still "running" our experience in our current incarnation on the earth plane.

Life in the Barn

In my twenties my past life selves were definitely directing my current life choices. They provided gentle and not so gentle urges from my unconscious to do things that my present self probably would not have chosen to do. These urges seemed so real and relevant to my current life. I never considered that I might be caught in an old karmic pattern.

One of the major karmic themes I played out was an intense need to live in the wilds of nature. My soul was crying out, desperately yearning for its place in the woods away from civilization. After spending a day in the woods I would feel a profound sense of loss when I had to leave, often bringing me to tears that surfaced from a vague sense of indefinable grief.

Ithaca is a magical, mystical place filled with natural power spots. Sitting in front of one of Ithaca's many waterfalls entranced me and allowed my consciousness to merge into the millions of droplets of water cascading over rock. Nature became my haven, my church, my temple. I relentlessly searched for beautiful places with great views or deep rich woods, dreaming of someday living permanently away from the confines of society, except when I had to come into town for supplies.

At twenty-three years of age I moved to the woods with my ex-boyfriend, both of us agreeing as friends to independently "do our own thing." There was a small rundown cottage on the property that he minimally restored enough to call his home. My only hearth option was to piece together the old barn behind the cottage.

Most of the barn had fallen down. There was one room in tact that I turned into my "haven in the woods." The 12' x 16' room had to house all my belongings, myself and my German Shepherd dog "Zorba" as well as serve as a kitchen, bedroom and dining area. Obviously there were no modern conveniences. I constructed a makeshift out-house near the barn, strategically placed in a fallen down out-building. The meadows, chaotically overgrown, served as my yard with the barn nestled among new saplings, tall weeds, and overgrown brush. While this was not the most beautiful spot that I could envision, I felt compelled to make it home.

I was driven by distant memories of past lives spent at subsistence level during the pioneer days as well as earlier American Indian lifetimes in the woods. Intuitive recollections suggested that I was primarily alone in many of these lifetimes propelling a current life need to prove to myself that I could survive in the wild on my own. At the time I was still opening up to the idea of reincarnation, unable to recognize these impressions as past life memories. They seemed to be vague urges, desires desperate to be played out. My rational modern self could not withstand the seduction of these intense promptings from my soul.

So I surrendered, allowing myself to move into an unlivable barn, alone with my ex-boyfriend who was away most of the time, with no plumbing, electricity or heat—just as the nights in upstate New York start to cool down. I spent all of August making the barn livable, padding the walls with insulation and covering the insulation with orange, red and yellow Indian print bedspreads.

I bought an old, but beautiful wood stove. It was tall and silver with a carved door. The stove, so elegant, was oh so impractical. Starting a fire was difficult enough, but keeping the fire going was almost impossible. There was no regulating thermostat on the stove. I either suffered from too much or too little heat. The fire inevitably died during the night forcing me to break through the top layer of ice in my water bucket in the morning to access water for brushing my teeth and washing up. September, October and November flew by while I remained possessed by this past life passion to prove myself in the wilds.

I continually struggled with the wood stove, wondering how I could possibly stay warm in the dead of winter. The outhouse became so cold that I dreaded using it, postponing the inevitable as long as possible. Despite the inconveniences, inside the barn was beautiful with my elegant wood stove and colorful wall coverings. My ex-boyfriend helped me construct a built-in single bed and a small table for eating and writing. Some of my hippie friends thought I was so "cool" to pursue this adventure. However in my heart I began to wonder exactly why I was there.

The property was in upstate New York, in a small provincial area outside of magical Ithaca. The town was known for its spiritualist community, a group of people who often met at midnight in the adjoining woods to invoke the spirits. Sitting alone in my barn room late at night listening to them chant scared me to death! My beloved canine friend, Zorba, reassured me that he would take care of any invasions that might occur. I put great stock in my dog's ability to rescue me from whatever harm might come my way out there in no-man's land. Not having a phone made calling for help impossible. Nighttime, under a kerosene lamp for reading with no company, TV, or stereo, extended forever into a boring, frightening and lonely experience. Once again, I wondered, "Why am I doing this"?

Finally it was Christmas. I had been surviving in the barn for five months. I was now very cold, lonely and broke. When I had quit my job the previous summer to live in the wild somehow I thought that money would be no problem. Ah, the innocence of youth! My karmic memory convinced me that I could magically live off the land in this rent-free barn. Being a young woman in 1972 did not prepare me to eat nuts and berries like an Indian in the 1700s. I didn't have the slightest idea how to forage for wild food, much less discern what weeds or berries might be poisonous.

This is a perfect example of someone possessed by their past life self to the point that there is a collision between common sense and deep karmic yearnings. I had used up my money. The temperature often dropped well below zero, the barn encapsulated in several feet of snow. The roads were icy. The days were short and nights too dark. My leaky wood stove had a bad habit of smoking up the room. Even Zorba seemed tired of this experiment, looking at me with wise and loyal eyes questioning why I remained in a situation that created so much difficulty. Much to my relief, a friend brought me a message from my previous employer informing me that my old position was available, asking me to return to work. At the same time, another friend was going traveling and needed someone to house sit. I gladly agreed to do both.

Within a few days I found myself living in an elegant townhouse condominium filled with what appeared to be the height of luxury—phone, heat, toilet, bathtub, dishwasher, lights, TV, etc. I felt like a newborn baby, eyes wide as I explored all of these "modern" creature comforts wondering what time zone or dimension I had fallen into over the previous five months. I reveled in the EASE of modern life in spite of my guilt that perhaps I had failed the test I had set up for myself. I decided to face that test again someday in the future when I was better prepared. For now, I would relax in the warm tub, the apartment lit up with electricity as Zorba breathed a deep sigh of relief knowing he was off-duty from the demands of constant woods vigilance. Even thick-coated dogs get cold in the winter. He was so happy to snuggle next to me on the fluffy quilt covering the queen size bed. Together we rejoiced that it was 1972 and not 1772.

I began to think that maybe civilization was not so bad after all, although I knew that an ancient part of me would not be quieted until I resolved this strange need to break from society and become a feral child of the woods. I realize now that the angels and masters protected me through this experience, allowing me to explore, remember and appear to fail, without coming into harm's way. For their love, support and protection I am deeply grateful.

Building the House in the Woods

Four years after living in the barn my "karmic selves" began pestering me again to attempt to live in the wild, self-reliant and free from the confines of society. Now twenty-seven years old, I considered myself mature enough to make the decision to build a house in the woods where I believed I would be happy for the rest of my life. This time I had a boyfriend to keep the loneliness at bay. I had received a small amount of money from the court case with my stepmother the previous year. This money financed the leasing of five acres of woods from a local lumber company. This lease was perpetually renewing every five years allowing us to live indefinitely in the middle of hundreds of acres of woods without having to purchase the land.

Remembering the discomforts of my previous attempt at wilderness survival, I resolved this time to have more creature comforts. This included state of the art kerosene lamps for extensive lighting, a substantially built out-house sealing off most of the cold winter drafts and a well-insulated expansive open living space, 24'x16', along with an 8'x16' sleeping loft affording enough room to ward off cabin fever in the dead of winter. What more could one ask?

My relationship with my boyfriend was strained by his alcoholism. His addiction caused him to be an unreliable partner. In my naivete I assumed that once we built this dream home in the middle of nowhere magically our relationship would improve. And he would stop drinking.

Aside from my slight financial windfall we were barely earning a living, his job as a house painter bringing intermittent income and my job as a rental manager filling in the gaps. I strongly believed that if we could only hang in there until we were settled in the woods our money and relationship problems would end. I was possessed by a karmic urge to get out in the woods no matter what, as if that would be the magic bullet for happiness.

Common sense completely eluded me as we started the insane project of building a house, just the two of us, in the deep dark woods. Digging the holes for the footers during black fly season was unbearable. Even wearing netting couldn't shut out those nasty little beings determined to eat us alive. This endeavor was already beginning to feel like torture even though I told myself I was supposed to be having fun. Due to financial restrictions we could only afford green lumber which weighed at least twice as much as seasoned lumber. The wood was unfinished, rough, wet and heavy. Splinters lodged themselves in my hands, arms, legs—everywhere.

I became extremely strong and lean during the four months it took to build our wood's estate. We were able to drive my boyfriend's old pick-up truck loaded with building supplies only so far into the woods. The hacked away dirt road came to an abrupt end forcing us to carry heavy supplies the rest of the way to the site, probably the equivalent of two long city blocks (even in the woods the New Yorker in me still thought in terms of city blocks). The dead weight of the green wood made this distance feel like miles, back and forth, as we dragged all the building materials.

I suffered from terrible vertigo, practically passing out in fear as I straddled the ceiling beam and nailed in the rafters. My boyfriend coaxed me out onto the ridge pole, reassuring me that there was nothing to fear. Our vision-driven cathedral ceiling design, sixteen feet in the air, was a long way to fall if I didn't hang on tight.

Completely driven during this process, I would not let any doubts challenge the rightness of our lifestyle choice. Karmic memories persuaded me that this was the solution to all of my problems—a good, safe home in no man's land where I could magically live in nature's lap held safe and sound. Friends urged us to camp out on the site before starting construction to see whether we would really be happy in such an isolated spot. But we resisted their advice, probably afraid to discover they were right.

Finally the day arrived in late August. We were ready to move in. The house was somewhat finished although we had not yet put the clapboard on the outside. Our friends turned out in good spirits to help us haul our belongings down to the site, including my upright piano. Filled with our furniture, the house looked beautiful. The piano nestled into the 5' divider wall with a window to the right of the keyboard, especially designed for musical inspiration. The treadle sewing machine sat squarely under the upstairs window offering me a beautiful view of the woods while I sewed. We even extended the floor boards out from our sleeping loft to create a small balcony affording yet another view of more trees.

After everyone left, my boyfriend and I sat around in our living room with a cathedral ceiling too high for the dimensions of the room. We tried to ignore the vacuous effect this created. Looking around, we took in the result of our hard labor. I smiled, trying to be pleased. But something sank within me as I wondered why I didn't feel joyful in this long-awaited moment. All the promises from my past life selves began to crumble. No, the woods wouldn't magically save us from our problems.

Our relationship became more strained as he drank and I cried. He escaped to the local bar in town, a forty-minute drive. I sat alone in my strange new home, wondering once again what I was doing there. I tried to play the piano but quickly the musical muse disappeared. Sewing upstairs offered short comfort knowing there weren't many things needing mending and having no heart for new creations.

Daily I walked around our wooded yard beginning to feel as if I was losing my mind. Everywhere I looked there were trees, trees and more trees. After days of this I began to hear the trees talking to me, but not in their usual sweet manner, rather in mockery of my bad judgment. They told me how foolish it was to think I could happily survive in their world so removed from humanity. This was their domain. I was only to be a visitor. At times it seemed as if the trees were actually moving closer to the house, filling in our small clearing almost to the point of suffocation.

My rational mind accused me of going crazy. Perhaps I needed counseling. I talked to friends trying to gain perspective on this emerging madness. Meanwhile, my boyfriend was spending more and more time in the bar, also unhappy with our "white-picket fence" life in the woods. I felt abandoned by him and betrayed by nature. Where was the solace I hoped to achieve in this environment? Why had I chosen to live ten miles from town with no human conveniences in sight?

As my mind began to crumble, so did my relationship. Within one month of moving into our dream world, we moved out—desperate for other people. I learned that nature has very strong energy, a world of its own. Without humanity around life can become terribly bleak. Previous lifetimes in the woods would have forewarned me if only I had been conscious of them. Perhaps blindly replaying karmic impulses was the only way that I would begin to access past life memories. My boyfriend and I somehow lasted another year after our woods experiment and then parted ways—he with his alcohol and me with my restless yearning for something I could not describe.

Power

The thought of being fully empowered, as a necessary step for enlightenment, used to make my stomach sink, throat tighten and head fog. I have a deep cellular karmic imprint around the issue of power that automatically impacts my body. My instinct for survival is triggered whenever I approach the threshold leading to new levels of power within my soul. Consequently, power has been associated with unconquerable fear, the kind of fear that ripples right under the skin, causing the body to shudder and the breath to shorten. Perhaps this is an indication of the extent to which I held back my power, wishing it would disappear, to avoid the responsibility accompanying an empowered state of consciousness.

It is useful to observe childhood models of power. They usually provide a picture of our karmic beliefs about power. My stepmother serves as an example of the abuse of power. She reflects the awesome power parents hold over children. The potency of parental impact on a child carries an enormous responsibility. A stepparent has the great challenge and opportunity to love a child not of their own flesh.

I was constantly afraid of my stepmother, even as a young adult. She was larger than life, filling the entire household with her power. Her narcissism demanded constant agreement and applause. Completely self-absorbed, all the energy in the house had to return to her. Consequently, she gathered a tremendous force field around her. Only as an adult was I able to understand that this force field was her protection against a terrible feeling of insignificance.

I was entrained by her power. My desperation for a loving mother seduced me into compromising all expressions of self in order to feed her self-image. In short, I gave her my power. She became stronger, larger, more intense and expressive, while I slipped into invisibility. I learned that power has no allegiance to the "good." Power is simply energy—gathered, issued, expressed.

At forty-three years old, when I too became a stepmother of a five-year-old son, I was able to appreciate the difficulty of step-parenting. I also relished the great rewards of carefully raising a child with compassion and love. Awareness of my own inner child's needs has been integral to this process.

The issue of power begins at a very young age. Childhood was designed by Source to be an experience of heightened vulnerability. Although this can be a magical adventure, it is a time when children are totally at the mercy of parental figures.

My brother responded to the power issue very differently, trying to match my stepmother's force with his own. However his anger, still undeveloped as a young child, did not hold the clout compared to the force of my stepmother's rage. Consequently, my brother was perpetually locked in a state of frustrated disempowerment—pouting, sulking and seething peppered with occasional bursts of yelling. This did not serve him, but only fueled his sense of defeat.

Looking to my father as an appropriate model of power was equally disappointing. He seemed to lack power, or was unwilling to use it to ward off my stepmother's verbal cruelty. He handed her full power to raise us, never intervening. Intuitively I sensed his power, held within, as a deep emotional undercurrent silently snaking its way around the house slithering around my stepmother's dramatic demonstration of self. I never trusted his silence. Even as a child my psychic attunement alerted me that my father was not a kind man. Highly sensitive to his cynicism and suspicion, I felt his silent power drain my joy.

My first initiation into power occurred in an actual trial. At twenty-seven I took my stepmother to court for inheritance fraud. My father had died six years earlier.

Even as a young adult in my twenties, still completely intimidated by my stepmother's power, I shrank in her presence. Continuing to comply with everything she said, I took issue with nothing. Impossible to take a stand with her, repressed self-assertion built up inside me for years. Eventually I had to literally take a stand on the "witness stand."

At the time of my father's death my stepmother informed me that Dad had disinherited both my brother and me. That seemed very strange. My father, in spite of his secrecy and emotional distance, had generously provided for our material needs. After thirty successful years of practicing law in Manhattan he was an expert in estates and wills. It seemed improbable that he would legally withhold provisions for our financial well being after his death.

During his year long battle with bone cancer my stepmother nursed him at home, seeing to his every need. She passionately fought for his life, introducing vegetable juice drinks long before they were widely recognized for their healing properties. My brother and I were away at college, unavailable to participate in my father's dying process. Participation would have been impossible even if we were living at home due to my stepmother's controlling and possessive nature. She created a steel bubble around her relationship with my father that was impossible to penetrate.

My stepmother's possessiveness, coupled with my father's closed-off personality, sealed the wall between my father and me leaving no room for real communication. There was so much I wanted to say to him. His dying process mirrored the way it had always been between us, small talk in a climate of emotional distance and distrust.

When my stepmother reported that my father, displeased with my brother and me, had left nothing in his will, I believed her. It illustrated the distrust I had of my father. In spite of sensing his love for me, I never knew what he was thinking. The imagination has a field day with this kind of uncertainty. Not sure in what way, I believed I had let him down. Ironically it was he that had let me down. I wanted to believe my father was perfect. Therefore, it had to be my shortcomings that created the wall between us.

This confusion was fertile ground for my stepmother's deception. My grief-ridden vulnerability allowed me to believe anything. Under my stepmother's direction I dutifully signed legal documents, neglecting to read them. My father, the attorney, frequently asked us to sign papers manipulating stocks, bonds, etc. As a child I had no idea what these mysterious papers meant. I simply signed on the dotted line. These legal papers of my stepmother's seemed more of the same. Little did I realize I was signing away my inheritance.

Examining my income tax records six years later with a friend, a Cornell Law School student, I realized something was wrong. I had finally snapped to my senses. In response, I called an aggressive attorney on Long Island referred by an old high school friend. The attorney didn't believe my story. I had to travel five hours to meet in person to convince him of my honesty.

Yes, I as a twenty-one-year old college graduate had indeed blindly signed away my inheritance. Why? Fear! At the time of my father's death I could not fathom standing up to my stepmother. Her word was truth. I had no sense of personal power.

Eventually the lawyer, seeing the truth in my eyes and accepting my story, agreed to take the case. A year passed in negotiations with my stepmother's attorney. I prayed that the case would miraculously be resolved out of court, dreading the act of physically facing my stepmother in court. As karma would have it we did end up in court.

Sitting on the witness stand I felt the internal heat of the fires of transformation. All pretense and hiding in childhood burned away in the intensity of that moment. I was exposed, not only to my stepmother but to the public in a court of law. Under cross-examination the minutes seemed to elongate into hours. Time stood still. My voice bounced off the walls as my truth rang out in the large courtroom.

I had finally broken the unspoken contract with my stepmother mandating that she dominate and control my reality. At that moment my entire karmic imprint started to rearrange itself. I began to feel my strength at long last.

My stepmother gave a theatrical performance on the stand, sobbing about how hard it was for her to raise us from the age of five as the Catholic judge melted in response. The attorneys negotiated a settlement. The judge called my brother and me to his chambers to attempt a reconciliation with my stepmother. Her "performance" continued, as she embraced us, took our addresses, and proclaimed her desire to stay connected with us. Sensing the emptiness in her words, I recoiled. That was the last time I ever saw her, the woman who raised me from early childhood. How strange life is.

The next day after returning home to Ithaca, I sat by a creek in the woods with my German Shepard, "Zorba." Together we contemplated the movement of the water. I felt victorious. I had faced the dragon and spoken my truth. In that moment it felt like I would never be afraid of anything in life again, realizing how fear dissolves in the face of self-love and self-advocacy. For a few seconds I actually felt enlightened! Inner peace and deep self-trust began to take root. I would never retreat back into that frightened empty shell again.

My stepmother grabbed everyone else's energy, absorbing it to make herself feel large and powerful. My father clung to his cynicism and shrewdness to convince himself that no one would get the better of him. These are fear-based stances of power. Because they are fear-based the element of power is compromised and weakened. If only I had the perspective then that I do now. I could have saved myself years of hiding.

I finally began my path of service during my Saturn return at age twenty-nine. At that point I allowed myself to outwardly express power. I had to.

I started a position working in a maximum security lock-up facility for juvenile delinquent girls. The first day on the job felt like a collision course with power. I had come fully prepared, wearing my "all-loving, soul-rescuing," identity. I was the "good person" who really cared and would make it possible for these lost teenage souls to get their lives together. However, I had no power to back me up.

Completely fearful of power, I arrived as a loving shell, unable to match the energetic demands of the fierce population with which I had to work. These girls, mostly street kids from Harlem, had been around the block with drugs, prostitution, burglary and assault, all before the tender age of seventeen. Within the initial few hours of my first day on the job I knew that I had to either exercise power or be destroyed by the intensity of the girls.

I spent the next sixteen months obsessing over this job. It allowed me to begin the process of claiming and expressing power in tandem with love, caring and service. The girls had a nose for fear. Smelling it on you, they would go for the jugular vein without mercy. Immediately they knew I was not lined up with the power that resides in the guts, the visceral power of survival, clarity, uncompromised boundaries and a strong statement of self. I was afraid of this statement of self because my fear of being a narcissist like my stepmother prohibited me from claiming a self. It took many years to differentiate between the deep self-confidence and inner authority that accompanies true power versus the ego-inflation and extreme self-involvement springing from a wounded and disempowered self.

During the initial six months at the juvenile facility I was tested and retested by these well-seasoned kids. The girls embodied battle, rage and viciousness. They had little regard for societal regulations. Daily, as I drove along Cayuga Lake to work, my stomach was in knots. The girls knew I had no internal power base.

My testing period involved several humiliating episodes of intensive verbal abuse. There was also an incident of physical struggle when I attempted to restrain one resident from smashing another over the head with a pool cue. Fighting back, she pushed me on the ground, pulling out my hair. I realized that being the "goody, goody, loving I never hurt anybody" personality would not take me far in life unless I retreated, cocooning myself from the mainstream. That was not an option.

As a young girl I had visions of working with street people, wanting to experience the collective soul at all levels. My upbringing took place in an affluent setting, living in large mansion-like houses with live-in black maids. I had never encountered these "kinds of people." True education had finally begun!

I quickly shed the skin of the sweet, white, blonde, blue-eyed, do gooder out to save the messed up violent, uneducated blacks. I came to respect these girls' intensity, ferocity, assertion and defiance. They were very creative and expressive in their "bad" language. As I began to feel my own power, my birthright of strength and self-assertion, I was able to truly love them. Looking into their eyes revealed the depth of their wounds, fears and needs.

After six months some of the girls offered to "watch my back." In this offering of protection they let me know I had passed the initiation. I was now part of the clan. The next ten months at the institution were filled with profound experiences of sharing life perspectives. We taught each other. I gave them an experience of love, nurturing, light and a safe person to trust. They gave me the opportunity to find strength, wisdom and a connection to my instinctual self. Sixteen months later I knew that my training with these wonderful teachers was over. I had found a piece of my soul in their eyes and discovered an internal power that would protect me in all situations no matter what the threat. I am forever grateful to them for this gift.

Often, in contemplation of my enlightenment, I have been immediately confronted with issues around power. Afraid to have power, my belief system associated power with selfishness, delusions, cruelty and destruction. In order to evolve into my true potentiality I needed to embrace the constructive, healing, truthful and loving aspect of power. Although I understood this intellectually, I recoiled at the prospect of allowing the full thrust of my empowered self to flow forth. Past life memories of overtly or inadvertently abusing power, hurting others as well as myself haunted me.

It is metaphysically baffling that regardless of our level of evolvement power is always available to us. Power is a neutral force, non-discriminating of the vessel it flows through. Consequently most of humankind has experienced, in one lifetime or another, having power before they were mature enough to direct it wisely. Inevitably, disastrous events followed. How many of us at least vaguely remember being overwhelmed, inflated, or deluded by our sense of power? Has Source given too much creative juice to those of us who are still naive and unconscious about life on the earth plane? While power can be gathered relatively quickly, wisdom, depth, understanding and discernment all require many lifetimes to develop.

My unresolved karma regarding power involved impossible self-expectations. My soul believed that if I had enough power I could save others. In one lifetime as a village witch with great healing powers, I took on tremendous responsibility for the well-being of all the villagers. When a plague wiped out 90% of the children I was certain that it was my fault. After all, I had been the designated "powerful" one. Why wasn't I able to stop this tragedy and save my beloved village family?

I began to distrust my power, seeing myself as a fraud. I felt unworthy of the trust that I had received from others and was angry at Source for betraying me. The feeling of betrayal came from the illusion that I had accepted as truth: "If you have enough power you can do anything." My unworthiness deepened into despair. As a final act of penance and purification for my shortcomings I turned myself in to the Inquisition engineered by vicious men who were eagerly burning women at the stake because they feared their power. My hope was that the fire would burn away the dross, the illusion of being powerful.

Looking back on that lifetime, I see a young soul eager to please and serve. I see a woman who wanted to be perfect in the eyes of others. I see a frightened woman. I see a woman who hadn't yet realized that regardless of one's power, Source's Divine Will can supersede all of our efforts if necessary for the collective evolution. In that lifetime I was both inflated and overwhelmed by power.

Licking my wounds from the trauma of that lifetime, I decided to lay low. It seemed safer not to have power, even if it meant being a victim. At least the victim can hide from responsibility. The victim seemed less likely to be a target. Consequently, I experienced many lifetimes of being victimized by others abusing their power. That seemed more righteous than using my power. At the very least I could get good karmic points for being a martyr. However, the lifetime as village witch/healer was not the first time I fell into confusion with power.

Life times prior to having been burned at the stake, I was a magician obsessed with uncovering the mysteries. I was determined to be a great alchemist who would prove to the world that I could change anything into gold. I would be the richest man alive. Blessed with a brilliant and penetrating mind enabled me to grasp the dynamics of the creative force. I understood abstract formulas for rearranging matter.

Passion for power was burning me up inside, leaving no time or interest in human affairs such as marriage or family. I was a mysterious loner who felt that I was above the human condition. Memories of previous lifetimes spent off the planet fueled me. Access to these memories offered the ability to witness the Forces at work from a galactic perspective. My "home" planet had been highly technological. Consequently the earth plane appeared primitive and coarse. I disdained the stupidity of humankind and had no tolerance for their emotional dramas. All that I cared about was magic, power and harnessing the Forces.

As the years passed I became a total hermit, reveling in my fantasies of power. Enshrouded in darkness, I never learned to love. Although power is not inherently a bad thing, it became a place of distortion. The acquisition of power became more important than reverence for Source. Any potential for identification with the divine was obscured by this obsession with power. I made the fatal mistake of claiming that the power was *mine*, not a gift from Source. That mistake encased me in a hardened shell of self-absorption and bitterness as I struggled in vain to outdo Source in His displays of power. Over the years my heart blackened from suffocation, completely cut off from the light. Finally one day my heart simply stopped beating, and all the power and alchemy in the world could not get it to start again.

That lifetime as a magician was the result of unresolved karma from an earlier lifetime in Atlantis. During that lifetime I held myself at a lofty level, self-identified as an offspring of the God race (the root race of the human race). Nothing could touch that. Caught in my ideals and expanded vision, I did not see disaster coming. I was inflated by the refined and sophisticated level of higher mind power. I was total scientist and had taken my mission as co-creator with Source very seriously.

In my vision, Source and I were collaborating in our scientific pursuit of the ultimate energetic grid. The potential of this grid would allow us to harness enough raw power to create another planet. Ironically, instead of creation, power led to destruction.

Once again, I had overlooked the importance of both the mysterious aspect of Source's Being and the crucial impact of the heart on the mind. I will never forget the moment, the cataclysm of Atlantis, when I realized the great mistake and abuse of power in which I had participated. I had been so certain that what I was doing was right. The shock of disillusionment rippled through my body like an electrocution. I was stunned and paralyzed to witness the explosions around me. Unable to move, the embodiment of incredulity, my physical body was atomized.

The impact of that disillusionment carried over into all subsequent lifetimes. Getting close to realizing any level of power infused me with paralyzing disbelief. My lifetime as a magician reflected a determined effort to shake off that disbelief. The magician's ego battled against false beliefs indicating I would never be worthy of opening to power again. Using my ego's will to override this false belief disconnected me from my soul. I became a small, desperate man, running from my karmic past. The more I ran from my fear, the more my power became distorted.

It has been a long journey from distortions of power to the experience of true empowerment, one that we all face. It challenges us to courageously open to power while simultaneously acknowledging that all power ultimately belongs to Source.

Past life Regression with Inger

Remembering a past life seemed impossible until my early thirties. I wondered how my present self could move out of its paradigm into another reality distantly connected through the Higher Self. At the very least I thought it would require deep hypnotic work to even approach that realm.

The ego has an amazing ability to convince us that its reality is the only "real" reality and everything else is illusion. In spite of this ego dominance, my logical mind accepts reincarnation as common sense from an overall metaphysical perspective. The belief that we each have only one lifetime on earth in which to evolve ourselves through matter is difficult to accept due to the challenging assignment of mastering our divinity on a plane of duality. Our gifts are inheritances from hard work accomplished in previous lifetimes. The opportunity of multiple lifetimes makes it possible to accept the inequities of our collective human experience. While we are not all born to equal circumstances and fortunes, in the eternal aspect of ourselves we all have identical opportunity for enlightenment.

On my thirty-third birthday a good friend introduced me to a woman, Inger, who offered past life regressions. Knowing that our soul energy is extra charged during our birthday month, I decided that this would be a great time to attempt to access blocked aspects of my soul. New to the frontier of past life work, I doubted that anything of real substance would occur. But I was open to experimenting, especially since Inger emanated a special angelic quality that made me feel both safe and inspired.

It was a bitter cold January night in upstate New York when I arrived at Inger's apartment. The warmth of her home along with the sweet smell of hot cider relaxed me as I anticipated our work together. At this point I wondered why I had agreed to do something so strange with someone I barely knew. However those gentle, persistent proddings from my Higher Self literally walked my legs through the doorway of her apartment preventing me from turning on my heels and running. Inger showed me into her meditation room filled with crystals, burning candles, sweet incense and a massage table draped in purple satin. Attempting to relax on the table, I had to once again chase away the negative voices cautioning me that this was either going to be a total waste of time, or I would not have what it takes to access a past life.

Within moments Inger's sweet but firm voice was ushering me through a deep relaxation technique. Simply taking the time to individually relax each part of my body was delightfully satisfying, introducing a new experience of rest into my busy, breakneck speed life. When I reached a state of deep relaxation Inger instructed me to expand into my subtle body—imagining myself becoming larger and larger. She then guided me to a bridge that once crossed over, would land me in a past life.

My imagination had no trouble wrapping itself around this guided imagery. Soon enough I was on the other side of the bridge. Inger had me look at my feet, and lo and behold I saw beaded moccasins. Clearly I had very easily slipped into a past life, current ego trying ineffectively to resist, but now as if from a great distance.

As I moved throughout the different phases of this past life, I discovered that I had been an American Indian woman who had initially lived in a village. However, once the community discovered that she had psychic healing powers they assigned her the role of "medicine woman" and segregated her to prevent the activity of daily village life from depleting her energy. Although she was pleased to be honored as a medicine woman and supported as a healer, her heart grieved for the life she was not allowed to live—no husband, children or daily communion with other women.

Eventually she exiled herself to the woods, initially finding the company of nature more nurturing than the isolating exclusivity of her position in the tribe. She built a small hut protected by great oak trees near a stream. Clairaudient, she heard music emanating from the trees as they spoke to her, intermingled with messages from the bubbling brook flowing past her front door. The words in the winds also carried wisdom and insights as they whistled through the tall trees. She received great knowledge from nature's teachers, often dancing to the harmony of these orchestral sounds. The woods were rich and deep, easy to get lost in. However, her psychic attunement to nature's energies allowed her to easily navigate unchartered pathways among the trees.

Several years passed as she matured into her late twenties. The wild animals and birds loved her, protecting her from harm's way. The villagers sought her counsel and healing. Often she was found seated under a great oak tree in a trance state. They approached her carefully with utmost respect for her connection to the other dimensions and showed their gratitude with skins, food, supplies and pottery. She was thoroughly supported in her lifestyle and imagined herself content during these years.

However, the painful impact of isolation began to take affect. The natural human craving for companionship was starting to scream inside of her. She knew that the tribe would never allow her into the community to live an ordinary life. She was both honored and imprisoned by her position. Ultimately her only choice was to live out her identity as a medicine woman or suffer total exile by her people. In spite of her efforts to resign herself to her fate, the loneliness began to break her heart.

As her heart suffered, her psychic abilities became distorted. Instead of rejoicing in the music of the trees, water and wind, she began to feel overwhelmed by them. The previous harmony turned into a cacophony of disturbing voices as she lost the ability to attune to natural resonance. Years of helping others work through their health challenges left her exhausted and empty. Unable to feed herself through human relationships depleted her ability to sustain a positive perspective on life.

The imbalance became too great. Her inner walls came crashing down. Nature's voices seemed to be screaming at her. Without a strong and happy heart for guidance and grounding, her psychic abilities became a curse that eventually led to madness. Her ego fragmented into a thousand pieces leaving her to wander about the woods bewildered and disoriented.

Initially the members of the tribe were pleased with her madness because it indicated that she was even more open to being used as an instrument for the great forces. However, as her condition deteriorated she was unable to speak coherently, much less remember her role as healer. Finally, on a sunny fall morning she fell on the leaves covering the forest floor under her great oak tree, and allowed her heart to break completely. This attack of the heart freed her from her body at the age of thirty-five.

At the moment of death she sailed out of her body in the shape of a huge black bird. Using her great wing span to propel her to the spirit plane she sought solace and understanding about the purpose of this lifetime of severe isolation. She learned that her deep love of nature could not take the place of human interaction. Her soul wanted her to understand that the heart's wisdom is the central matrix for human evolution. An undernourished heart can lead to madness. Once again, my Higher Self's monadic wound of abandonment was played out by the medicine woman's fellow villagers. This lifetime forced my soul to look at Source's love and to contemplate the creation of joyful relationships and trust in future lifetimes.

Surfacing from this past life journey, my head felt expanded fifty times its normal size. Two hours had passed. Sitting up on the massage table, I felt dizzy, disoriented, open, and transparent. I mumbled deep appreciation to Inger for opening a door to my soul in a way I never could have imagined.

After a warming cup of cider to bring me back into my body, I hugged Inger goodbye and returned to my apartment. Grabbing my German Shepherd dog, Zorba, we walked for two hours until 1:00 a.m. The streets were cold and empty, allowing me the crystal spaciousness I needed to begin to integrate what I had just experienced.

I realized that my yearning to live in the wilds was related to this lifetime as a medicine woman. As Zorba and I walked, I still felt the moccasins on my feet, walking like an Indian that knows her beloved earth. I resolved never to isolate myself through nature again. No longer would I need to challenge myself with wilderness living. I vowed to make a greater commitment to my humanness and the need for relationships and community. Determined not to recreate the monadic imprint of isolation, I quietly thanked and blessed that Indian woman who was self hundreds of years ago. She taught me so much. I would be forever grateful to her. In that moment I was released from a compulsion that had driven me throughout my twenties and early thirties. In my reconnection with the wild medicine woman of my past, I was now free to join society.

THE WITCH AND THE TIBETAN: A LOVE STORY

The Golden One

My first psychic/channeled reading happened during a visit to Ithaca when I was thirty-four years old. I had heard that my friend, Inger, who had guided me through my first past life regression, was beginning to channel. Always a believer of messages and support from the "other realms," I was eager to hear what guidance might come my way.

My first husband, two other friends and I gathered around Inger as she sat on her bed. Eyes closed, she filled with an energy that softened her features, erasing all previous stress. I was fascinated with the sweetness and love that fell across her face as she opened to the guides. When my turn came to ask questions my heart was racing. This was the first time I had ever experienced tangibility within the invisible connection to the next dimension.

The year before this visit my brother had experienced a profound opening to Jesus as his teacher. In childhood we had no formal exposure to any religious teachings, never even attending a church or temple service except for weddings and Bar Mitzvahs of friends. Consequently it came as a shock when my brother was "born again" into a fierce Christian faith. My own relationship with Jesus felt vague and illusive. Influenced by my brother's spiritual rebirth I asked the guides via Inger if I should try to open to Jesus, hopefully to experience the same joy and infusion of faith in which my brother was rejoicing.

Inger's face took on a warm, knowing smile as the guidance came through. I was told that although it is always beneficial to allow Master Jesus into the heart, another teacher was working with me. I had spent lifetimes with this teacher in Tibet as his student. The guides indicated that I was not yet ready to know his name. However, I had always called him "the Golden One" in our previous relationships. They encouraged me to tie threads around my wrist and open to the presence of the Golden One as much as possible.

The guides also told me that eventually I would be a channel as well. Hearing this statement made my blood run cold, fear shooting through my veins in response to this future mandate. I couldn't imagine doing that kind of work. It terrified me.

Returning to my studies in psychology safely back in Boston, I thought from time to time about this mysterious teacher called the Golden One. The name gave me a strange sense of comfort and warmth. I wore the threads around my wrist for awhile until the demands of starting my counseling practice swept me away from such exotic notions of foreign teachers from a strange land working with me on the spiritual plane.

It would be three years before I would actually consciously meet the Tibetan in this lifetime and realize that the guides were right. I would become a channel. However, at the time those threads opened my soul to receive the Tibetan through the dream state, allowing him to work with me in preparation for our service work together.

Relationship with Djwhal Khul

My love for the Tibetan grows in leaps and bounds. I have been consciously working with Djwhal Khul since January 1986. Our relationship has radically shifted my consciousness. Djwhal Khul's presence within me has expanded all aspects of my life. Our relationship is a marriage, a working partnership, an apprenticeship, and a love affair. He has touched all levels of my soul and is infused throughout my being.

I was awe struck when we met. A friend phoned a few days after my thirty-seventh birthday to inform me that a channel from Colorado, Kathlyn Kingdon, who channeled an ascended Tibetan master, was currently visiting my neighborhood in Newton, Massachusetts. Kathlyn had just had a cancellation, leaving her an open slot for a reading. I love receiving messages during the month of my birth. Energy is particularly strong when the sun is moving through our birth sign each year affording heightened opportunity. "Coincidentally" the available appointment was exactly the same time that had just opened up in my schedule from a client who canceled earlier that morning.

Driving to the reading I told myself to be open to the information and not be afraid. Channeling was quite new to me, having experienced only one brief reading from Inger three years prior. I knew at some level that I had been waiting for this reading. Hungry for guidance, I had been calling out for a teacher for many months.

In my spiritual search I had enrolled in Dyhani Yahoo's Peacekeeper Mission, a nine-month program for spiritual alignment, earth attunement and service. After attending the first two meetings of the program I knew that this wasn't my spiritual path, despite its popularity. I needed something different. In spite of several past lives as an American Indian, my soul did not need a program filled with American Indian symbology/ spirituality. However, the American Indians and Eckankar were the only pathways that I was really familiar with. The eastern approach to spirituality was foreign to me. I wasn't even sure geographically where Tibet was!

When Djwhal Khul spoke to me (through Kathlyn) I was speechless. I couldn't find my words. He chuckled, teasing me that it was OK to talk. I couldn't get over how strange it was to experience this foreign energy from the spirit plane talking directly to me through another person. Djwhal Khul was intense, penetrating, direct, funny and powerful. I felt exposed, loved, challenged, and highly stimulated. His first words to me were "When are you going to let me in?" I was compelled to say "Now" even though I had no idea how to do that. I sensed that something major was happening to me that required surrender, although it was beyond my ego's understanding. I realized immediately that Djwhal Khul was the teacher I had been calling for.

What I didn't bargain on was our agreement that I would become a conscious channel for him in service to others. However, by the end of our hour-long conversation I committed to opening my channel, letting him "in." He enticed me with the promise that he would improve, expand and enhance my work with clients.

Djwhal Khul informed me of one hundred false beliefs needing removal in order to clear the channel. These beliefs reflected karmic fears of possession, losing control and betrayal. He said "You won't have any trouble channeling; the difficulty will be in trusting it." How right he was. I struggled with the trust issue for the next ten years, always questioning the validity of my channeling. When I began giving readings I told myself that after one hundred successful sessions I would know that my service work with the Tibetan was valid. One hundred successful readings came and went. I was still plagued by doubt and suspicion, wondering whether I was making the whole thing up. Was I completely deluded or mad? Was I incredibly good at copying Kathlyn Kingdon's style? How real was this?

After this initial consult with Djwhal Khul I drove home in a daze. What had I just committed myself to? Why me? Was I worthy?

Dutifully I used the Tibetan's technique for clearing, releasing one hundred false beliefs. The technique involved imagining each false belief as a stone in my body that had to be removed by a light-filled hand reaching in through the crown chakra. The stone was then to be thrown against a concrete wall to explode. This seemed simple and straightforward at the time Djwhal Khul suggested this technique. However, when I tried to release them, some would elude me. I did not realize the impact of the complexity and ferocity of my attachment to these beliefs.

This process flushed up my terror of possession by dark psychic forces. I became aware of how much past life material had to be cleared in order for me to trust that I would not be overpowered by Djwhal Khul's energy. Often the stone would move away when I tried reaching for it. If I was able to grab and throw it at the wall, the wall receded and the stoned failed to explode. I was struck by the stubbornness within my psyche. Convincing my psyche to innocently let down psychic defense structures securely in place within my soul for lifetimes was not easy. But something deep inside urged me forward with this process. There would be no going back on my commitment to this strange Tibetan teacher.

Several false beliefs centered on the issue of worthiness. This lifetime's karma orchestrated a childhood in which great levels of unworthiness were generated, enabling past life material to surface for clearing. Despite having done a tremendous amount of work and healing, internally I was still on shaky ground. My private practice as a psychotherapist was successful in spite of this inner turmoil around personal worth. The idea of channeling an Ascended Master exceeded the scope of my self-perception. After all, I was a "loser." Isn't that what my stepmother concluded? I wasn't good enough to keep my real mother from killing herself. Certainly my father's absence proved that he had more important things to do than to waste time focusing on me. This childhood package neatly wrapped up my soul's self-negation and unworthiness into a crystallized ball that the Tibetan was trying to convince me to simply "toss" away! The effort of trying to stretch the parameters of my self-image to include the magnitude of bringing through a great teacher sent me reeling into a sea of resistance. I realize now the perfection in this process. It was only my immediate love for Djwhal Khul and developing trust that enabled me to harness the determination to push through walls of unworthiness, clearing a space for our work together.

I sat alone in my office, night after night, releasing false beliefs and trying to clear out my heart chakra. Djwhal Khul had indicated that it would be best to receive him through the heart chakra. However, he said that the back (intake valve) of my heart chakra was sealed over with "scar tissue" from lifetimes of betrayal. He instructed me to imagine a small flashlight of cosmic light shining and burning away the layers of protection and fear.

Finally, after six months, all layers were released. I felt energy pour into my heart, struck by its power once the blockage was discharged. My heart instantly expanded, rejoicing. In meditation I positioned my awareness in the middle of my heart chakra calling Djwhal Khul to me. He appeared in his light body, white light. (Later, during readings, Djwhal Khul came to me as a blue light shimmering in my third eye.) Approaching me, we sat together, sweetly content in each other's love. After repeating this exercise many times I gradually began to trust his presence.

Allowing more of his energy to merge with my body often frightened me. The physical body knows when a "foreign" energy is within it and reacts protectively. I experienced physical responses acclimating to the current of Djwhal Khul's energy such as rocking or swaying. Sometimes my head jerked backward. The kundalini was strong. I wasn't used to it. The Tibetan's frequency felt like 1000 watts as compared to my 75-watt orientation.

Still reacting to past life issues around possession, often I immediately ordered him to leave as soon as he had entered. He complied instantly. I gradually began to trust that I was in charge of my own body in this process of opening to channel. Djwhal Khul would only come and go as I requested, demonstrating absolute respect and reverence for my process. He never became angry or impatient, consistently showering me with gratitude for my willingness to cooperate with him in this endeavor. Eventually I grew more comfortable with his frequency and its impact on my physical body.

I often need to sway in a circular fashion when the Tibetan is coming through. My body dances to a heightened frequency that compels movement. It is within this circular movement that our frequencies mix and resonate together, each one modifying the other into a mutually beneficial flow.

Protection

The issue of protection has always confused me. As a "psychic" I have often been advised to protect myself. Working in the energetic, therefore invisible realm, carries its own unique set of challenges. We know how to protect ourselves from bad weather with appropriate clothing. Protection from physical attack or abuse can also be addressed by withdrawing from the abuse or defending oneself physically. However, to protect myself from invisible "negative" energies and psychic attack can feel like trying to shield myself from inhaling an odorless gas leak or radiation.

The impact of insidious negative energies is powerful, difficult to recognize and track. Many times I have retreated into the innocence of Persephone picking wildflowers, oblivious to Pluto's presence and impending seizure of her. I, too, have tried to numb myself to the impact of these invisible energies, cultivating my innocence as a form of denial, hoping that miraculously angels and masters would offer protection from any encroaching dark force.

Opening to channel requires just that—openness! Open, open, open is the message we get from the New Age community. The only way we can align with our Higher Self is by opening to its energy. However, openness brings a sense of heightened vulnerability. When we are open to our higher self, and/or the masters, are we not also open to negative forces as well? How do we know that we are safe? How do we know if there is toxic energy present when we cannot measure, touch, smell or see it?

THE WITCH AND THE TIBETAN: A LOVE STORY

I repeatedly question Djwhal Khul about this issue. He teaches that our fear attracts negativity. As long as we have unresolved fears about being attacked, we must use some kind of psychic protection because our fears serve as magnets for the dark force. He adds that eventually we reach a level where those fears are dissolved. Then we become empty enough to allow negativity from others to move through us and out the other side without harm. It is only our fears (and unresolved past life trauma) which create the stickiness for the dark force to attach to and feed from. The more we energize our fears, the more susceptible we become to negative energies. As always, our fears and false beliefs create a self-fulfilling prophecy.

Wholeheartedly accepting the Tibetan's wisdom, I have been determined to work through this process around protection. My past lives were filled with issues of good vs. evil. To trust that I will be safe in the physical world and the astral energies surrounding it is a continuing challenge.

The process of opening my channel required diligence in removing false beliefs around the dangers of the dark force: possession, loss of control, and violation. My soul lesson in this lifetime is to learn trust. Working as a channel has been an excellent opportunity, however painful, to work on this.

I had been practicing channeling for five months, removing false beliefs, clearing out my heart chakra, establishing a new (in this lifetime) conscious relationship with Djwhal Khul and meeting with a support group of close friends to keep me from sliding off the "deep end" during this expansion process. To receive input on my readiness to give channeled readings professionally, I decided to see a well-recommended psychic in Newburyport. The psychic told me I was not yet ready to give readings because I needed to deal with the issue of protection. She insisted that I contract and tighten up my chakras like "little rose buds" to prevent the dark force from attacking me, emphasizing that this was especially important when I was in motion, as in walking or driving. She added that this protection was also necessary while sleeping. In short, it seemed there was no safe time to be relaxed and fully open. Constant vigilance was required to maintain protection.

I was deeply churned up inside as I left our session. The psychic's advice was the exact opposite of the Tibetan's perspective. Yet, she was a successful psychic with twenty years of experience. I was simply an innocent novice in the world of "working with the invisibles."

The psychic managed to push every karmic fear button I carried stemming from the false beliefs: "To be open is to let self be extremely vulnerable to attack. If I open to the Tibetan's energy I will be contaminated and possessed by dark forces. I have no control over my psychic body when I am open. It is not safe to trust anyone, even the Masters." What a challenge it was to receive such a wonderful invitation to channel an Ascended Master, such an honor. This honor would force me to eventually face all my inner demons.

For two weeks I struggled with fears and confusions, torn between following her "expert" advice or opening to trust with Djwhal Khul. Finally, exhausted from the endless inner turmoil, I surrendered to my destiny with the Tibetan. I knew in my heart that I had to learn to trust him. Trusting Djwhal Khul would enable me to trust my Higher Self and finally complete the alignment process.

I also recognized an agreement, made prior to this incarnation, to serve the Masters as efficiently and productively as possible. This agreement felt like a subtle but persistent "nudging" in my heart, almost a longing to complete something begun lifetimes ago. To postpone our work together would allow fear and illusion to stifle my soul's progress. I had to face it.

Dismissing the psychic's warnings, I decided I was indeed ready to give readings and carry the torch wherever it led. In spite of feeling stripped of my defenses there was no turning back. I had given my commitment to Djwhal Khul in our reading. My karmic bridges were burned. There was no choice but to move forward with our work. The collaboration with the Tibetan would teach me about my own internal darkness and demons. This endeavor would eventually allow me to "empty my vessel" in order to meet Djwhal Khul's energy with assurance, strength and inner peace. Most of all, I had to learn to TRUST!

Distrust

I continue to be astounded by the impact the emotional body has on the physical body. The body isn't solid but permeable, easy to fall prey to the potency of the emotional plane like a sponge absorbing water, saturated and dripping out the excesses of the psyche.

My emotional body is filled with pockets of distrust, deep caverns in need of root canal work. Is it the distrust that eats away at the fabric of my psyche like acid? These areas of distrust strip the richness from my emotional body just as acid rain browns and dwarfs the trees, leaving them lifeless and barren.

What are the effects of distrust, lack of openness, on my physical body? How do I protect the physical body from these deep acid pockets in my emotional body? I don't want that acid to touch my flesh.

The rest of my emotional body is beginning to heal, taking on the fresh pinkness of a newborn baby's trust of the universe—rose quartz pinkness revealing the power of regeneration. If my emotional body can heal so can the woods, rivers, and oceans of our beloved earth.

However, the more the radiance emerges in my emotional body, the more painful the acid pockets of distrust become, revealing deep dark veins of stagnant energy dwelling within bank accounts of hurt, disappointment, rage, and vengefulness sprouting from soils of perceived betrayal from Source, from those higher initiates who **should** have known, who should have warned me. Are these acid pockets ever refueling themselves like black spring water giving rise to new levels of distrust? This keeps my emotional body well pock-marked with scars of sorrow and determination not to be fooled again.

Yet I hear the Tibetan's response, "*It is time to dare to trust again. Without the fresh innocence resurrected from the smoldering ashes of wisdom, self cannot reclaim the magical child - the child who spontaneously opens her heart to creation.*" So attached am I to the swirling patterns of distrust—webbing and cocooning my emotional body—that I am profoundly reluctant to offer them up for transformation. At long last I must expose the purity within my emotional body to the bright, bright light of the Divine, truly knowing that rather than be burned I will be spun into ecstatic wonderment, allowing the true nature of my emotional body to take its place in my soul.

Moving into the Mystery

"How long can you sustain the not-knowing?" asked my mentor, Rich Borofsky, at his Cambridge office in 1983. I was eager to become a therapist—a good one. I had found a wonderful teacher with whom I studied intensively for two years. While I had confidently placed my apprenticeship in his care, I couldn't help but balk a little when he suggested that I take his four-month course on "Not-Knowing." I wondered how I could possibly sit through sixteen weeks of learning how to suspend my "knowing." Little did I realize at the time that those sixteen weeks would liberate my orientation to counseling work, channeling and daily life.

I had always relied heavily on a very active mental body, filled with information and theories that quickly produced powerful insights. My mentor asked me to suspend my "working hypothesis" when in session with a client. He insisted that I take the risk to simply stay in the mystery for as long as I could stand it rather than grabbing on to the known and perhaps prematurely calling it the truth. While this initially appeared to be an easy assignment, it proved to be far more difficult than I ever would have imagined.

THE WITCH AND THE TIBETAN: A LOVE STORY

As soon as I applied his teaching to my work, I began squirming in my therapist's chair within moments of attempting to sit in session in a state of not-knowing. It left a space for all of my insecurities and self-doubt to surface. My mental ego immediately attempted to regain control—grabbing onto any thought or idea that could give me something to hang onto in the great sea of mystery. This was an internal process that my client knew nothing about. Outwardly I appeared to be as competent and "knowledgeable" as ever. It would take years before I would be able to totally let go of knowing while in session. Eventually I learned to be able to say "I don't know." to whatever questions my clients tossed at me that left me blank. I realized that competence, intelligence, and authority are not based on how many truths or pieces of knowing one has accumulated. This allowed me to begin to experience the deep inner knowing that comes from fully embracing the mystery.

Opening to the not-knowing has been key to my evolution. After initially applying this process to my therapy work, my next challenge was to apply it to opening my channel. Attempting to get my ego out of the way in order to let in the Tibetan's vibration, I had to empty my mind and release all expectations of what would happen. Once again I found myself flailing around in the sea of Great Mystery. I had to practice sitting in the void and waiting, suspending all notions of what Djwhal Khul's energy would feel like and what he would say. Every time that I would try to fill up the not-knowing with familiar ideas, my channel would contract, and I could feel Djwhal Khul's vibration begin to fade like a radio station that gets crackly in the car as you drive away from receiving range. With my channeling it wasn't a case of spatial distance that caused the interference but rather my attachment to knowing. I had to learn to allow myself to be surprised at the words that came out of my mouth. Surrendering to the unknown placed me squarely in the mystery, the most fertile place in the universe.

After years of channeling, I have grown quite comfortable with the experience of suspending knowledge. Even jumping off a high diving board blindfolded gets easier if you do it enough. Now my cutting edge challenge involves applying the mystery to my everyday life. One would think that after all of these years of opening to the mystery that the application of that openness to my daily experience would be no problem. Wrong! It was one thing to suspend my knowing for an hour in session or when channeling, but quite another to attempt to suspend it as a way of life. It seems that the need "to know" is hard wired into my energetic field. Do I have to melt down the entire computer system called my mental body in order to step into the not-knowing just as one steps into a deep dark pond at midnight on a new moon?

How many of us say to ourselves upon awakening in the morning, "I have no clue what today is going to bring me?" It seems instead that we usually lunge for our daily calendar or appointment book to refresh our knowing of an already planned-out reality, usually orchestrated down to the very last minute of our precious sixteen waking hours. The busier we get, consumed by the known demands upon us, the farther we drift from the sea of mystery that laps at the edges of our consciousness. As time goes by the idea of opening to the unknown becomes more and more frightening. Our threatened ego's quiver at the prospect of being suspended on the edge of the precipice without sight, sound, touch or smell. Familiar reference points are dissolved by the unknowable, leaving us feeling very vulnerable, unprepared, defenseless, disoriented and strangely open.

"What is going to happen now?" These words have become my mantra. Repeatedly I find myself saying it, sometimes even out loud. Although I have consciously committed to opening to the mystery, I still resist it at every turn. My desire to know gnaws at me like the deep hunger that sets in after three days of fasting. Keeping my mind from "filling in the blanks" is like keeping an appetite-driven teenager from the refrigerator door. While my mind understands that we never really know what is going to happen from moment to moment, I still prefer the illusion that lulls me into the comfort of thinking that I have it all figured out.

The Tibetan responds to my wrestling match with the Great Uncertainty with a twinkle in his eyes. In my attempt to stretch into the unknowable, he showers me with love, encouraging my efforts, cheering me on from the sidelines but not interfering with this necessary next step that I can only make on my own. He exclaims:

The Mystery is the land of Great Secrets—cosmic puzzle pieces fitting together into the great Matrix that is Creation. To open to the mystery is to have a glimpse at the wonder that is held in the Unknowable. For it is in this Unknowable that all possibilities are held—unformed potentialities of the Divine. When students allow themselves to sit within the mystery, without struggle or defiance, a profound feeling of inner peace emerges. To know nothing is to experience everything.

The universe expresses itself through riddles that carry the Great Mystery like emissaries of the twilight dimension. It is in this dimension, where light merges into dark, that the mystery anchors itself into the human experience. At this profound point of contact with life-not-yet-manifest humankind is transfixed, momentarily released from the web of illusion emerging through the past which projects itself as the known.

The mystery is the gateway to go beyond time and space. It ushers in the eternal. As the student touches the mysterious, all is possible.

The unknowable rests the mind from its never ceasing efforts to control life. To bathe within the mystery is to cleanse the soul from the burden of expectations. The mystery is the underpinning of all realities, either on the earth plane or off. To work with the mystery gives the student great gifts of expansion, depth, connectedness, universality, and magic.

Do not fear the mystery. It is the safest place around! Not only can't it hurt you, but rather it heals for in the not-knowing one reaches into the Netherlands of the Great Being called Source and draws from it all that is needed.

Learn to breathe in the mystery as it is carried on the air currents. As the student takes in the unknown with every inhalation, the cellular memory is activated to a time when the mystery was experienced as the Voice of Great Guidance. There are no disappointments in the mystery—no losses—no failures. There is only the vast fruitfulness of unformed potentiality.

Magnificence is in the void. Let the mystery creep into your soul and guide it forth as it cultivates true faith in the knowing that it is impossible to go off-course. The mystery wraps itself around all beauty and gives the unfathomable nature to the exquisite creation of Source's imagination. Drink it in. Celebrate it. Play with it. It enables humankind to release all attachments. There is no danger in the unknown, only the unformed Love that surrounds us all.

As I listen to the Tibetan, his teachings feel like an invocation of the Great Mystery that is my life. I am awed by this opportunity to enter the Domain of the Unknown and grateful to sit at the edge of this vast precipice as I sing the song of my soul into the ethos of limitlessness not yet touched.

Dreams: The Gateway to the Unconscious

I don't know what I would do without my dreams! They map my inner world, buffering me from the ever-present chaos looming in my unconscious. Through their images I make contact with the myriad of sub-personalities within. Dreams come bearing messages, however obscure, teasing my knowing out into the daylight of waking consciousness. They evoke the detective within me as I hunt for clues in their maze of incongruity and ridiculousness.

These clues, disguised as pointless stories and colliding images capturing only the absurd, nonsensical, random loose ends of my inner life, reveal the psyche's wisdom as it valiantly pulls out all the stops to get my attention! It knows what is going on with me at deeper levels even if I don't. My responsibility is to learn how to listen to my psyche and make sense of its unique language. The dream language of images and symbols is both mysterious and obvious. Sometimes our dreams are downright corny as our psyche works to show us the blind spots right under our nose.

It is fascinating how Source created such a complex creature when It created humankind. I have wondered why Source split our psychic structure in two parts—one to be so easily experienced at a conscious level and the other to be forever just out of reach in the deep waters of the unconscious. It seems like "mission impossible" that we have to integrate our unconscious into our consciousness in order to be fully aligned. How can we integrate something that is specifically designed to be unknowable? Why didn't Source simply allow us to have full conscious reign over the unconscious?

The Tibetan is often referred to among the Great White (Light) Brotherhood (the group of enlightened Masters working with the earth plane) as the Great Psychologist. He and I share a fascination for the workings of the human psyche. He reminds me that if we had full conscious access to the unconscious terrain, our egos would have a field day censoring our inner life. Any "unacceptable" aspects of self that our egos might judge and disown would be cut off from our psychic juice and allowed to wither away. These aspects of self are therefore banished to a distant corner of our psyche (the shadow) where all the "undesirables" are corralled off in order not to contaminate the "righteousness" of the rest of our being.

So our shadow must live, unthreatened by our conscious belief systems, far below our waking knowing in the underbelly of our being.

In this world of shadow land our unconscious fosters the growth and development of all aspects of self not yet acceptable to our current identity. If we were to have full exposure to this underworld reality, we might be thrown off balance. No one is eager to claim his or her darkness and wear it like a badge. So we keep it neatly tucked away from the boundaries of our conscious self.

However, as night falls (even our persistent egos need rest) then it is the witching hour. This is the hour when our censors punch out on their time clock as they leave their days work, all defenses checked and working—ego in tact. Then the hobgoblins from the dark shadows within start to shout out - to voice their concerns—to make noise—to move about. Now it is their time for full expression as they bring forth our soul through shadow. If we are "lucky," we are completely unconscious of this activity. We are simply sleeping the night away, eager to return to morning's light, unthreatened and secure in our known self.

However, Source gave us one foolproof linkage point between the unconscious and the conscious—our dreams. Upon waking up to the rising sun we bring back with us evidence of our bizarre journey into shadow land. We bring a story, one that usually makes no sense upon initial recall.

If we are willing to lovingly hold that story almost like one would hold a vulnerable alien being in the palm of one's hand, we can learn to listen to this entity who speaks so strangely to us. The more we listen, the more we begin to understand dream language. While we may often recoil from their messages desperate to write them off as foolish nonsense, if we allow ourselves to digest what we are being shown, we are alchemized. Our conscious self finally embraces the unconscious. The Tibetan teaches:

> *The heart's capacity to love and accept human nature allows one to receive the full impact of the unconscious material as it pushes up into full awareness. If one can accept one's shadow,*

so richly expressed through dreams, one can accept the full human condition and all of the apparent aberrations of Source. As the student lovingly embraces this dark material, he/she realizes that what appears to be a distortion of one's divinity is actually a poetic, imagaic description of soul material that lands outside the confines of one's belief system.

In this terrain the soul is free to unleash its wildness, uncivilized or untamed by the expectations of the ego—rich in passion—in juice—in life force. Without this realm, conscious life would be a desert, dry and lifeless. It would reflect too much light, blinding the student into the illusion that light is all there is. The deep, dark waters that lubricate and cleanse the soul are essential to the Divine Feminine and must be accepted and embraced. In this embrace, the light and dark unite in mystical harmony.

Trying to remember dreams is like fishing with one's hands. Dreams are slippery, wet and illusive. They tease our consciousness as our logical mind tries to capture their stories in recognizable language and story line. Most of our dreams slip away like secret messengers, revealing the impossible line between the world of the awake and the world of the asleep. If we are lucky enough to catch a dream, we must immediately rush to save it in our dream journals, scraps of paper dedicated to honoring these fleeing moments of contacting the unknowable within.

When we wait too long the dream may vanish, leaving us with a vague sensation that we dreamt something but can't quite put our finger on it. Ironically, if we decide to ignore our dream, the dream often continues to swim along side of our waking consciousness, vague and blurry but annoying us with a distinct feeling that there is something there that needs our attention. It is the same annoying feeling when we stop mid-sentence, having just forgotten our thought. Oh, how we hunger for integration at that point, for just a momentary opportunity to connect the dots within our soul and see the big picture as it is reflected through our underground friends—the characters that live in our dream world.

I first began to take my dreams seriously when I was thirty-nine years old. I was entering my mid-life crisis, deep rumblings beginning to resound in my soul. I had been channeling the Tibetan for three years. This period had been one of light, light and light. When we open our channels we are often infused with heightened light vibrations as we access realms beyond the earth plane. These realms are etheric in nature—lighter, finer, and more rarefied in frequencies. While this is initially experienced as highly pleasing, expanding and uplifting, eventually there may be a counter-reaction in the psyche.

As I was bathing myself in the heightened light factor known as Djwhal Khul, this higher vibratory rate was flushing out dormant shadows in my soul. Consciously I was focusing on spirit, love, compassion and other "spiritually correct" qualities while unconsciously my dark side was beginning to stir with a vengeance! I was able to keep a clean separation between these two worlds for three years. Then my unconscious broke loose. I could no longer resist the internal pressure from my own shadow.

My dreams were filled with dark, frightening images. These images pushed up into my mind screen even when I was only momentarily closing my eyes. I felt barred from the angelic realm as the forces in my underworld caught my soul and began to tug it down, down, down. Night after night I was tormented by fearful images both personal and collective. Several months of nightly terror through a repeating nightmare of being pursued by Nazi's drove me into Jungian dream analysis. I wanted to get away from these "bad guys" and return to my light-filled "high-level" reality. However, these "bad guys" would not loosen their grip. Now that they had my full attention they weren't going to let go. I began to wonder what was wrong with me. Was I being possessed by the dark force in retaliation for all the light work I was doing?

THE WITCH AND THE TIBETAN: A LOVE STORY

Within the first month of dream analysis these nightmares receded. Finally psyche had both my attention and commitment to exploring my shadow lands. I soon realized that it wasn't the dark force taking over my being but rather my own unique underworld drama trying to participate in my transformational process. Light magnetizes dark. It was time for me to dig into my dream life and bring the hidden aspects of myself into full consciousness. I was amazed at their potency. Within each dream were characters, real beings, who carried strong emotional charges. These characters were highly differentiated, specifically created to carry energies that my soul had cast off earlier in this lifetime or perhaps in past lives.

With my channel opened and higher self accessed it was time to tie in all the old threads, leaving no stone unturned in my efforts toward complete wholeness. Initially I felt embarrassed and exposed by these dark dream beings. They reflected parts of me that my ego refused to accept. I teased myself that perhaps these were someone else's dreams, surely not mine!

With the encouragement of my analyst I began to claim these aspects of my soul, accepting each character as myself. My curiosity and flair for drama moved me into their reality, wondering what their message or teaching might be. As I embraced each one, they gifted me with heightened energy that had been bottled up in the dark recesses of the basement within my soul. As I allowed the dream characters full expression, I realized that there was nothing wrong with any of them.

I learned to appreciate their divinity as much as I appreciate the divinity within a bouquet of flowers. Allowing my underworld sub personalities to have an impact on me, I saw them as raw gems waiting to be polished. Polishing them with love and acceptance, I began to embrace this bushel basket of jewels within my psyche. Soon I began to hunger for my dreams, eager to see what gifts I could pull up from the rich, dark fertile lands of my unconscious.

So, daily I eagerly awake, dream journal close at hand, hoping each morning I will be given another story revealing the next layer of my soul. Deeper and deeper I go in this quest for soul-knowledge. Working consciously with my dreams creates a feeling of connection and integration. I no longer fear the monsters deep within my psyche. I welcome and celebrate my internal mystery through the stories told by my psyche's brilliance.

Dreams guide me into the most profound levels of my passion. No longer do I fear being blinded by the light. With my awareness firmly anchored and rooted in the soil of my uncensored self, I am free to stretch out into greater and greater realms of light. Spinning stories of the evolving self and releasing our fears, dreams guide us into our deepest truth. Dreams are the rainbow bridge between the known and the mystery—moving us into the land where soul and spirit become one.

The Descent Experience

"It's the small, small things in life that create the descent experience." Cutting edge Jungian pioneer James Hillman spoke these words in a lecture that I attended on a balmy summer night in Cambridge in 1989. At the time I delighted in Hillman's brilliance and humor but didn't particularly relate to what he was saying. I was still holding the belief that the descent experience was a huge ordeal catalyzed by trauma, loss, existential crisis, etc. I referenced it as an overall spiritual crisis that might occur in a midlife shock, job loss, financial disaster, divorce or death. I couldn't imagine how an insignificant, petty moment could really bring us down into the underworld. I believed the energy required to pull us into the vortex ushering us into Pluto's underground shadowy realm would have to be very powerfully triggered.

I have had many "opportunities" to apply Hillman's teachings to my own experience. Perhaps the big events in our lives blatantly vivify the descent experience so boldly that we can't ignore it. These overt descent experiences allow us to know what it is really like to go down into our inner basement. However, we don't need a major crisis to experience a descent. On a daily basis we can watch our psyche take the elevator up and down as we fluctuate between ascending and descending.

What is it that makes our mood positive? What is it that robs us of that positivity in a flash? Just as Persephone in Greek mythology goes merrily picking wildflowers in a meadow, carefree and innocent, we too may be going about our daily business without a care in the world. Persephone is suddenly taken down by Hades, the Lord of the Underworld. He grabs her by the foot before she has a moment to realize what has happened. She is taken down, down, down with her little bouquet of flowers tossed aside. Her reality changes instantly from one of light to one of dark.

We all have a Persephone inside of us. It is that part that expresses a fresh positivity, trusting, perhaps oblivious to the "underbelly" of reality. From Persephone's perspective life is like a meadowland, flower-filled and gloriously colorful. We expect to be in a good mood all day long. There are no overt crises going on, no demons after us. But all of a sudden, something very small and insignificant can yank us out of our bliss-filled song into the pits of despair. How many of us have said, "I was having a good day until I couldn't get the ingredients I needed to make that special dish for company, or when I made myself late for work in order to pick up coffee only to spill it on my lap in the car, or when I called the phone company and they put me on hold for twenty minutes, or I put on my favorite outfit, looked in the mirror and I looked horrible, or some guy yelled at me from his car because I forgot to put my turn signal on... There are endless small events, inconsequential scenarios that have the power to ruin our day. Why?

The Tibetan jumps in to answer my question. I am continually amazed at how ever-present he is when I have a question. He teaches:

Humankind must learn there is no real difference between ascending and descending. When the student is able to be non-

attached to the direction that their psyche takes them, they are free to experience their divinity in all of its expressions. A pathway is established between the "higher" aspect of self and the "lower aspects of self." As the student moves fluidly back and forth between both, he/she begins to understand and accept Source's creative initiative in establishing the earth plane.

To incarnate on the earth plane requires a "descent" into form from the higher etheric realms. The soul goes from the rarefied atmosphere of pure spirit into the density of physicality within the human condition. Often humankind views this as a punishment as if Source were angry at or displeased with them and therefore banished them to a lower realm.

The quest is to realize Source's exquisite light factor as it is amplified through form and density. The earth plane does not diminish spirit. Rather it enhances and celebrates it. The physical dimension focuses the spaciousness of light into a crystallized state that vivifies Cosmic Love. While this may appear far-fetched to most of humanity that experiences earthly life as heavy drudgery, from where the Masters and Angels dwell the earth appears as a magnificent star of brilliant light emanating oceanic waves of love. It is a great opportunity to incarnate into the wondrous human condition. The descent therefore becomes a gift to the soul.

Listening to Djwhal Khul makes me wonder why we dread our descent experiences. The small things in life offer us daily, if not hourly, opportunities to fall deeply into our selves. At a subliminal level we may be negatively remembering our soul's descent experience of incarnating on earth from the heavenly realms. Perhaps if we can accept the idea that a descent is not a bad thing but rather an opportunity to enrich our self-awareness, then we would gladly allow Pluto to transmute our Persephone innocence into deepened wisdom.

Djwhal Khul teaches that the descent is an experience of gliding down Source's "Ladder of Love." If we don't resist it, it is relatively painless and highly informative. If we do resist it, we suffer unnecessarily. Most of us, including myself, instantly resist our descent as it begins to draw us downward. My little ego clings to anything to keep me from taking the "great fall." The resistance starts with fear, moves into desperation and ends in futility. It is no wonder I conclude that it can ruin my good day! Ironically, it is only my fearful response that turns the descent into a nightmare.

Djwhal Khul reminds me that mastering the earth plane involves our willingness to flow up and down at random. If we can do that, we can just as easily ascend—bring up our vibratory rate, as descend. Our eventual non-attachment, or fearlessness of this process, allows us to joyfully move through the different striations of density from the highest angelic realms and down to the deepest caverns within our soul and back up to the cosmic rooftops without flinching. Our souls' become acrobatic as they dance along the vertical axis. If we go beyond our fear of the descent, then we can move ever more fully into our truth. The deeper we can dive, the higher we can fly. Eventually we realize that the "small, small things" that create the descent experience are emissaries of light—gifts of travel—keeping us fluid, adaptable, resilient, elastic and ever so wise! They can't ruin our day or our mood. Rather, they bring us dimension and the memory of how we got here.

I'm a Witch!

It was an enjoyable shock when at forty-one years old I realized I was a witch. The word "witch" gives me great comfort. It seems to cut through all the spiritual expectations that burden my psyche.

The witch has the freedom to play with magic and be outrageously wild. She is totally sexual. Her eyes twinkle as they reflect her vast appreciation of the absurd. The witch boldly challenges and invokes the Forces. She dares to hold the poles in their full fury, dark as well as light. Her "ugliness" is as sacred to her as her beauty. Imperfection of the physical form, such as her crooked teeth, heightens her primordial wildness. She often forgets the difference between being human and being animal. To be devoured psychically by her beloved totem animal—wolves—is a joyous tumble into her blessed underworld.

As a witch I forget the spiritual pain of my impurity and imperfection. All that matters is the magic. I am caught in a passionate embrace with the Earth.

I am a child of magic, not of spirit. Perhaps there is no difference. My childhood was immersed in solitary wandering through the dimensions of magic, masked as fantasy. Mother Earth wrapped her arms around me with the help of great oak and maple trees. This was my nurturance and sustenance, allowing me to trust the Divine Mother.

The magic initially expressed itself through sound—the subtle whisperings of the wind and deep, tonal messages emanating from the trunks of old gnarled trees. A great comfort would seep up my spine as I lay on the dirt. These were my roots—solid—of the earth— immersed in natural magic—always with those invisible arms encircling and holding me through my fears and isolation.

In the throes of a mid-life crisis at age forty I took a two-year break from channeling the Tibetan. Curious about earth magic, I apprenticed to a wonderful old crone to learn about the forces of nature. Through her mentorship memories of my childhood "knowing" of the earth magic surfaced. She also taught me numerology and the tarot, important tools for any skilled witch.

During that time I had a dream of being immersed in orange fire burning from the trees. The blue spiritual glow I associated with the Tibetan appeared to have been replaced as the earth put her magical claim to my soul, the way any protective mother would do if she sees her child wander off. The large boulders peppering the woods of Gloucester, Massachusetts reminded me of an ancient commitment I had made to the earth's soul. I experienced a sexual communion with these stones that caused me to wonder if a man could ever completely fulfill me again.

At times the intensity of my involvement with this realm scared me. Would the potency of these forces take me away from a normal life? How could I reconcile the realm of earth magic with the rarefied realm of the Masters? I decided that if I had to choose, I would choose the earth realm where my roots first took hold in this lifetime, and probably many others.

Lifetimes of martyrdom and self-sacrifice made me question the apparent demanding nature of the spiritual plane. Why not dive deeply into the lap of Mother Earth. Her constancy, simplicity, substance, depth and richness, not to mention her wild magic, eased the pain in my soul.

And yet, I knew in my heart that ultimately there is no separation between Earth's magic and the high refinement of the spiritual plane. I realized that I was suffering from lifetimes of judgment from the *human* representatives of spirit, priests, as they had condemned my magical ways. Yet, why would the Tibetan pick a "wicked wild witch" to assist him in bringing forth the Teachings? Perhaps this is the lifetime of integration. Heaven and Earth become one.

Past Life as a Witch

Entering the third millennium, we are told that the planetary poles may be shifting their axis. Djwhal Khul teaches that we are moving from a third dimensional reality into the fifth dimension which exists beyond the plane of duality. This involves a process of intensification of the polarities as they are propelled into an extreme state. They appear to be going in opposing directions but are actually coming around full circle to meet each other. This union of the opposites alchemizes our current bifurcated plane into the fifth dimensional state of oneness.

This intensification of the duality is often experienced in radical swings as we seesaw between feelings of ecstasy and depression. The pathological clinical term for this is manic-depressive. While the accelerating energies produce symptoms that appear to be a reflection of imbalance, they are simply a necessary by-product of our healthy spiritual emergence.

We are exploring all the ramifications inherent in our plane of duality. Some days we are positive—active, energetic, inspired, initiating, excited. Other days we are negative—passive, tired, confused, ineffective, discouraged. Humanity has always toggled between the poles. However, today's heightened energetics send us rapidly swinging back and forth, often many times during the day. It feels like a roller-coaster ride that doesn't end.

In reaction to this intensification of the poles, many of us are using chemical means such as anti-depressants to smooth out our emotional bodies in order to "stabilize" ourselves. However appropriate this treatment may be in extreme situations inevitably we have to confront the way in which we each explore and express the experience of duality through our unique focus. It is a grand process of integration.

According to the Tibetan, we are on a "crash course" in mastering the earth plane. We are challenged to move through all aspects of the human condition in its dual focus. Fully exploring ourselves through all our dark and light levels frees us up to move into our mastery.

All of our karmic issues regarding the light and dark force, as well as our issues about duality, are flushed up as part of our mastery process. There is a tendency to attach to the "positive" experiences of our divinity: joy, excitement, happiness, contentment, optimism, creativity, etc. When the impact of our "negative" aspects present themselves: fear, disappointments, anger, depression, confusion, rage, disorientation, loss, etc., we try to push it away. These emotional and mental states are judged as unworthy of our ultimate divinity.

Djwhal Khul teaches:

> *Mastery involves perceiving and appreciating divinity in all aspects of the duality. Humankind must welcome all expressions of the poles in order to evolve beyond them. Welcoming the duality means learning from it, allowing it to have a strong impact. Surrender to the negativity and let it bring wisdom and depth. Bask in the positive without becoming attached. Know that the student will continue to swing from one state to its opposite until he/she is united in an experience of Oneness. When the student is firmly anchored in the Oneness, the polar flows move unimpeded, shaping and strengthening one's being.*
>
> *Most students find fault in Source's decision to create duality. Rather than seeing the richness in it, humankind perceives it as a punishment. Moving from happiness to unhappiness is like being given toys to play with and then having them heartlessly taken away. Until the students are ready to create universes of their own, perhaps they need to suspend their judgments around this design of bifurcation and learn from the magnificence of Source's creation.*

This brings me to an exploration of my issues with duality. For many lifetimes I have struggled with the concept of evil. Many religions teach of evil, or of a fallen angel, that represents a distortion of the light. These demonic forces are seen to be the anti-Christ, the opposite of Source's Being. Evil, the extreme of the negative, is an entity fueled by lovelessness.

In the middle of the night, when I sometimes awaken to a free-floating sense of anxiety, I wonder just how present the dark forces are in my spiritual life. My own shadow hovers around, encircling me in doubt and fear. At these times I feel particularly vulnerable to the demons within my soul's history and to the collective demons energized through our human condition. I call out for reassurance from the Tibetan that I am safely anchored in the light. He says that I am, but that I must accept the full range of the duality within myself. He reminds me that I see my own darkness as separate from my spiritual self and challenges me to allow the darkness to have as great an impact on my soul as the light.

The Tibetan instructs: *"Break all attachments to your preconceptions about spirituality. Let the entire universe reside within you. Accept the earth plane as a gift from Source. Welcome the light and the dark as they dance together within your soul."*

I am temporarily quieted by Djwhal Khul's teachings, although it is still confusing to try to perceive the Divine in the despair, fear and rage of humankind. That seems to be a tall order for any student! It brings me back to a past life regression that I experienced during my training in April 1991 with Roger Woolger, a Jungian analyst specializing in past life regressions and author of *Other Lives, Other Selves*.

This lifetime took place during the early days of the Great Inquisition. I was trained as a witch, carrying my family's lineage in our community. We lived in a large, bustling village in Europe. A woman in my late twenties, I was respected by the community and offered healing to all in need. Having trained in the herbal arts, I knew how to create potent potions that could rebalance the physical, emotional and mental body. I was confident in my skills and in the genetic make-up that allowed me this position of honor in our hamlet. While aware that the Inquisition was dangerously gathering more momentum, I felt protected by the village and their loyalty to the old wise ways.

I was deeply in love with my partner, a young wizard who was also schooled in Merlin's magic. He was from a neighboring village. We had met at a pagan festival honoring the Great Mother. He seemed to have all that I needed in a mate—handsome, sensitive, strong, intelligent, loving and very passionate about the alchemical practices. However, he was younger than I by six years, and still filled with innocence. I resolved to teach him all that I knew in order to enhance our magical connection. We performed many rites and rituals together, calling the great Forces to us under the light of the full moon. We invoked these Forces in our sexual embrace and heightened the impact of our occultism.

One cold, gray November afternoon he came to me with his usual big smile. When I looked into his eyes I sensed that something was wrong. There was a disturbance there that I had not previously seen. Even though he was smiling, I knew that his soul was not. It seemed as if something negative had gotten inside of him even though my initial impressions weren't definite.

Over the following three weeks he became increasingly agitated, short-tempered and gloomy. From my training I recognized that somehow the dark force had internally grabbed him. Although I had taught him the practice of protecting the sacred space created when we opened the magical circle, I was concerned that he had not closed his energetic field carefully enough after our rituals were finished. In his youthful impulsiveness he had moved too quickly into his role as male witch, wanting to keep up with my level of expertise.

I knew painfully well what happens when we open prematurely, leaving ourselves prey to the invisible dark force. It is only too happy to capture the open heart of the innocent. The dark force looks for as many channels for its work as does the light force. Three months passed as I watch my lover grow darker and darker. Soon he was unable to look me directly in the eye. His averted gaze was smoldering with a resentment and disorder that he could not control. I fought to exorcise these negative elements but they were well anchored in the fissures of his auric (energetic) body.

My heart broke as I realized that I did not have the power or the knowing to save my beloved from the clutches of this black force. Our hearts were still one, but his eyes fell upon me as it from a great distance. Days went by as he slipped further and further away. Weakened by despair, I did not dare to penetrate his energetic field with my will fearing that I too would be overtaken by the same dark currents running wild within his soul.

Meanwhile, as I struggled with my broken heart, a sickness was beginning to devastate our village. It was a flu-like plague that was particularly deadly to newborns. Our babies were dying at an alarming rate. While I was able to prescribe effective herbs for the adults' full recovery, I knew of no remedy that could save the infants. Mothers looked at me pleadingly, imploring me to somehow find an answer to this nightmare. Every infant death seared into my soul. "I failed them." Confused, overwhelmed, frightened and helpless I watched the babies slip away. I saw the anger and disappointment in their parents as they questioned my abilities.

The elders understood that there are times when the great Goddess takes her children for no apparent reason. They urged me to surrender to Her, to cleanse myself of guilt and responsibility, and perhaps go into retreat for a month to renew my strength and vision. In spite of their kind counsel, deep inside I felt that there was no one to turn to. It seemed as if the dark force had won its battle against the light.

My lover was completely lost as the darkness enveloped his soul. My service had failed as I watched our precious young being devoured by a dark and mysterious sickness. I turned against myself, feeling that I somehow had caused all of this. It seemed that everything I touched became contaminated. I wondered if there was an evil place within my soul that was over-taking my life. While I had worked hard to be worthy of my position as healer, perhaps the required initiations of purification were not extensive enough. I could not hear the supportive words of the elders. The torment of my beloved seemed to be yet another reminder that I was unclean in spirit.

Finally, before the sun rose on a cold mid-December day, I slipped out of the village unnoticed. Although my stomach was churning in fear, my will drove my feet forward. I walked several miles to the nearby city and went directly to the Inquisition headquarters. The guards looked at me curiously, wondering why I would freely enter this dreaded domain. I boldly turned myself in, stating that I was a witch practicing sacred arts. One of the guards, disgustingly unclean, responded with a vicious gleam in his eyes. "This is the way I like it—nice and easy!" He roughly grabbed my wrists and dragged me down the stairs to the dungeon, pushing me onto the frigid stone floor. In the dark I waited, alone with my thoughts of failure and impurity: "I deserve to be punished. I need absolute purification. I am nothing. The dark force is eating me alive. I must burn it out of my soul."

Days passed, how many I don't know. Weak from starvation, isolation and grief, I lay on the cold damp floor, listening to the sounds of rats hovering close by. Suddenly bright light shot through the room as the door opened and the same two guards dragged me out into the bright frosty winter afternoon. Hundreds of people were gathered around the burning post awaiting my agony. Their faces were a blur as they shouted insults and threw rotten garbage at me.

None of this mattered. All that I cared about was my intense need to be cleansed, to let the fire burn away my darkness, contamination, failure and guilt. Bordering on insanity, I was almost giddy with anticipation as the smoke began to encircle me. The flames started to consume the bottom of my feet as red-hot agony shot through my entire body. I released only one scream, unable to control my body's reaction to this torture. The scream pulled me right out of my body as my heart stopped, overcome by the shock and pain.

After leaving my body, I traveled very quickly to the spirit plane, not lingering to look down upon the dreadful scene of my last moment in that lifetime. I called the Tibetan to me, asking for guidance. What had I done that was so wrong to have caused so much hurt? "Teach me about the dark force," I pleaded.

Djwhal Khul stayed present with me as I wailed. Then he began to teach: *"The dark aspect of Source, the void, is no worse that Its light aspect. To pit self against either pole is to create inner conflict and block the integration process."* Illustrating his point, Djwhal Khul dramatically displayed himself in his dark aspect. I could barely look at him, so afraid that I would lose my long-term trust in my beloved master if I could not reference him as only light. His dark aspect appeared powerful, intense, mysterious and large. However, *it did not appear evil.* It was neutral energy with an absence of light. I bowed to him, awed by Source's expression of Itself devoid of illumination. I realized the vastness of Djwhal Khul's soul, his magnitude, whether dark or light. My respect was unbounded.

I understood that it was no longer necessary to fight the dark force. I would stop judging the tragedies of life as a reflection of my own unworthiness. I would learn to accept the duality and use both forces as opportunities for wholeness and enlightenment.

I realized that it was humankind's fear and illusion that filled the darkness, the Great Void, with images of evil. I would not participate in those collective false beliefs again. I became clear that my obsession with being pure enough to serve was as distorted as the Inquisition's obsession with routing out aspects of humanity they considered unworthy of God.

As a result of this awareness I knew that my wizard lover's soul would eventually heal from the dark "possession" as he resolved his confusion about the apparent split in our human condition. The Tibetan flowed effortlessly from his dark to his light image, unattached to either reflection. From his perception on the etheric plane duality is simply part of the Cosmic game called evolution, an opportunity to reflect through opposition one's true essence. I will never forget Djwhal Khul's mysteriousness, his dark magnitude and how it honors the Great Void within all of us.

Relationships with Invisible Beings

For many years I was uneasy and anxious about having relationships with non-physical beings, fearing it was inappropriate to spend too much of my time with them. A stern inner critic admonished me for not focusing more on the immediate physical plane with its incarnate beings. Struggling with myself around this issue reflected the struggle one wrestles with when having an illicit affair that may be discovered.

Perhaps this has been an issue of loyalty. By nature a loyal person, I have often been confused as to where to direct my fidelity. Although instinctively other-worldly, I was concerned that I might be neglecting earthly homework if I didn't ground myself in strictly earth-plane relationships. My fear declared I was escaping or using my relationship with spirit as a crutch. In addition, I also feared abusing the power available to me through spirit, especially in alignment with the Tibetan's force.

When others exclaimed how fortunate I was to have this "gift," inwardly I shrank from the complement, feeling guilty for using this gift to my own advantage. Was I exploiting my relationship with the Tibetan in order to expand my therapy practice, receive attention and applause, or increased income? Exploring the motivation for channeling has left me confused, guilty, curious and frustrated. After all, it was Djwhal Khul who first invited me in, enticing me with gifts of increased awareness to enhance my soul work with clients. How could I resist that?

Perhaps my strict beliefs about sustaining only an earthbound reality was an attempt to balance out my strong magnetic pull to spirit. I frequently scolded myself for being too "out of body," using self-recrimination to prevent myself from leaving the earth altogether. My ambivalence toward being left on the planet after my mother's suicide made it all too easy to consider departing as well.

What is our mandate for growth and mastery of the physical plane? Do we have to put 100% focus on earthly matters in order to fulfill our curriculum here? How do we integrate spirit and matter if we are not allowed to be in communion with our spirit in equal amount with our humanness?

When I took my first break from channeling at age forty, I spent two years focusing fully on self—my physical body, emotional life, dream life, identity, ego and relationships with other people. I established a full sense of self, apparently "uncompromised" by the demands of the spirit plane, and reveling in my ego—in me, me, me! I was convinced I would never channel again.

Little did I realize I was AWOL from the Cosmic Army of Light. Once you are drafted, you are drafted! Nothing matters aside from the fulfillment of one's soul contract. Thank God I love the realm of the Masters. Their spiritual wealth makes this assignment so worthwhile.

I now understand how being a channel has been an opportunity to bring up past life memories of the dangers of mediumship and the responsibilities of the role of the oracle. Daily I have asked myself what is the impact of living the life of a psychic? How do I deal with the power that others project upon me? Can my personal energy sustain and ground the demands of interfacing with higher frequencies?

In spite of the confusion and uncertainty surrounding these issues, my greatest concern has centered on the issue of evil. In my darkest hour I have wondered if there was anything "evil" about my channeling. Was this entire "mission" a great delusion? Was the "devil" involved somehow? I now recognize that these were karmic issues flushed up from an ancient belief system established lifetimes ago.

Most of these concerns were unconscious until I had to make the decision to tell my brother, a born-again Jesus devotee, about my channeling work. I had hidden it from him for eight years. Finally at age forty-five, I was emotionally strong enough to fully reveal myself and my calling. I wrote him a confessional letter stating that I could no longer hide my truth. It was unbearable to continue living with the fraudulent feelings accompanying self-misrepresentation.

In response, he sent a book, *The Beautiful Side of Evil,* with the intent to "save" me from the devil. My brother was convinced I would be in severe danger if I were to continue channeling. Blinding rage flooded me as I realized the snap judgment he made without any inquiry into my spiritual experience as a channel. He was dismissing the loving and caring sister he had grown up with and replaced her with a wicked stereotype. The entire "fur ball" of past lives of persecution, torture, exile and death in the name of Jesus rushed forth registering themselves energetically in my physical body. So complete was my fury, I felt like breaking every bone in his body with my bare hands.

This was a subliminal recall of a lifetime where he had inflicted that identical physical torture on me during the Great Inquisition. My brother's determination to make my power and knowing "wrong" in the eyes of God was as great in 1994 as it was lifetimes ago. This process demonstrated the precise nature of karma. While we don't have to play out a tooth for a tooth, energetically we respond, detail for detail, in our impulse for energetic balance and cosmic justice. This painful and dramatic encounter with my brother resulted in his decision to sever me from his life, refusing all contact. The wall currently still stands, thick and impenetrable, unyielding to love and forgiveness.

Perhaps my lesson was to dismiss all past life fears related to being a medium, an oracle, who lets spirit speak through her. In contrast to the extreme of my brother's judgment, I realized how great is Source's unconditional compassion for all those who seek to know their divinity. Witnessing my brother's delusion, I was set free from my own. Past life fears around abuse of power and the dark vs. the light were flushed out and cleansed.

How could Source help but rejoice in our efforts to embody light, spirit, and wisdom? The question of "evil" still remains ponderous and indecipherable. Yet, I know that ultimately it is nothing but a great illusion, an inversion of our Truth. Slowly I heal as I release the daggers shot into my heart by my brother's venomous words. As the wounds soften, yielding to love, my heart recognizes more than ever vast reservoir of its potential for universal embrace, a true blending with the Divine.

Soul Emergence

My psyche reacts to the heightened energies impacting our beloved earth these days with a deep feeling of agitation. Responding to this uneasiness, Djwhal Khul says: *"Within self create a center pole around the heart chakra to serve as a pivotal point for the rest of self to flow around as it yields to the bombardment of the chaotic vibrations."* My soul is distressed by this because it deeply yearns for a life that is solid, stable and predictable, offering some semblance of security.

My daily rituals of chi gong and walking in the woods create an internal anchoring of my psyche's process. This routine grounds me deeply within and temporarily evokes the sweet stillness emanating from true inner peace. However, an inaccessible internal itch parallels this momentary bliss. This itch presents itself as restlessness, dissatisfaction, and unsettledness that leads to discouragement and fear of failure. This triggers a core fear of not completing my mission in this lifetime.

My sense of mission includes being a teacher/catalyst for others to open up to their enlightenment process. This reflects my belief that enlightenment, more than an illusory concept, is a conscious process that is truly attainable in this lifetime. I often deliver the message to my clients, "Go for it." However, when I feel the internal itch, I wonder if I have truly "gone for it" myself. At that point I assume there must be something more I need to do for others as well as myself. Yet, I don't know what that is.

The accelerated and intensified energy continually alters my perception of life's purpose robbing me of the luxury of pinning down future visions of fulfillment. Without these reference points for a projected future self I am left anxious and uncomfortable. How will I be able to manifest a larger expression of my potentiated self if I cannot settle into a plan permanent enough to commit to on a daily basis? How are we to master the art of manifestation when things are changing so rapidly that any attempt to anchor form requiring long term cultivation seems futile? Many students have directed these concerns to the Tibetan.

I work to resist the temptation to give up and simply allow myself to be bounced along these changing currents without direction. Our perception of time is speeding up. Simply accomplishing minimal daily chores requires all of our time, energy and focus. Time seems as if it is slipping through our hands leaving us feeling impotent, unable to control or direct our destiny.

Djwhal Khul offers motivation, *"Do not give up or allow feelings of discouragement to energize false beliefs indicating that this is yet another lifetime when you have failed or let others down. While these are indeed challenging times, as humankind reorients itself to a new energetic truth it has the opportunity to ride the acceleration that is speeding the clearing of individual and collective blockages. Self's negative thinking is a form of resistance to the new that is emerging."* When I ask him how to scratch the deep "itch" within, he smiles and teases, *"That 'itch' is your soul's emergence into full conscious embodiment within self."*

My ego reacts to that soul push, perceived as an undermining disturbance that makes me cranky, confused and uncomfortable. I have often fantasized that when finally making contact with my soul it would be a blissful, miraculous feeling of well being. I did not count on the agitation that comes before birth, the disturbance that creates the opening for one's greatness to emerge. It feels like something large is happening internally. Yet, I can't put my finger on it, unable to claim it with my ego. Feelings of loss of control surface as another larger reality appears to bombard my "small" world that is Moriah.

I experienced similar issues during the five months previous to consciously meeting the Tibetan in this life. During that time I sensed that something of great magnitude was going to occur within and tried to ready myself. However, the practice of touching the mystery is like trying to clean one's house blindfolded. I had no clue how to approach this preparation.

In retrospect I understand that my psyche and Higher Self knew exactly what was needed. They were subtly aligning with my personality so that when I was formally introduced to the Tibetan my conscious mind would be able to connect with the experience without going into destructive forms of denial. How challenging it is to prevent the repressive function in the psyche from pushing down all realities that don't fit into our ego's well-contained perspective.

My initial meeting with Djwhal Khul required total focus to sustain the encounter without running away from this event that would completely change my life. Oh how my ego wailed for control. As soon as I left the reading and was safely seated in my car driving home, my ego tried to invalidate the experience. But by then it was too late. I had made the leap into a greater commitment to the Divine Plan and was entrained by the Tibetan's heightened vibration.

All the ego ranting and raving would have little or no affect on the strange new hold this invisible teacher seemed to have placed on my soul from the moment we made contact. I later realized it was not that Djwhal Khul had a hold on my soul. Rather, my love for him and recognition of our soul's commitment to each other would take precedence in all areas of my journey from that instant on.

Djwhal Khul gently nudges me out of my reverie about our first encounter. He reminds me: *"Learn from the past. This cycle of restless preparation for the unknown is no different from what occurred in 1986. It is just happening at a deeper and more comprehensive level. The same negative and fearful thinking springing from the same false beliefs is happening now as it did years ago. Perhaps self might grow tired of, and even bored with, the self-negating scenarios created and recreated for lifetimes."*

I laugh, responding that these are indeed my favorite scenarios, and I will be hard put to let them go, even as a tradeoff for liberation! The Tibetan shakes his head, feigning bafflement at my stubborn human inclination to hold on for dear life to belief systems supporting nothing more than an empty shell of memories. He adds: *"The part of self that arrived at these mistaken conclusions lifetimes ago is now long since merged into a greater consciousness with no need whatsoever to energize old karmic assumptions that were only illusion anyway."*

THE WITCH AND THE TIBETAN: A LOVE STORY

It is the twinkle in his loving eyes and his unbelievable capacity for acceptance that melts my heart, helping me to open, just a little, to the possibility that all failures are behind me and that this great restlessness is the gift of my soul's fire. Yes, once again the Tibetan reminds me to celebrate this process with him as he turns on his heel and walks off to tend to other celestial matters leaving a trail of soft, magnetic light behind him.

THE ORACLE AND THE GOLDEN DISCS

Greece Trip

Turning forty-one years old brought a great hunger for a pilgrimage. I could feel my soul calling to me, but couldn't access a form for this calling. It felt like a vague pressure and deep yearning for something I couldn't pinpoint. I desperately needed a vision.

My pre-midlife self was slipping away as I began to contemplate my magnitude. What would be the most expansive way to express my soul? What was my destiny? Who was I becoming?

The internal pressure increased as I began to look through catalogues offering journeys for the soul. I knew this wasn't simply a matter of traveling somewhere far away in order to experience a larger perspective. In order to access a vision of my soul's evolutionary pathway I needed ritual and initiation.

Perusing a new-age travel catalog from California, I spotted a trip to Greece offering a reenactment of the Eleusinian Mysteries. The decision to embark on this trip was purely intuitive. I had no prior interest in Greece and had no clue about the Eleusinian Mysteries. I called the woman offering the program, Deena Metzger, to feel out her energy before committing to something completely unknown. Immediately her warm and gentle voice, maturity, and responsiveness poured out to me through the phone. I knew I would be comfortable with her and felt assured that my fellow travelers would probably not be too "weird."

Nonetheless, I found myself at Kennedy Airport munching on a muffin at the snack bar trying to push down my anxiety about what I had gotten myself into. Whatever possessed me to travel with a group of strangers to a place very far away in order to go through some unknown ritual that was supposed to help me find a vision for my soul's calling? I had never flown overseas and was not used to traveling alone. I knew it was too late to turn back in spite of feeling prickly all over from my body's electrical response to moving into the mystery.

Meeting Deena at the loading gate, I immediately liked her, and felt relieved. As other travelers gathered around I noticed that most of them had that California look—lots of wild hair, crystals, colorful clothes, and unique self-presentation. My northeastern ego reacted with curiosity as I registered that this would probably not be a dull trip!

I arrived in Athens excited and disoriented. My internal feeling of chaos heightened when I picked up my luggage and discovered that the zipper of my brand new canvas traveling satchel had broken in flight—clothes, toiletries—everything—was spilling out onto the airport floor. A fellow traveler found some rope to tie the suitcase together. Already the anarchy of the unknown was expressing itself as I resigned myself to traveling through Greece, moving from sacred place to sacred place with a suitcase that couldn't close. The message was to let go of control and trust that I was doing the right thing.

During the next two weeks in Greece I experienced an ecstatic state far beyond anything I had known. In the past I had touched that ecstatic place for moments, or if I was lucky, for hours. This trip elevated me into the rarefied realm of the ecstatic and sustained itself at that pitch for the full two weeks.

During the journey, and hanging on for dear life, I rode through a series of descents and ascents. Deep emotional outpourings mystified my ego as I moved through the rituals of the Eleusinian Mysteries.

Thousands of people participated in these ancient Greek Mysteries long before the birth of Christ. This great ritual involved the process of facing death, moving through rebirth while keeping the secrets of these initiations to oneself. I marveled at a culture that would support so many of its citizens in this quest for immortality. Everywhere we traveled, we brought the sacred with us. One's intention "magicalizes" one's experience. My intention for heightened soul alignment coupled with Greece's exquisite wonder catapulted me into what I would now call the fifth dimension.

A few days after consulting the oracle at Delphi, I had a dream. In this dream I witnessed an oriental woman spinning two long stalks, like bamboo shoots, one in each hand. I called them "yarrow stalks." She spun them faster and faster as I watched, spellbound at the beauty of her movement. Suddenly the stalks turned into discs—large golden discs engraved with ancient symbols. They kept spinning and spinning in their golden, mysterious glory. Next I found myself driving a car with a fellow traveler in the passenger seat, moving downhill too fast, feeling completely out of control. I awoke from this dream knowing that I had received my message from the Oracle. The eastern aspect of my soul, reflected in my practice of tai chi for twenty years as well as my deep resonance with the Tibetan's energy, was merging into my karmic history in Greece.

Three years later the Tibetan taught during one of our group Chats about the tablets brought to this planet in the early days before the human race was seeded by the God race. These tablets were golden round discs imprinted with strange and undecipherable symbols. Djwhal Khul said that the tablets, buried deep in the earth, contained the creative matrix for the greater mysteries governing our planet and beyond. Within the center of the earth these tablets energized alchemical fires. He said that as we enter the new millennium these tablets were programmed to release the mysteries contained within, allowing the human race to access the wisdom and knowledge required to makes its evolutionary leap.

My dream brought me the realization that these golden discs were my calling—my mission—to assist in this great process of bringing forth the ancient teachings catalyzing our collective transformation.

Vision crystallized, I saw myself establishing a mystery school with these dazzling golden discs of knowledge as its foundation.

While my soul rejoiced in this awareness, my solar plexus recoiled in fear as in the dream I found myself driving at high speeds, ultimately losing control. Going downhill away from the rarefied atmosphere of the Eleusinian Mysteries and bringing back my golden discs to everyday life would be a stretch for my ego who wanted to be safely driving a car at slow speeds and in full control. Tapping into my soul meant no more control—only surrender to the Divine Plan.

Upon my return to Massachusetts I chose not to bring this dream to therapy with my Jungian analyst. This particular dream was a gift from my soul, not to be worked and analyzed - only to be received with deep humility. I began the process of telling my friends of my intention to start a mystery/magic school. It would be called "The School of The Golden Discs." At times when the entire idea seemed foolish and unrealistic, I would remember the sensation of watching those yarrow stalks turn into golden mysterious discs and my resistance would fade, leaving me to bask in the wonder of the Great Plan that guides us all.

Tablets Revealed

According to Djwhal Khul:

Ancient tablets were buried deep within the earth thousands of years ago. These tablets were brought to the planet by the original race that seeded the human race. This Root Race was made up of highly advanced beings able to use heightened brain power resulting in clairvoyant, clairaudient and mental telepathic abilities. These beings came forth from the archetypal realm bringing the matrix for the collective consciousness of humankind. They were very tall with elongated heads. Their bodies were less dense than human's because they resided between the physical and etheric dimensions. The Root Race served as the rainbow bridge to usher in human form. It is through their extreme brilliance and heightened light factor that humankind knows its potential as spiritual beings. These great beings stayed on the earth plane only long enough to crystallize the blueprints for humankind. Their evolution did not take place on earth. Their earth mission was a pure act of service to Source. Once it was completed, the Root Race had no further need to dwell on such a dense planet. Their parting gift to humanity was the tablets.

These tablets are large, disc-shaped objects covered with mysterious symbols. Contained within them are the Greater Mysteries, the ancient secrets of life. These teachings were kept secret while humankind was in its infant stage, not yet ready to deal with the power held within these tablets. Now humankind is ready to receive all the teachings and allow the mystery schools to open their doors to any and all that want to learn.

In the ancient past to be allowed to study at a mystery school involved specific levels of initiation. The prospective student was assessed quite closely to make sure he/she was worthy of entrance to the archives of the universe. Now, collectively, it is time for us to receive these teachings. We are going through a collective initiation granting humankind the right to access the blueprints of our original make-up. No longer is it necessary to hide the keys to the universe, as one would hide the car keys from a toddler. We are at least at the stage of being awarded our learner's permit! The Tibetan teaches:

The tablets are filled with time-activated capsules of information pertinent to mastering the physical plane, especially as it interfaces with the etheric plane. This information is best accessed through one's intuition, self's individual channel at a conscious level. However, the students who are blocked in their readiness to receive this material consciously will access it through the dream state. It is important to look at one's false beliefs regarding power, worthiness and responsibility. These are the areas of blockage in the collective unconscious preventing humankind from consciously taking in the vast amount of knowledge currently available from the etheric plane. To access this knowledge, the students must clear their channels and heighten their vibratory rates.

This is analogous to picking up a distant radio station. If we are finely tuned, we can receive it in all of its exquisite refinement. If we aren't finely tuned, we are lucky if we can even pick up static. Djwhal Khul reassures us that the matrix of the human condition duplicates the matrix within each knowledge time capsule. Therefore, we have a unique affinity to this information being released. The Tibetan teases that it should be easy to hook up to receiving this energy. It is exactly like our energy only more refined and vibrating at a quicker level. He says that as we purify ourselves of our chronic self-limiting thought patterns, making this connection will be as natural as breathing.

This is profoundly exciting because we finally have access to **complete** knowledge. While we may all receive this information in our own unique interpretive way, we equally have the wonderful opportunity to master our human experience in a highly accelerated manner due to the release of this tabloid energy.

In addition, the tablets were implanted in the earth to catalyze the earth's transformative process. As their energy is released, the earth's vibration is heightened as she experiences her "earthness" at a completely new level. In order for us to cohabitate harmoniously with the earth, we must be able to reside upon her at a new energetic level. As the earth sheds her old density, so must we. The earth will not be able to sustain beings of the old world order due to the energetic discrepancy. So, we lighten up together and open to the knowledge of the universe as it emanates from the activated tablets.

Djwhal Khul cautions us not to worry about whether we will open fast enough to align with the heightened vibrations. He lovingly encourages us to simply continue to clear out false beliefs and old karmic baggage. The Tibetan teases that even if we tried we couldn't totally block out the new knowledge that is coming forth. If we are only able to receive it on an unconscious level, it will still affect our thinking as it liberates the lower mind from the old collective patterns of perceiving the world through suffering and separation.

In sensing the knowledge from the tablets, I register a heightened sense of potentiality. While I cannot always language what I am picking up, I experience this tabloid energy as very, very old and sacred. I feel awe and reverence when in contact with it and realize more than ever that the Divine Plan is truly at work in my life. When I am in channel with the Tibetan, the information from the tablets radiates out to me in crystal clarity. However, returning to my ego self reduces my ability to decipher the tablets' teachings. In spite of this, I know that this energy is making a tremendous impact on the connection between my lower and upper minds. The Root Race really is the rainbow bridge between the collective lower and upper minds.

This Root Race bridge has always been in place, but not activated until now. Because of the dawning of a "New Cosmic Day" upon the planet, the current is moving dramatically through the rainbow bridge within us stimulating our awakening and ancient knowing. Djwhal Khul gives us the assignment to:

> *Visualize the rainbow bridge connecting the upper and lower mental bodies. While visualizing this connection put forth the intention to pick up the energy from the tablets and register it in such a way that one's lower mind can interpret and language it. Then the students can teach what they are discovering to each other, each one holding a piece of the*

mystery revealing itself at long last. Do not be afraid to open your channels. They are your natural birthright. Create group channels to heighten the reception of the divine that already resides within. The original karmic agreement states that when the tablets release their wisdom, humankind will be ready to receive it. It is now your collective responsibility to tap into the great Knowledge Bank and dare to share it with others. It is no longer time for one teacher to point the way but rather for all of humankind to guide itself through the portals of enlightenment through its innate connection to the spiritual plane.

Greek Oracle Lifetime

In this lifetime I have found the calling to be an oracle very compelling. What an honor it is to sit in front of a group of people as a channel, while allowing the divine flow to overtake my being, pouring out energy, love and wisdom to all in need. The responsibility of this work has also been overwhelming. Acknowledging this position of power and the potential to unconsciously abuse it has often left me anxious and tentative about unleashing the full impact of my gift. I carried into this lifetime deep veins of guilt and failure running through my psyche. It has been my personal work to resolve and release this karmic debris.

My past life experience as an oracle preceded my lifetime as a solitary American Indian medicine woman who sat under a great oak tree providing guidance and healing to fellow villagers. It originated in ancient Greece when thousands of people flocked to the Temple of Delphi to listen to the Oracle.

I was one of many young girls chosen by the Temple Priests. I had just reached puberty when my family allowed me to live on the Temple grounds and be trained for the honorable position of oracle. Initially I was overjoyed by this opportunity, feeling very special and important. I dreamed of being a true messenger for the Gods and Goddesses. In my fantasy I would have Athena's brilliance and Aphrodite's beauty; Apollo would smile upon me with pleased approval; I would live in the rarefied realm of the Gods and Goddesses and be blessed by their immortality; I would be a star.

I assumed this greatness would more than make up for the loss of normal life of a teenage girl in Greece, spent preparing for her wedding and childbearing experiences. Despite my youth, I was in love with a young man, captivatingly handsome with dark Greek curls circling his refined face. I treasured the way he took me in through his deep brown eyes, cherishing my beauty. When he learned of my temple appointment he was deeply torn between his joy for the possibilities this opportunity afforded me and his despair over losing our option to marry. Because our families had not yet officially approved our union, I was still available to accept the position of oracle priestess. In spite of the temple laws that would prohibit us from marriage, in our innocence we pledged our undying love to each other no matter what the external circumstances. I was so excited by this thrilling turn in my life that the sting of not fulfilling my relationship with my beloved faded behind the light of this great opportunity to devote myself to the Gods and Goddesses.

In a matter of days I was taken to the Temple grounds to be trained. I quickly discovered that the Temple priests were harsh disciplinarians, ruling our daily life with strict, unrelenting sternness. The loss of the warmth of my family and touch of my beloved fed a sadness beginning to grow deep within. Yet, I could not allow myself to question my destiny. After all, I had been chosen! What an honor! What sacrilege not to appreciate this divine grace. I was determined to be the best oracle, truly allowing the Gods to speak through me. I would sacrifice my own soul to make sure the needs of the collective were met. I chided myself that nothing else should matter other than complete devotion to my service. This was the highest possible pathway I could ever hope for. I must rejoice in it.

However, my human needs fostered questions like: "How would I be taken care of? Who would love the personal me? Why must the sacrifice be so great?" We were trained to take our attention off of self and focus it on the Temple priests at all times. They were the real links to the Gods and must always be unquestioned and obeyed. Anytime I had an individual thought, interpretation, or idea, it was squelched. I was punished for being rebellious enough to cultivate my own intuition and wisdom.

After a year of indoctrination and ego-stripping, the priests introduced me to an herbal potion used to open the channel to allow full access to the realm of the divine. This potion was hallucinogenic, scrambling and disorienting my mind, and creating an intense state of inner chaos. Instead of clarity and insight I experienced fragmentation and deep confusion. After several ingestions of this herb I began to lose any sense of self. No longer able to maintain coherent thought patterns, I felt weak, vulnerable and idiotic. This weakness led me to feel more dependent on the Priests, seeing them as my only connection to sanity. Even though they were the perpetrators of my mental breakdown, I needed them.

I began spending more time secluded in my quarters. It was a small space about eight by ten feet with one small window. The dirt floors were a cooling relief from the hot Mediterranean sun. My only furniture was a sleeping pallet, wash stand and small chest housing my oracle dress.

The sacred days of high ritual drew crowds swarming in by the thousands hungry to hear messages from the oracle. I was given the required herbal dose a few hours before the event. It took affect quickly. Psychically altered, somehow I managed to dress into my gown. Parting the draped covering of my doorway, the intense sun would hit my face, temporarily blinding me. Servants assisted me to the center seat as I peered at the sea of faces swimming before me. The drug fragmented my psyche into thousands of little pieces making it impossible to focus my eyes or thoughts. I desperately wanted to speak clearly, but all that I could do was babble incoherently. The priest stood next to me in full formal attire looking powerful, in control. It was his role to interpret my babbling so that the crowd could understand.

Visions of great service had degenerated into a hypocritical nightmare. My babbling was not an offering of counsel from the Divine. It was the uncontrollable madness that comes from burning out one's light centers in the brain. I knew that this entire situation was a sham as the priests, exploiting their power, manipulated the desires of the crowd. Yet, I still felt responsible. I could not believe that my dreams of sacred glory had shattered into a bizarre drug-induced haze. I blamed myself for not being stronger, more capable of controlling the affects of the herb without letting it undo me.

The priests, scolding and punishing when I objected to taking the drug, shamed me as an insolent ingrate. There was no one to turn to for help. Everyone assumed my babbling was truly the Divine pouring through my being. They wanted the priests to interpret the voice of the sacred for them, taking no responsibility to make their own individual connection to the Gods and Goddesses. I was a pawn in a game of spiritual power. The drug so confused me that I too began to believe that the Divine was actually speaking through me in a babble that only priests could understand.

My only support was my precious young lover who sneaked into my quarters at night. He knew of my torment but was in no position to rescue me from this waking nightmare. Due to his youth and low societal status no one would believe his story of my distress. He ran the risk of being judged and severely punished for disobeying the way of the Gods. His only recourse was to hold me, soothing my soul, and validating my reality as I clung to a last strand of sanity. His love was a lifeline preventing me from being completely absorbed into the twilight of a hallucinogenic madness.

Two years passed. I was terribly weakened from the demands of my position. Eventually the herbal potion had taken its toll. I suffered from an unbearable swelling in my mouth and throat. A severe dryness made it almost impossible to swallow. The drug was finally suffocating me. My beloved held me in his arms as I took my last breath, still reassuring me that I was not crazy. The crime was not mine but the priests. I am eternally grateful to him. Ironically, he was my lifeline to the divine, not the priests.

My current lifetime reflects the affects of my trauma as a Greek oracle. I have struggled with dry coughs and sudden catches in my throat. Once during a channeling session my entire throat suddenly closed up. I was unable to breathe for several seconds. There I was, the channel, the oracle, sitting in front of a group of people seeking messages from the Masters, from the Gods, and my throat was as shut as if I had swallowed the drug hours before.

I was struck by the immediacy of our karmic material. It surfaces as quickly as if that previous lifetime had just happened. The right combination of events and people sets up familiar circumstances that resonate with a past life, activating a time capsule releasing one's karmic energetic imprint. This explains why I have been more comfortable channeling to small groups.

Infinitely patient, Djwhal Khul waits as I struggle to dislodge the distrust and humiliation of this Greek past life. My past life self still feels exposed, shamed, manipulated and used while my current self rejoices in the pleasure of basking in the Tibetan's vibration when I am blended with him in channel. This has created significant internal conflict resulting in limited exposure to the world as a channel. While my current self deeply desires to serve the divine plan to the full extent of my potential, my past life self limits the possibility of channeling to *too* many people. Slowly the congestion releases. Frequently I have had to clear my throat when teaching and counseling. The effects of my oracle lifetime, thousands of years earlier, still had its grip on my throat chakra.

The Tibetan gently reassures me that the gift of his willingness to work with me as a channel will allow me to go beyond past life torment and realize the joy, honor and empowerment of the oracle as my vessel fills with his light and we blend together in a dance of *true* wisdom and love, offering ourselves to all who are open and ready to take responsibility for their alignment. My husband Zayne, who was my young lover so true to me when I was the Greek oracle, still holds and grounds me as he sits by my side when I channel to groups. This time he is not going to let me out of his sight, protecting me from negative energy that might be absorbed from my very open state. This heightens his empowerment process as he releases the frustration and helplessness of his past life "failure" to protect me from the priests and demands of the crowds. Together we heal and respond to our true calling: to use our union as a platform for the Masters. We are deeply graced in our service.

Chiron and the Virgo/Pisces Intercept

Astrology has always been a powerful vehicle of insight and self-revelation. My library of astrological books waits on the shelf until the appropriate time when a specific type of guidance is needed. Then miraculously one of the books almost whimsically calls to me. The angels and masters have a way of reaching out to us concretely, their invisible hands practically pushing a book off the shelf just when we need it the most.

My book on Chiron, by Barbara Hand Clow, was "pushed" off the shelf one September Saturday afternoon in 1996. Chiron is an asteroid that is currently energizing the collective consciousness. Chiron is the mythological story of the wounded healer. As more alternative healers serve the Divine Plan the issue of the wounded healer intensifies. I have long struggled with the "Chirotic" aspect of myself when I am simultaneously providing insight, guidance, wisdom and healing love to my clients while personally moving through the deep layers of my own psychic wounds. The deeper I go with my clients the more my own woundedness is stimulated. This has created a push/pull in my attitude toward service. It would be so much easier to have a vocation that never touches my inner pain. Of course, that wouldn't bring me to my cutting edge, but the "safety" of it certainly is appealing.

There was information in the Chiron book on birth charts that have an intercepted Virgo/Pisces axis. People with this astrological configuration had an opportunity to bring their soul into the body in a past life and refused to do so. As a result others were damaged by this refusal. These people with the Virgo/Pisces intercept reincarnate with intense feelings of guilt and failure. Consequently, in their current life they are forced to deal with this issue of ensoulment for once and for all. There will be no getting around it this time.

Recognizing this intercept in my chart made my heart race. I could feel energy streaming through my body as cellular memories were activated. I felt excited, agitated and disturbed. My entire being experienced the truth of what I had just discovered. Simply the awareness alone of this insight was liberating, flooding me with understanding.

In this lifetime I have always been haunted by feelings of guilt and failure. I assumed that this was because my inner three-year old child felt responsible for her mother's death, as if somehow she could have stopped it if she had just been good enough. That level of trauma for a child is enough to create quite the guilt/failure complex. However, this new insight into Chiron allowed me to realize that this lifetime was just the tip of the iceberg. Suddenly I understood why I could never say "no" to the Tibetan. Karmically there was no choice. I knew that I had to channel him (serve the Masters) even if it meant self-sacrifice.

At age forty I "gave up" channeling the Tibetan. My inner life was exploding with aspects of self long buried in my unconscious. As a "wounded healer" the scales had tipped precariously in the direction of my woundedness. Every act of service was painful, especially the channeling. I just wanted time to find myself, reassert my identity and be selfish. Djwhal Khul gracefully and lovingly backed away, giving me the space that I demanded.

I spent the next two years deep in Jungian analysis, sorting through the debris from the mid-life explosion, healing from my divorce, and seeking new visions of my potentiality. I believed my channeling days were behind me. However, during my soul pilgrimage to Greece I was reminded that my contract with the Tibetan was still binding.

An important stop among the sacred sites that I visited during my trip was the Acropolis. As our group was walking up the steep stairs to the Acropolis I suddenly experienced intense vertigo. The crowds of people around me became blurred and swirling as I clutched onto the metal handrail to keep from falling. Desperate not to make a scene and pass out, I finally had to sit down on those ancient stone stairs while the swarm of tourists walked around me. Eventually sheer willpower carried me to the site of the Parthenon at the top of the stairs. I sat alone in the ancient ruins and sobbed.

The leader of our group noticed my upset and walked over to lend support. Not knowing why I was upset she said, "I have to mention this Tibetan teacher that you say you used to channel. You know, you can't say no to the Gods. You're going to have to deal with him." I was stunned that she would bring him up out of the blue at this time, and with such firmness. It was as if he was talking through her. Suddenly my energy cleared. I was grounded and filled with a sense of spaciousness. I felt as if I were on top of the world and knew that it was time to begin again with the promise I had made lifetimes ago. Six months later I "reopened" the channel.

My second attempt to say no to Djwhal Khul occurred three years later after having channeled a tremendous amount. I had offered weekly groups with the Tibetan for two years as well as completed an intensive, channeled nine-month Core Program for his students. Increasingly, I was experiencing severe migraine headaches. Eventually I became so sick from the migraines that it felt like I continually had the flu. My body was out of control as I kept vomiting, holding on to my screaming, pounding head. I was a wreck and wondered if I would ever fully function again.

In desperation I went to a healer and was told to stop channeling immediately. My crown chakra was off kilter. I was terribly out of balance. My energetic system was completely depleted. It was shocking to hear her insist that I stop. I had readings booked in advance and groups of people depending on me to bring in the Tibetan. However, the truth of what she said was obvious when I wasn't even able to make it through our healing session without throwing up in her office bathroom. Somehow I made the thirty-five minute drive home and collapsed. I didn't channel again for a year and a half. I thought my channeling days were well behind me for sure this time. After all, nothing was worth sacrificing my health.

Despite this conclusion, after eighteen months I realized how much I dearly missed the Tibetan—his presence, energy, wisdom and love. I knew he was always inside of me. However, that was still not the same as channeling him for others, running his powerful current through my body. This realization struck me, once again as a shock, that it was time to begin again our strange, compelling and karmic relationship in service to others.

Sacrifice: Willing vs. Unwilling

We all make sacrifices in our lives. How many of us accept these sacrifices willingly, coming to terms with the "need" to make sacrifices? Most traditional spiritual teachings include the concept of sacrifice as a high virtue. From this standpoint sacrifice is supposed to lift us into a transcendent place free from personal gain or desire. According to these teachings the more sacrifices we make the closer we are to God.

My own experience has shown me that sacrifice refines our ego's natural inclination toward selfishness and self-centeredness. However, sacrifice as a vehicle for purification only works when it is a *willing* sacrifice. An unwilling sacrifice fosters resentment and the burnout of good will.

I often wonder how many sacrifices I make that are unnecessary. Do these self-imposed sacrifices drain my positive charge leaving me spent, exhausted, angry, confused and discouraged? How did I originally latch onto the concept of sacrifice as a necessary part of my spiritual path? If I have made wrong sacrifices, have I also overlooked or resisted making the required sacrifices?

A wise friend once told me that the Divine Mother always exacts a sacrifice from us when She gives us something. I have puzzled over that thought for many years. Do we have to "pay" for our gifts and fulfilled desires through giving something up? What is the energetic exchange required for our right to be here on the earth plane? Djwhal Khul repeatedly tells me that it is our natural birthright to have our needs fulfilled. Yet, throughout life we are continually being presented with demanding sacrifices. Our spiritual conditioning is deeply wrapped around the concept of sacrifice. Most of us may not even register that yet another sacrifice is being demanded of us. We automatically expect to make sacrifices for our jobs, children, parents, lovers, friends and our dreams calling for manifestation.

While we may make sacrifices automatically, or unconsciously, how many of us are secretly resenting these sacrifices, inwardly disagreeing that sacrifice should be a requirement for transformation? The quality of energy fueling a *willing* sacrifice is quite different from the energetic reaction to surrendering to an unwilling sacrifice. Making the statement, "I would gladly give up my free time to make sure this important job gets done," reflects that we are fulfilling a needed sacrifice with love and a positive attitude. This energy returns to us ten-fold. The sacrifice feels like a bargain, a reasonable cost for the something special we wanted, and we willingly relinquish whatever is required. How many of us have prayed, "Dear God, if you give me this one thing—health, money, love, career, etc.—I will give up something that I'm really attached to—addictions, negative emotions, etc. While it may be difficult to keep our end of the bargain, it is with a healthy conscience that we give over the promised sacrifice.

What happens when sacrifices are thrust upon us, much to our annoyance, frustration and despair? Examples of unwilling sacrifices are: being the only one available to take care of an ailing parent who was abusive to us when we were children, staying late at work night after night for endless paperwork that goes unacknowledged and underpaid, having our lunch break snatched from us by a needy co-worker who cries on our shoulder about the endless crises they perpetuate making it impossible to extricate ourselves in time to relax before the demands of the afternoon schedule bear down upon us, or more tragically having to take care of a mate who has suddenly just been paralyzed from the neck down. These sacrifices, not consciously chosen, are handed to us by Lady Fate whether we like it or not. To abandon these sacrificial mandates would be to shirk our learning curve, our course requirements for enlightenment.

In addition, there are unnecessary self-imposed sacrifices. Martyrs are spiritually advanced people—so we are taught by the great religious traditions. We look for ways to humble ourselves through selflessness, making sacrifices because we feel we must if God is going to smile down upon us. Meanwhile we are muttering complaints under our breath, secretly resentful that the Divine is so demanding. Caught in the false belief that God would want us to make sacrifices that are not resonant with our evolution, we never glean the satisfaction that results from fulfilling the appropriate sacrifices in life. We continue to pile up more and more sacrifices perceived as required. Eventually we are drowning in a sea of "unwilling" sacrifices, painfully burned out and devoid of faith. We have to ask ourselves, "Whose idea was this anyway? Does Source really want me to give all this up? If so, why?" If we can't answer these questions, then these sacrifices are usually misdirected and fruitless. Djwhal Khul teaches:

Not all sacrifices promote the soul's evolution. Sacrifice is not a generic process that works for everyone, regardless of who they are or what the sacrifice. Most of humankind makes far too many unnecessary sacrifices. This reflects the collective's scarcity consciousness. It also demonstrates humankind's inability to allow in the fulfillment of all needs lubricated by the ease factor. Humankind still feels as it if needs to "pay" for whatever it receives. How can one pay for the gift of divinity which is inherent in all creation?

However, the sacrificial process is a necessary one for purification. The student's ability to willingly surrender something important in order to selflessly provide for another requires the practice and perspective of Universal Love. The ego must be temporarily set aside in order to truly sacrifice one's desires. The ability to set aside the ego then allows the student to open to a greater reality—to the Higher Self and beyond. To be able to make appropriate sacrifices is to be flexible, adaptable, willing, and generous in spirit. The student realizes that the true Self is never really sacrificed. It is only enhanced through this process.

Source never requires sacrifices that negate the soul or cause needless suffering. Necessary sacrifices are inherent in the exchange between spirit and matter. The soul gives up the high lightness of spirit to come into form. Spaciousness, formlessness, expansiveness and the infinite are temporarily "sacrificed" in order to experience density, solidity, form, limitation and the finite. This exchange of energetic realities serves the soul well as the student applies metaphysical principles to the application called the human condition. At death the soul then sacrifices its rich and sensuous earthly form to return to spirit. And so the cycle of giving up and taking in continues.

Inherent within each true sacrifice is a gift, a precious jewel. Empty sacrifices motivated by illusions springing from false beliefs leave the student hungry for more, resentful of the "unfairness" of the demands of the universe. It is not that the universe is unfair but rather that the student has given up too much; oh so much more than what was originally required. In this handing over, the student misses the true generosity of Source's love.

Sacrifice is not really a giving up but rather an exchange of energy, a change of form. So, choose your sacrifices carefully. The appropriate sacrifice goes a long way on the evolutionary scale. Don't burden yourself with too much "selflessness." It only leads to a contracted heart chakra. As students understand sacrifice to be an alchemical process that ultimately trades in one level of consciousness for a heightened awareness, they will rejoice in the occasional "true" sacrifice that presents itself along the path.

"MAY THE FORCE BE WITH YOU"

Tibetan Past Life

I am filled with emotion as I explore memories, reminiscing about sitting at the feet of the Masters asking for clarification on the paradox and absurdity of earthly life. Reflecting on my initial experiences with the Tibetan, I was so young in the human condition, fresh off the "cosmic press," more etherically than physically oriented and still adjusting to the density of a physical body. I treasured my time with Djwhal Khul. His goodness, humor and tenderness enveloped me in a sweet cocoon of gestation and potential.

Remembering the early days in Tibet, I am filled with a deep sadness. I know that somewhere along the long line of subsequent incarnations I let him down. At least, that's the way my emotional body remembers it. What did I do? How bad could it have been? Why is there such deep emotion when I ponder my connection with Djwhal Khul?

I don't feel this way about the other Masters. In my connection to them the energy feels fluid and clear. My relationship with Saint Germain excites, stimulates and delights me. However, the Tibetan is my true cosmic love, my divine consort, my divine parent, my divine mentor. What is it that makes me feel so strongly for this being?

When moving into channel, I am immediately swept into an embrace with the Tibetan. He feels like a powerful, dynamic and creative dance partner, swirling me around the cosmos as we collaboratively search for meaningful ways to penetrate, cleanse and enlighten my clients and groups.

This brings me to my initial incarnation with Djwhal Khul. I was an adolescent boy, eager, vital, pure and incredibly curious, always running around near the teacher trying to find ways to make his work easier. Oh how I wanted to serve him. He would softly chuckle under his breath when he saw me coming.

It felt as if we had made a very special promise to each other. My promise was to bring forth his teachings in subsequent lifetimes, thereby watering the seeds he had planted in the collective consciousness. His promise was to hold, nurture, protect and liberate my soul.

In 1991 I attended a powerful past-life regression training with Roger Woolger, author of *Other Lives, Other Selves*. As a Jungian analyst, Roger's style is deep, emotionally and physically intensive. The past life currently being explored is experienced as if being drawn directly through the physical body because the cellular memory is activated. Prior life content stored in the unconscious streams through the body into full consciousness.

Once we consciously move through a past life we can no longer close the door of awareness in an attempt to seal off that lifetime. Just as if we had lived it yesterday, it is strongly present in our consciousness. Although the regression is processed through our subtle energy body (the causal body), the experience does not have the ephemeral quality of a dream difficult to remember upon awakening. Currently my past life selves remain as vivid and real as when I initially encountered them during the training.

Psyche offers us the most immediate and urgent material needed for integration. The ego or will cannot orchestrate which lifetime will surface. It is necessary to surrender to the process of temporarily setting aside our current ego. This allows whatever past life issues currently impacting this lifetime to have an opportunity to present themselves. Whatever lifetime presents itself is exactly what is needed to be re-experienced in order to free up our creative flow in this incarnation. This requires trusting the innate wisdom of our soul to select the past life offering us the greatest opportunity for present day healing.

The initial past life I "fell" into during Roger's training occurred in Tibet hundreds of lifetimes ago. Upon entering this past life regression I found myself as an eight-year old boy walking up a long set of stairs. To my little legs, these stairs felt endless. The monastery was been built into a steep mountainside. Waiting for me at the top of the stairs was an older monk with the kindest face I had ever seen. He embraced me as I reached the top, holding me while I waited for my heart to stop racing from the climb. When I looked into his deep brown eyes I knew we would be friends forever. (This wonderful soul is my dear friend Nancy Howe who has been a soul-sister to me in this lifetime since 1977).

I soon acclimated to life at the monastery, loving the daily routines of meditation, work, chanting, meditation, work, meditation, sleep. I did my fair share of cleaning and scrubbing the vast floors insides this beautiful temple, happily taking on my responsibility as an opportunity to honor the sacred space that was my home. I enjoyed the other monks and developed a loving sense of camaraderie in our mutual quest for enlightenment. Cocooned in a field of safety, in a spiritual home which felt blessed and protected by Source, ten wonderful years passed.

During that time I was gradually given the opportunity to have short sittings with our great teacher. Initially awed by his presence, tongue-tied and shy, I looked down at my feet in order to avoid meeting his penetrating gaze. He was able to look through me, seeing the full range of my foolish thoughts and fantasies. However, soon I realized his enormous capacity for love and compassion. This great teacher spoke to me with a twinkle in his eyes, often teasing me along as I struggled through my daily concerns. I called him the "Golden One." He seemed larger than life, sitting cross-legged on his carved and painted throne-like chair placed on a stone platform. The Golden

"MAY THE FORCE BE WITH YOU"

One was like a giant being who knew all there was to know about life and Source.

Maturing into my early teens allowed me to talk freely with him, less shy and unworthy in his presence. More than a teacher, he was a father whose presence filled me with respect, reverence and profound gratitude.

During my teenage years I rebelled against the monastic rules and kept a lost puppy that I had found wandering around the grounds. We were strictly forbidden to have any animals on the premises to avoid distractions from our spiritual practices. My heart fell in love with this puppy. Unable to bare the idea of giving him up, I kept him in a small cave up the slope from the main building, slipping away unnoticed every evening to bring him dinner scraps. We played and frolicked in the cave, two youngsters reveling in the joy of being alive. It was hard to tear myself away from my furry friend to return to the never-ending chores before my absence might be noticed.

After a few months of caring for my puppy, during one of my scheduled sittings the Master looked me directly in the eyes and asked me what I had named my dog. My knees grew weak as I dreaded the disapproval of my beloved teacher. However, his twinkling eyes and smile expressed to me that he would keep my secret, allowing me to experience this wonderful new relationship with an animal. From that moment on I knew that the Golden One would never judge or criticize. His compassion poured over me like a waterfall as we laughed together over Source's magnificent creatures.

Two years later, healthy and strong at the age of eighteen, I was working in the great kitchen, washing dishes and pots from our afternoon supper. Suddenly, I heard loud crashing noises, the sound of heavy boots stomping through the halls breaking glass and smashing sacred objects on the stone floors. Chaos erupted as hundreds of Mongolians attacked our benign world destroying everything in sight. From my peaceful upbringing, I couldn't comprehend what was happening. What could these militant people possibly want from us?

Blind with rage and aggression, they treated us like objects. Large swords and sabers slashed through clothes and flesh as the monks fell one by one. Blood covered the floors, walls, stairs and windows. My peaceful heaven had become hell within moments. Most of the monks fell quietly, unable and unwilling to defend themselves. We were not prepared for attack, not trained as warriors. Collectively we believed our monastic life to be protected by our Master. No harm could possibly come to us.

I managed to hide, waiting for a moment to slip away and run toward the Golden One's great chamber. I arrived there just in time to see my beloved Master mysteriously transform his physical body into a light body and disappear. There were other monks present, surrounding him as he completed this form of departure. We never had a moment to say goodbye. When I realized that he was truly gone my heart broke, feeling completely abandoned. The pain of this apparent abandonment betrayal was far greater than the white-hot sensation exploding through my stomach as a Mongolian saber ended my life.

Death allowed my consciousness to escape my body as I hovered on the ceiling looking down at my corpse. Profoundly bewildered, grief-stricken, angry and confused, I witnessed the monastery, our sacred home, and all of my brothers destroyed. My spiritual family was gone and so was the Golden One that I had entrusted with my soul.

I spent lifetimes struggling to resolve the devastation in my heart from that tragedy. Through past life work I was able to communicate my soul pain to the Golden One, whom I have come to know in this lifetime as Djwhal Khul. He reassured me that I was never abandoned, his magnificent aura of love unceasingly surrounding me through all lifetimes. I realized that this trauma was an expression of my monadic imprint (the original illusion created through our initial extension from Source). My particular monadic illusion constellates around the myth that Source could abandon us. This Tibetan lifetime stimulated the question: can I trust Source and Its Masters to faithfully parent me, to offer safe harbor in a chaotic universe and to hold back the dark force from harming all whom I love?

The Tibetan reminds me that just as Source never abandoned or betrayed my monad, neither did he desert his beloved student. Djwhal Khul stressed how I had to experience that devastation to be able to move into an understanding of how our false beliefs create illusion. My illusion of safety in monastic life was destroyed but my love for the Golden One and his absolute commitment to me endures for all eternity. Nothing can come between us because we are truly united in our divinity, in our oneness. Today I can be grateful for that lifetime, even for its devastation, because that was the precious time when I met my teacher, my beloved Master. As a result of our union, I truly know the love that Source has for me and all of Its children.

Hungry Ghosts

The Tibetans and shamans call them the Hungry Ghosts. We all know them quite well—too well! They are the voices of undoing—the "sirens" from Odysseus' journey who would seduce us off course on our journey homeward. They are the demons who surface when we suddenly awaken in the middle of the night filled with doubts and fears. They are the nagging worries like flies buzzing around our mental bodies looking for sticky places to land. They are powerful and convincing, tempting us into believing that we can't grow, heal, transform, change, or awaken. They feed off our negativity like turkey vultures feeding off dead carcasses. They would devour all of our positive energy if given half a chance. They are on the job twenty-four hours a day, always on the alert for times of vulnerability that create openings in our auric body like invitations to "set up shop," distributing fearful messages. They are like gnats or black flies so small that even the finest screen mesh can't filter them out of our energetic reality.

We often don't realize we have been bitten by them until the damage is already done. When we awake in the morning depressed and discouraged—thinking that our life is a joke—they have left their mark, just as if we were covered with minute bee stings leaving us swollen, toxic and hurting. Perhaps Source created the nasty bites of insects to mirror the energetic impact of the hungry ghosts on our emotional, mental and spiritual bodies.

Some of us try to pretend they are not there. The oblivious innocents merrily go through the woods of life with no bug spray, assuming they are invulnerable to the swarms of energies hungry to dine on the human spirit—devouring its light as quickly as possible. These people are quickly brought to their knees, undone in their optimism. Here comes the spiritual crisis: "What kind of God would create a reality like this? Surely this God does not love us." The hungry ghosts love this kind of thinking. For them it is food for a week as they whisper to us that we can't possibly know our divinity.

The hungry ghosts are particularly activated when we make a conscious commitment to transform or heal an aspect of our souls, especially if our intentions are heightened through ritual. Bringing out the heavy artillery, they are ready to battle our determination to liberate ourselves. Working with the magnetism between the positive and negative poles is required to master duality.

Gathering the positive force needed for self-healing simultaneously activates the opposite pole. This activation sounds an alarm in our energy body as the ghosts close in, ready for the kill. They would destroy our inspiration: "How ridiculous to think that life could be so good. Who do you think you are to dare to consider enlightenment? Remember the pain that you have suffered? Don't think that it could possibly stop because you are doing some stupid ritual or saying some sniveling prayer. Get real! This is all there is. If you try to make it better it will just get worse—better to leave well enough alone. Let your fears make your decisions."

Intentions to grow heighten vulnerability as we momentarily allow our vision to reflect our true potential, invoking the challenge to let go of our familiar self-limiting parameters. Releasing the known pushes us to the edge of the cliff, teetering on the brink of our faith, daring to believe for one moment that more could be possible. Into this delicate space the hungry ghosts swarm, trying to distract us as they bite at our convictions and visions. If they succeed, we are thrown off balance and fall into the abyss of our illusions. They win, we lose.

The Tibetan smiles at my melodrama around the "Forces of Undoing." He challenges me to open to the possibility that the hungry ghosts might have a divine mission. At first all that I can think of is that their only purpose is to make us miserable. Djwhal Khul laughs, reminding me about the two different kinds of faith. The first springs from life filled with joy and opportunity. It is easy to have faith when all is well. The challenge is to hold steady with one's faith when life starts throwing major obstacles in our path. The second faith is hard earned through inner strength and persistence. If we can sustain faith when our external reality seems to make a mockery of our ideals, then we are truly rooted in our faith.

That's where the hungry ghosts come in—to tempt, torment, ridicule, and undermine our faith. If we can survive their attacks and remain centered and aligned, we are truly strong in our spiritual body. This spiritual conviction makes it possible for us to allow the physical, emotional and mental bodies to go through whatever intensity is integral to the transformational process.

Ironically, the hungry ghosts are really spiritual coaches in disguise. Just like strict drill sergeants in boot camp, their job is to toughen us up, whether we like it or not. All of our fluff is stripped from us. Although believing we never signed up for this tyranny, deep in our souls we can sense the rightness of the overall process. We cannot possibly bushwhack the cutting edge of our magnitude if our core star (our soul's center) is not strong enough. Still breathing after an onslaught from the hungry ghosts indicates we are all ready for action—the action that sweeps us through the gateway into the fifth dimension. So, let us welcome these messengers of the negative pole as they create the very resistance that propels us into our divine destiny.

As a psychologist I am keenly aware of the alchemical cycle of transformation. Initially when metal is alchemized into gold there is the blackening stage. Emotionally and spiritually the blackening phase demands a journey to the underworld resulting in a dismemberment process. This is not a physical, but a psychic dismemberment. We leave the world of order, certainty and knowing, and fall into the vortex of chaos, not-knowing and fragmentation. This is a necessary part of the alchemical process of breaking down old forms. At this point the hungry ghosts lunge forward, eager to pick apart our certainties as they introduce doubt, disturbance, fear, bewilderment and judgment.

While intellectually I understand all of this, when the hungry ghosts come after me, I'll run faster than anyone to get away from them. Of course, they always catch me, shrieking in delight at my dismay. As they pull me apart I wail at my predicament, losing all sight of my overall process. Rarely, when particularly centered, I manage to faintly remember that this is a very necessary part of the process. However, it is hard to be comforted by that thought when the experience becomes painful and discouraging. Sometimes I try to block out the process until it is over, struggling to invoke "psychic anesthesia." But that doesn't work. We can't sleep through the hungry ghosts. They are just too noisy. They demand interaction. Attempting to push them away just makes them stronger. Surrender is the answer—surrender with awareness.

Oh how mature we have to be to hold this perspective, allowing ourselves to be momentarily devoured by our karmic past. In the long run it's easier to be mature than to throw a temper tantrum which only wastes the precious energy needed to survive the alchemical fire.

Memories of past skirmishes with these ghostly devils help me to "hang on" during this process. I have survived and flourished in spite of their history of relentlessness. In my twenties I could not name this process, feeling at the mercy of these potent adversaries. Bringing me to my knees, I would cry, rage and wonder whether life was worth living, thinking that it would always be this bad. I believed every lie the ghosts told me. Caught in a place of inadequacy and failure, I would let them win—"postponing" my transformation. However, even in those dark nights, the subtle voice of guidance emerged telling me that eventually I would have the strength to go forward, allowing my true self to flourish.

Over time I have learned to recognize the usual insults and criticisms of my personal hungry ghosts. They always say the same thing. This allows me some measure of perspective to keep going. Every time I dare to be more than I have been, the hungry ghosts will immediately spring forth, undermining my positive outlook. I try to remember to breathe. They have never been able to completely take away my breath. Physical movement helps. A moving target is harder for them to attach to—tai chi, chi gong, yoga, walks—whatever it takes to keep the energy circulating. The more the energy moves, the quicker this process is completed.

It helps to remember that birth resides within death, and so too does gold reside within the blackening. Patience is essential. Eventually the clouds part and the sun shines again. Hungry ghosts don't like the sunshine, especially when it radiates out from the soul. I now trust that my natural light will burn away the veils the "ghosts" tell me are real. So, I surrender, ego unwilling, to this spectacular process reminding myself that transformation is possible for all beings—no, not possible—probable. The gold within always emerges victorious.

The Force
Dedicated to the Count de Saint Germain

When I first saw the film *Star Wars* years ago I was enchanted by Yoda, Luke Skywalker's teacher. As I watched Yoda teach Luke about the Force, something deep within me stirred. Subliminally I was remembering similar teachings received lifetimes ago. These teachings were passed on to me through levels of initiation within the various mystery schools in which I participated.

As I watched Yoda, I felt a strong desire to be once again blessed with teachers that would show me how to use the Force. I tried to remind myself that Yoda was only a fictitious character in a science fiction movie. However, I knew at an archetypal level, that Yoda was reminding us that we are all apprentice magicians on the path to earth mastery, and that the Force was available to all of us anytime, any place.

My analytical, logical mind cautions me about this kind of thinking. "Don't let your imagination run wild. Get real. Don't let others know how delusional you are. Keep your feet on the ground. All of this is too impractical."

Consequently, over the years since I saw *Star Wars*, I have struggled with wishing I could actually work the Force. Then I would typically shut myself down from such foolish yearning. When I opened my channel, I realized that I was finally finding a way to interact with the Force. This satisfied me for many years.

At forty-five years old, I experienced my Saturn opposition. Astrologically this is a difficult midlife passage, highly challenging to our life's vision. During this time I did some shamanic work with my dear friend Nancy Howe that involved journeying to the lower and upper worlds.

On the upper world's journey, I immediately connected with Djwhal Khul at our usual etheric meeting spot. This place is a large library on the causal plane, filled with akashic (karmic) records as well as massive volumes of teachings on the Greater Mysteries. I usually find the Tibetan waiting for me in front of this library. We often talk on the steps. The library looks like a giant sized version of the public library on 42nd Street in New York City.

Sometimes Djwhal Khul takes me into the library. I am honored to be taken through the archives. This is a rare occurrence usually in

"MAY THE FORCE BE WITH YOU"

response to times when I am at a critical juncture in my process that demands powerful intervention. However, simply standing in front of this great place of learning fills me energetically with my own magnitude. I am keenly aware of the great treasures that lie within this building. These treasures reflect the divine plan as it has played itself out in our collective evolution for millenniums.

During this particular journey the Tibetan had brought the Count de Saint Germain, his fellow member of the White (Light) Brotherhood (also known as the Saturnal Council, comprising a group of advanced beings on the spiritual plane who serve as teachers committed to the evolution of humanity). Years ago I was told by Djwhal Khul that I had studied with most of the Masters in my past lives. He reminded me of rides that I took with Saint Germain in his glorious chariot driven by six horses. I remember the Count to be a dashing young man, dark haired with vivid blue eyes, wearing a black floor length cape with a high stand-up collar. I have always been struck by his handsome appearance and the excitement exuding from his dramatic expression.

Saint Germain is the master who works extensively with our western civilization. He is known as "The Magician" and teaches us on the soul level about alchemy. Many of his lifetimes were spent in Europe. Therefore he is resonant with our western orientation.

I am immensely attracted to him, but also perhaps a little intimidated. My unworthiness takes over in his presence as I shy away from deeper conscious contact with him. However, this time the Tibetan insisted that I talk with the Count.

As I connected with the Count I was immediately whisked away in his chariot off to a distant region of the galaxy to explore the mysteries from a larger vantage point. During this time Saint Germain held my gaze with his brilliant blue eyes and said very emphatically, "USE THE FORCE!" He was so strong in his message to me that even after I returned to "normal consciousness" from my journeying trance state, I could physically hear his words ringing in my ears.

For weeks afterward, I wondered, "What does he mean, use the force? How do I do that? Why was he so vehement about it? Why did the Tibetan turn me over to the Count when he is usually in charge of my instruction and guidance? Was this journey simply my imagination bringing up memories of Yoda years ago?" In spite of this questioning, I knew in my heart that something real and significant had happened. I wanted more contact with the Count, but nothing at a conscious level ensued. I knew that in the dream state I was probably studying quite a bit with Saint Germain. However, my waking state left me with only those few words—USE THE FORCE!

It has been eight years since the shamanic journey that led me to the Count. During this time I have immersed myself in the practice of chi gong. These physical movements have greatly enhanced my awareness of chi, the life force. At times when I am particularly open, I can see trails of energy streaming from my finger tips as I move through the forms. My physical body is lightening as the chi opens my channels. The life force is breaking down all obstructions in my emotional body as well as my physical body. Sometimes this process is difficult and uncomfortable as the debris is released. This debris leaves waves of toxicity being discharged and transmuted. I know that this is a powerful process of using the Force.

As I have these thoughts, I can feel Saint Germain leaning into my awareness with his reminder that this is only the beginning. He tells me that I am still exhibiting some hesitancy in fully issuing the Force when needed. He reminds me that past karmic mistakes are well atoned for, to be shy and fearful at this time will only incur more negative karma.

I am struck by the notion that we incur negative karma not only for inappropriate behavior but also for **not** doing what we came to the earth plane to do. I fear that I will inadvertently hurt someone or something if I unleash the Force. Like Disney's Mickey Mouse in the animated film, "The Sorcerer's Apprentice," I don't want to get carried away with the power of the Force.

"MAY THE FORCE BE WITH YOU"

Saint Germain reminds me that I now have the wisdom and am well seasoned in my understanding about the inflation that power brings. He indicates that if I don't apply my knowing, I will still be caught in past life patterns of confusion about power. He offers me simple suggestions for remembering my attunement to the Force:

1. Remember that the Force is everywhere, within and without. You can't get away from it, even if you try.
2. Your energy field is constellated by the Force and therefore instantly resonates with it.
3. Simply bring your conscious awareness to the Force, at all times opening your mind to the way the Force works within the physical plane. Let your mind be filled with questions about the Force. These questions automatically activate their own answers.
4. Upon awakening, tell yourself that you will consciously use the Force today to bring out your highest level of Self in form.
5. Before going to sleep state: It is now safe to use the Force.
6. Remember that alchemy is not possible without the fire. The fire is the Force.
7. Use your imagination to paint a picture of yourself using the Force. What does that look like? How do you work the Force—through dance, music, speaking, silence, nature, creativity, relationships, etc? Describe to yourself the specific way that you most naturally attune to the Force. Commit to a form that you can use to actively work the Force.
8. Write down all the times when you have felt the Force. What is that experience? Is it changing? How?

I realize that Saint Germain is quite serious about this assignment. There is no getting away from it now! He smiles at my response, blue eyes flashing sharp delight. He says as he gets ready to leave,

When you have mastered this, we will create chariots that fly through the dimensions lighting the world on fire. May the Force be with you!

My heart leaps in delight, excitement, wonderment and deep gratitude for all the resources available to us as we play in the cosmic garden of the Great Forces of the Divine.

Russia

My father's parents were Russian immigrants, Orthodox Jews who quickly changed the family name from Leipschultz to Luria. My father and his brothers Sol, Macy, Bucky and their sister Grace, rebelled against their orthodox tradition and became modernized Jews no longer observing Jewish high holy days. The event of their father's (my grandfather) sudden death on a high holy day in the temple must have made quite an impact on them. However, it appeared that all they cared about was becoming financially successful Americans.

Although I grew up on Long Island near these relatives, I never felt connected to them. They all seemed distant and unapproachable. It was fascinating to witness the four brothers kissing each other hello or goodbye on the lips. This exchange suggested a deep loyalty and bond even though they were not particularly warm people. They seemed imbued with an old Jewish mystique despite having long since severed their connection to their religious upbringing.

Although our family was unscathed by the holocaust, there were often hushed conversations about bigotry and the dangers of being known as Jewish. Although as a child I didn't fully understand what they were talking about, I secretly relished the fact that I was half Irish.

"MAY THE FORCE BE WITH YOU"

If I had to, I would be able to hide my Jewish roots behind my cute, little, freckled non-Jewish nose, blonde hair and sparkling Irish blue eyes. I took great comfort in that thought when sensing my family history of persecution.

At age forty-two, I felt compelled to uncover the mystique of my father's background. I had to go to Russia to feel the past. Although my father had been dead for twenty-one years, I hoped to connect with him through the Russian soil that his ancestors had worked. The universe made this very enticing for me with an international conference in Moscow offered in the area of psychology that most intrigued me—dreams! The fact that my Jungian analyst, Robert Bosnak, had organized this cutting edge symposium clinched it for me. The universe wanted me to go to Russia!

Three weeks before departure I had trouble sleeping. Electrical jolts rippling through my body interrupted my sleep repeatedly during the night. I felt like a Mexican jumping bean bouncing all around the bed uncontrollably. Spiritual emergence experts would probably have called it a kundalini awakening. Yes, it was kundalini energy, but also I knew that the Tibetan was having an impact on me. It felt as if my entire system was being charged for something mysterious. I asked Djwhal Khul to please inform me what this trip was supposed to be about.

I had remembered Russian past lives during the training I received with Roger Woolger. Perhaps I was to deepen the healing of that fragment of my soul, tormented as it was. But while I knew that Russia would enable me to work on my personal soul's journey, I intuited that Djwhal Khul knew something that I didn't, something that he was not telling me. Every time I asked him about the larger purpose of the trip he was silent—loving, but silent. Unnerving as this mystery was, I knew there was no turning back. I had made my commitment.

The most compelling global piece of the pie was this opportunity to possibly network with Russian witches, perhaps sharing magical secrets, experiences and support. I knew that Russia was a very magical place.

Most European witches/shamans originate from Russia. Astrologically, Russia is a Scorpio, and what a Scorpio it is! They are highly advanced in psychic healing and the exploration of paranormal experience. In spite of the repression from their government, in secret they managed to pursue their innate knowing of the Force and Its magical application.

I boarded the flight to Russia prematurely jet-lagged, having had only three hours of sleep the previous night. As I waited to change planes in the Frankfurt airport I noticed the news flash on TV stating that a coup was occurring in Moscow. My stomach sank as I watched the news report of armored tanks rolling into Moscow. I desperately hoped our conference would be called off, sensibly sending our plane back to the States. I couldn't believe we were indeed going forward with our plans to land in a country with political crisis filling the air with a sense of unpredictable danger. Anger flooded me as I realized that Fate was pushing me into an experience I never would have consciously signed up for. So, this is why the Tibetan was silent with me about the Russian agenda!

Landing in Moscow, jet-lagged and disoriented, was surreal as I witnessed tanks driving into the city. Registering the foreignness of this world, Russia has a chill to it even in the height of summer. The countryside is filled with tall spruce trees creating a deep, dark wooded environment that adds even more drama to the gray skies. Russia has its own particular kind of magic that emanates from its intensity. Perhaps the northern realm creates a chill within that touches the soul. I felt the depth of this country, her people having known great hardship and a wailing kind of magic, like the distant packs of wolves baying at night.

The countryside is filled with villages made up of beautiful cottage-like dwellings as if lifted from a time one hundred years ago, the local men still wearing billowing pants tucked into knee-high boots and women with babushkas over their heads, long peasant skirts and boots. This was a soulful place that embodied the mysterious.

"MAY THE FORCE BE WITH YOU"

My first night was filled with anxiety as I lay in my bed at the conference center staring out the window at the tall evergreen forest illuminated under the full moon. I felt myself slipping into past life memories. I knew that I had spent many lifetimes in this unforgiving land.

The Tibetan told me that part of the purpose of my being in Russia in 1991 was to receive that part of self that was still living in Russia in a parallel reality of a previous lifetime. I was immersed in feelings of strange nostalgia, soulful mourning and yearning, political fear, and a deep sense of not-knowing. Russia has always had a way of forcing me to accept the depth of the mystery as well as my inability to know or control it. There is something so psychically rich about this part of the world. However, I was afraid my past lifetimes were still so magnetically charged within my soul that somehow they would create a current experience in Russia that would hold trap me there.

Having experienced many lifetimes of government oppression, my soul has been on a quest for justice. Lifetime after lifetime I have tried to create an experience of true justice or fairness often leading to experiences of oppression. Therefore, it was no coincidence to find myself in a politically charged situation far from home where justice has not been a top priority in the political arena.

Lying in bed that night, I painfully regretted my decision to be there. I raged at the Tibetan, demanding that he explain why he allowed me to make a trip that could be potentially dangerous. Why didn't he warn me? He smiled and said that if he had warned me, I wouldn't have agreed to go! The Tibetan reminded me that on a soul level I had agreed to help anchor light during a time when the energetic balance of the light vs. dark force was very fragile. He instructed me that working with the Masters did not only involve teaching or healing others but also physically being in places to heighten the vibratory rate during shifts in the overall equilibrium on the planet. *"Your commitment to the Masters is TOTAL. If that means being in a volatile country shining your light, so be it!"* I tried to take in what he was saying but could only focus on my safety and a burning desire to get out of Russia immediately.

The next day's sunshine soothed my apprehension in spite of the fact that our passports and visas were temporarily confiscated during the coup. In addition to not having travel papers, I was unable to acquire any rubles (Russia's currency) for over a week. A strange detachment countered my feelings of helplessness despite my lack of passport or money. I felt watched over and protected.

Sitting within our international group of psychologists, a quieting calm filled me as I watched others experiencing major anxiety about our situation. Either I had gone numb, or I knew that I was ultimately safe and supported by the Tibetan. Perhaps both! The heat turned up on our second day of the conference when the American embassy suggested all American's leave the country. At that point I was trying to figure out how to get out of Russia, fantasizing about spending time in the safe beautiful countryside of Austria. I felt an uncanny sense of lead weights attached to my body, pinning me in place, making me feel as if leaving was simply not an option.

I began to understand that when our souls have a commitment to fulfill, our egos really have no say in the matter. Our only choice is to decide how we will react to what inevitably must unfold. Djwhal Khul reminded me that there is no arguing with the Divine Plan.

On the second day of the coup I was getting acquainted with a group of female Russian psychologists. They were wonderful—passionate, spirited, curious, open, excited and highly interactive. In spite of the language barrier we were able to share about our work and ideals. Though most of them were mothers of young children, they spoke of their willingness to risk their lives for freedom. To surrender to the coup and return to political repression was not an option.

Outwardly I applauded their courage. Inwardly, I dreaded the significance of their words. Realizing that the Russians would not easily surrender their freedom, I was fearful of being caught in a political upheaval that would be a replay of many past lives ending in disaster.

Angrily I thought, "I don't care about your country's freedom. I just want to go home." One's ideals of global community can rapidly deteriorate under the pressure of personal fears. Although I wasn't proud of my uncaring attitude, I accepted my human limitations. That evening at dinner I overheard my American colleagues stating that no matter what happened they would participate in the political upheaval to lend their support for freedom. Apparently they didn't mind getting "trapped" there, and were glad to jeopardize their safety for a greater cause. Internally I said, "NO. My safety is more important than any political cause."

This experience humbled my idealistic, humanitarian, transpersonal self. How could I be so selfish? Djwhal Khul gently reminded me that I was working through old karmic patterns of self-sacrifice in the name of collective transformation. Those sacrifices were often non-productive and unnecessary. He said how honoring the sacredness and value of self is just as important as the sacredness of the collective. In the past I was all too eager to throw myself away through some dramatic intensification of noble spiritual ethics. In this lifetime I am supposed to be releasing the high drama, accepting safety and personal value, seeing no greater ethic as cause to destroy or abandon self. This karmic shift in my belief system has been challenging and humbling. In many past lives I have enjoyed the superiority that can come from feeling "above" the human condition with all its vulnerabilities and weaknesses.

In magic everything occurs in threes. Sure enough, on the third day of the conference the coup was overturned. People rejoiced in Red Square, once again reclaiming their precious freedom. Lenin's statue was overturned in defiance of future repression. Some of the conference members went to Red Square to witness this historical moment, in spite of the warnings to stay away due to threat of uncontained, frenzied crowds. The Americans were safe, some

Russians were hurt and one killed by the storm of the collective expression of righteous rage, passion and excitement. I stayed safely at the conference center, happily letting this great moment in history pass me by as I watched the Red Square event on television.

Needless to say, our conference was rich in bonding, debate, exploration, celebration, and communion as we explored our collective dreams, impressions of the coup, cultural differences and ultimately our oneness. The last evening of the conference was a banquet and party. Drinking very strong Russian vodka in large shot glasses in an attempt to keep up with the Russian constitution for hardy alcohol-filled celebration, I thanked my Higher Self for placing me in this wondrous adventure—to have the honor to drink Vodka in Moscow with Russians grasping once again their hard-earned liberation. Djwhal Khul sweetly reminded me that everything did turn out alright, encouraging me to deepen my trust in the divine plan, as well as in our relationship.

After returning to the United States I wondered what exactly this journey to Russia had been about. I knew something major had happened but could not put my finger on it. My travel colleagues were raving about the experience. I could only feel deep gratitude for having survived potential danger. I knew that my physical presence in Moscow during that time was assisting the Tibetan in anchoring stable energies and releasing possible disaster through the astral plane. While my conscious mind still wonders what that "mission" really was, my soul knows the sensitivity of the energetic balance thankfully preserved. My personal karma was healed as I experienced a "happy ending" to a story that reminded me of past disaster. I was challenged to open to a knowing of the true safety that is my birthright—a safety that would allow me to trust Source in a completely new way.

Grace

With time and life lessons speeding up and intensifying, we need all the help we can get. This brings me to an exploration of Grace. Djwhal Khul often reminds me to open to the Grace. The moment that I hear the world "Grace," I relax, feeling safe and warm inside.

I, like many people, often feel that I have to struggle with life, doing battle with all the internal and external opposition. I mistakenly believe that it is only will and determination that will get me through life's challenges. It is not in my karmic programming to consider that there may be "freebies" available.

My belief system states that, "Life is difficult. Everything has to be earned. One has to work hard for one's progress. One has to toil away at one's accomplishments in order to be worthy of them. You can't get something for nothing. There are no free rides." This makes for a "nose to the grindstone" reality. Always toiling at my enlightenment, I am forever chipping away at the blockages that seem to prevent me from true liberation.

While I appreciate the need to be willing to apply myself 100% to the alignment process, I wonder if I have been using the most potent mix of ingredients for my alchemization. Somewhere along the line I have forgotten perhaps the most important catalytic agent in my transformation process. This is the element of Grace.

Without Grace our human experience is just plain hard work, dense and dry. It is Grace that lubricates our efforts and carries along our intentions, like a fast-moving stream, into manifestation. When we open to Grace we are showered with EASE. Perhaps our biggest challenge is to accept this ease, releasing our attachments to struggle and difficulty.

This thinking makes me nervous. How will I know if I am making progress if things are too easy? What if I delude myself into thinking that I can effortlessly get away with the necessary requirements for progress? Would I be lulling myself into a delusional laziness and expecting the universe to take care of everything for me?

Ironically, it may be total illusion that the more I work, the further along I will be. Whoever said that continual hard work is the answer? Perhaps we reach a point of diminishing return when it comes to effort. If we use only effort, without the mix of Grace, we may just burrow ourselves into a ditch. Like worker bees, we tirelessly take things on; one task after the next, assuming Source will recognize and reward us for our industriousness. While this may be true, it seems that we fail to consider the big picture.

The big picture starts in the Garden of Eden, a place of Grace, where all needs were effortlessly filled from the Well of Great Abundance. Even though the human process seems to require an expulsion from the Garden of Eden, a loss of original innocence, this does not mean that we are barred from the experience of divine Grace in our lives.

Without Grace it is too hard to master the earth plane. Too much toil without assistance dulls the human spirit and extinguishes the imagination. While we may have to turn over the soil and plant the seeds, it is the Grace of the sun and rain that brings forth our eventual harvest.

Grace is the cosmic YES! It gives us our potential. It reminds us that we are not really in charge. Grace reflects Source's benevolence. It makes things easy and lightens the load. It speeds things up. It reminds us to surrender. Grace teaches us that if we simply show up, the rest will be taken care of. Djwhal Khul reminds me that if we trust Grace, our process will require half the work, half the concern, half the effort and none of the worry! It is Grace that truly beams Source's love back to us. The human process was not meant to be so difficult. Grace demonstrates that Source gives us days off, vacations, down time, and bonuses for our dedication. The Tibetan teaches:

"MAY THE FORCE BE WITH YOU"

Try to imagine that everything you do requires half the effort. Accept that the ease factor called Grace carries the soul forward like a magic carpet designed for wonderment and flight. Grace is the great dispensation agent forgiving humankind its elementary efforts at mastery. Grace washes away the mistakes and brings forward the gifts, making all things possible. Grace brings the teachers and guides, the protection, the insights and understandings, the big picture, the release of old burdens and the cleansing of wounds. Humankind is challenged to accept Grace—allowing it to inform the mind of the path of greatest comfort and delight. Open to Grace! When humankind accepts that divine gifts are given freely, then true freedom is experienced. One can only experience divinity through the flow of effortlessness. Opening to Grace is opening to the All!

This convinces me to make a daily ritual of receiving Grace, reminding myself that I can relax on a soul level as Grace washes over me, removing undue levels of difficulty. As I plant my intentions for the day and water them with Grace, I acknowledge my birthright to return wiser and well seasoned to the Garden of Eden—the Fountain of GRACE.

TRANSMUTING THE DARK FORCE

Shamanic Healing and Egyptian Past Life

In 1988 I attended a series of three workshops with Kathlyn Kingdon, the channel who first introduced me to Djwhal Khul. Kathlyn also brought through the being "Vywamus," known as the "Earth Logos" and teacher of Djwhal Khul. These workshops were taught by Vywamus. A wealth of information was provided about our monadic imprints. The last of these workshops was a day of initiation designed to heighten our soul alignment process.

The night before the initiation I had trouble sleeping. A migraine headache made me sick to my stomach. Seeking relief I took a long hot shower to try to relax and dissolve the pain in my body. The walls of the bathroom seemed to be moving as a profound feeling of dizziness drove me out of the shower, barely able to keep my balance as I stumbled to bed. Exhausted, I finally fell into a deep sleep. During the initiation the following day I had an opportunity to speak with Vywamus alone to ask him about my physical disorientation and discomfort the previous evening. He informed me that I was working through a distant past life in Egypt where all my toes had been cut off.

My mind received this karmic insight but not my heart or body. I felt curiously detached when Vywamus was speaking, wondering if he (or the channel, Kathlyn) was making up the entire story. It seemed so melodramatic. Due to my inability to absorb his words, I shelved the "story" for a later date. My skeptical mind was often ready to discard material that seemed too "new age" and far-fetched. It was challenging enough be open to an initiation from a channeled entity much less to buy into some bizarre notion that I was reliving trauma from a lifetime thousands of years ago.

Egyptian Past Life:

"...I can still see the rich emerald light glowing through the fertile green grasses growing thickly in front of the Great Pyramid. The pyramid towered majestically in the bright light of the afternoon, such a monument to grace, majesty and power. POWER—a word to be wary of—so much power abused. What a crime it is to use the power within the Sacred to feed one's selfish desires. Sacred geometry, sacred art, sacred dance all belong to Source, not to humankind. The Great Mysteries have given humanity many gifts. These gifts were to be honored and held from a place of humility and deep gratitude, not from arrogance and greed."

Source gives us free will to enter this playground called earth to exercise our divine creativity and apply universal love to all that we manifest in the name of our Creator. We are *free* to discover ourselves through form and duality. We give our children gifts to play with, for celebration and self-exploration. We don't give our children gifts to destroy and hurt each other. The reason we are given free will is to find ourselves, not for destruction.

As one of the youngest members of this "divine order" of brotherhood held within the sacred temple of the mystery school, I was eager and excited to be accepted into full membership at the tender age of eighteen. Despite my position on the lowest rung of the school hierarchy, requiring menial chores, to be part of this mystery school was an honor far beyond my wildest dreams. Joyfully I dropped to my knees in deep humility as the elders walked by, barely glancing my way. They had far more important matters to discuss than to notice my insignificance.

Everything about the mystery school was shrouded in a veil of secrets. One didn't apply to be admitted. Students were chosen unexpectedly. After a knock at my parents' door late one night, notice was given that I had been observed as appropriate for the "great training." Off I went, with barely a moment to pack my few belongings. My parents were excited and grateful, so proud of their son. Shock and wonder masked my disorientation and anxiety. Although I knew that the mystery schools sent out "scouts" to screen the local populace for the "priesthood," I never dreamed that they would consider *me*. Unbeknown to me, childhood school teachers who recognized my bright mind, curiosity and natural reverence had put my name forward for consideration to these representatives of the Temple.

Negative power feeds off secrets. When truth cannot be brought out into the open, a dark nest is created that fosters deception and distortion. Ironically the mystery schools were developed to keep the great wisdom teachings in the hands of the "evolved." This was done to "protect" the "ignorant" from inadvertently abusing sacred power. And so the great hierarchy was set into motion. This hierarchy described the universe vertically, up the cosmic ladder, placing superiority on those at the top, leaving the great masses at the bottom to reflect not Source's glory but an abstract unworthiness, as if Source's light did not shine on all of Its Creation but only the chosen ones. A major distortion in the divine plan came from assigning the Sacred into the hands of the few. The primary "oneness" uniting us all was shattered when this hierarchical perception of the divine led us down the road of fragmentation and disconnection.

During the next three years I flourished within the great walls of this mystery school. Eagerness, a positive attitude, and innate attunement to the teachings made it possible for me to progress rapidly through the doors leading to the inner sanctum of the Temple. My teachers were very encouraging and fellow students were equally supportive. Like a bright shining star, my light factor was heightened through devoted study and practices.

Basking in my own potential blinded me to the darker side of what was occurring in this sacred world. Jealousy grew rampant in the festering minds of some students who did not match my unusual capabilities. Wanting desperately to block my progress, they found an ally when the head of the school was mysteriously replaced by a man not of the light. The secretive nature inherent in the school gave no one warning or input into the political system of the school.

Little did I realize that the dark force had infiltrated our great mystery school of light. Gravitating to the powerful beacon of light radiating outward from our Temple in all directions, the dark force began to devour every last shred of light and love within our sacred home. I was one of the first to be "terminated."

My cosmic reverie was shattered early one morning as the door to my quarters burst open revealing angry priests yelling at me that I had betrayed my oath of secrecy. Rough hands grabbing my flesh, dragging me out of my illusion of safety, overshadowed my protests of innocence. Naked and cold, I was pushed down long stairways into dark maze-like corridors, each step taking me into a shadowy world I had no idea existed in this institution of light. Reeling from shock and fear I did not recognize where I was. I knew I had done no wrong but immediately sensed the futility of my situation. These men were not the familiar priests and students with whom I had been associated. My training enabled me to see their auras of swirling darkness, rage and ignorance. I instantly knew that the "dark force," spoken about in hushed whispers among the students, were circled around me, going in for the kill. Outnumbered and overwhelmed, I surrendered to their viciousness, praying that I would be strong enough to stay connected to my own soul no matter how great the physical pain they might inflict upon me.

My soul cried out for justice as they threw me on the cold dirt floor of the dungeon that I never knew existed in this beautiful Temple world. Cries of innocence and the need for understanding evaporated in the face of the head priest as he entered the room. This was the newly appointed high priest in charge of the entire school. I had not been able to warm up to him. I greatly missed his predecessor, a kind, wise and gentle man who suddenly withdrew from his position, declaring a need for rest. He was neither seen nor heard from again. Now I understood what was happening.

Although our school prided itself on its renowned reputation for teaching the full range of the Greater Mysteries, there was little exploration of the duality, the light and dark aspect of Source. Although we probed the alchemical recipes for transformation, transmutation and healing, we were not prepared for the full impact of our light work and the inevitable magnetization of its counterpart, the dark force. We were living in a time of direct connection to the "God race" that seeded the human race. Because of the purity and magnitude of the God race a relationship of absolute alignment with the divine pervaded our training. There was no consideration that malignant distortions of our great truths could exist.

The battle of dark vs. light is ancient in our collective memory. Was it Source's plan to create this awful aspect of Itself? Unanswerable by mere mortals, we are individually left to come to terms with the concept of evil. Is it real? Does it have its own intelligence? Are we under attack by the dark force when we heighten our light factor? How do we protect ourselves? What is the dark force? Is it simply distorted aspects of our divinity, our unclaimed parts of self? Or does it spring from a great intelligence geared for destruction, the "anti-Christ." Is this all part of the divine plan or did we lose our way somewhere along the pathway of evolution?

My soul has wrestled with these questions for lifetimes. It all started in Egypt, the land of wonder and power that links to distant planets and galaxies. Extraterrestrial assistance aided the formation of the Great Pyramids and the Sphinx. The God race knew that this would be the place where a new aspect of Source's evolution could develop. Humankind would anchor the advanced awareness of the God race within its rich texture of emotions and heart wisdom.

And so came forth the inevitable great resistance to this emergence of Source in earthly form—the dark force. Was it preplanned, as a necessary disturbance required for true alchemy? Or, was it a distortion, a cosmic mistake, an aberration taken from Source's generous gift of free will to humankind? Either way, the "evil" has existed and flourished side by side with the light, each running the race to the "finish line" where the outcome of this universe will be determined.

Lying on the floor, shivering from cold dread, I looked into the face of my persecutor. Sanctified darkness and righteous cruelty emanating from his cold, piercing eyes attempted to penetrate my soul. In spite of his dominance and my body's terror of anticipated agony, I held firm in the light of my Higher Self, knowing that no being, however powerful, can rob us of our spiritual integrity.

In frustration and focused rage he gave the order to amputate my toes. I discovered that it is possible to feel tremendous pain without blacking out. Perhaps it was my psychic training that kept me awake throughout the entire assault as each toe was slowly severed by a knife not sharp enough to mercifully cut through bone in one blow. Reeling in agony as the elongation of this black ritual extended my ordeal into infinity, I knew that this so-called priest was feeding off my pain and helplessness. His power grew as my life force ebbed into a sea of shrieking despair. Where was my God? How could Source allow this atrocity to exist within Its universe? Torture completed, they left me alone to die. All of my toes scattered on the floor, I glimpsed the bloody stumps that were my feet as my life force flowed out of my body into the ground. Grateful for the loss of blood, I knew that very soon I would be delivered through the death tunnel into the light.

This was the beginning of a long journey into the strange world of duality. Departing this Egyptian lifetime, I fell into the arms of beloved guides and teachers on the etheric plane and began the process of attempting to integrate and heal this horrific experience. How would I include this nightmare in my spiritual paradigm of Source as a Being of light and love?

So, I vowed to fight these "dark forces" for all of eternity if necessary, to stamp out their distortion of the divine. They had robbed my young soul of its innocence and purity. I would not be fooled again by illusions of bliss and universal compassion. My soul would be the sentry that sits up through the night, holding the vigil against the dark force that robs humanity of its birthright to dwell within the Garden of Light. I would not rest until this great battle was won, the evil ones banished to far corners of the universe to be alchemized into Source's only truth—The Light.

The Tibetan smiles sweetly as I write this account of my soul's journey into darkness. He applauds my determination and courage and yet reminds me that it is time to reexamine this vow made thousands of years ago. Perhaps things have changed. Perhaps it is time to rest from this endless psychic battlefield. He reminds me that this is the lifetime to bring resolution and forgiveness to the beings who would devour Source's light. Only then can true unity return to our beloved earth plane. I wonder how I can lay down my weapons and protection, declaring peace when there is no assurance of safety. The Tibetan responds:

Safety lies within your heart. That is the center of your divinity, the invulnerable core of Source's power and Its great love of all creation. Surrender to this love and no one can ever hurt you again. You have learned much about the duality within the worlds of darkness. Now it is time to surface into the realm of eternal beauty where the illusion of evil dissolves in the brilliance of a light that extends itself through and beyond this universe into greater and greater universes. The earth plane's time for wrestling darkness is ending. No longer serving evolution, the fallen angels rise up again into their radiant truth. The game of dark vs. light is coming to a close. Humankind is ready to learn unity, oneness, and liberation. Let your self re-describe your mission. Do not fight an ancient battle long outlived in its usefulness. Pioneer this new dimension of light, one that engulfs and devours the dark

TRANSMUTING THE DARK FORCE

vortexes of the past. Catch the great tsunami wave of magnificence called Source as it extends Its light factor in all directions, metamorphosizing the wonderment that is called humanity.

Inspired by Djwhal Khul I realize the need to integrate the dark unforgiving pockets in my own soul as I follow my struggle with "evil" through subsequent lifetimes. Only then will I be able to know the truth in his words. Only then will I be able to trust again at long last.

Little time was spent on the astral plane after I departed that shattering lifetime, just long enough to rest my soul from its ordeal and disillusionment. I couldn't wait to get back to the earth plane in order to launch my crusade against the dark force. My vow to war against darkness burned in my soul leaving me restless and pacing as I went through the necessary karmic procedure required in between incarnations—a short reorientation on the astral plane (the dimension immediately beyond our physical world) and then off to the causal plane where the Akashic records are kept. On this plane lifetimes are reviewed. Old karmic contracts are reinstated, revised or deleted.

Meeting with my teachers and guides I was cautioned about my rage toward the dark force, reminded that love is the only effective response to negative energies. They insisted that I delay my return to the earth plane, instructing that on a soul level I was still young and immature. "You won't be able to manage the powerful sway of human emotions with this vendetta imprinted so deeply within your soul. Not yet wise from ample previous experience of emotional body management, you will be swept away in the moment, making your efforts to stamp out the darkness ineffective and dangerous. This may retard your evolution."

The karmic board guides, informs and encourages appropriate incarnational decisions. However, ultimately the free will reflected in Source's Self-creation opens the door to the Great Mystery within Self-determination. I knew that the final choice was mine as I overrode their caution with a self-confidence not yet earned. "I can keep my head cool and fight that terrible force from a place of detachment. I know I can. I must not let even a moment elapse for they will grow in their dominance and all will be lost." Unable to stop my determination, they released me from the meeting. Barely hearing their loving teachings of protection, grounding and alignment, I charged off to wait my turn for incarnational assignment.

Shortly after my meeting with the karmic board I was back on the earth plane in Egypt where I had left off. This time I was female, insisted upon by my teachers in an effort to sensitize and soften my approach to the "mission." After an uneventful childhood, at age sixteen I was assigned the position of servant in the Great Temple of the Mystery School. My only task was to clean the great hall where the high services and rituals were held. There were many sacred objects there needing dusting and polishing. Simply sweeping the great floor itself took hours. Everything had to be meticulous, nothing out of place. I knew this would be my only position in life. People at my level were immensely grateful to be allowed to be anywhere near the Great Temple. Because of my humble status I would never be given any kind of training in the Mysteries held within these great walls. I was happy with that, never daring to assume that I could be worthy of more.

One afternoon a few months after my servitude began I was taking a momentary break from my chores. Stealing a long, curious look around the great hall I was overwhelmed with excitement and fear. The servants were not to look too closely at their surroundings as it was forbidden to open the mind to absorbing the energy emanating from the sacred nature of the objects being cleaned. I could not prevent myself from daring to explore this world of the divine. Filled with questions about the use of the sacred objects, I began to hold each of them, hoping for some insight into their function. Buried beneath my unworthiness was a yearning for the knowledge I had received in my previous incarnation. This yearning pushed me to break the rules as I looked into the forbidden.

Soon time was forgotten. My work break extended more than a few seconds as I was swept away by the sheer energy held within the hall. Dizziness overcame me as I looked at the carvings of sacred symbols etched in the high ceilings. I experienced a strong, tingling, electrical sensation throughout my body. Struggling with waves of nausea, I tried not to faint. My chakras were spontaneously opening. Unaccustomed to the high vibrational level held within the sacred objects, I was thrown off balance as the kundalini energy, usually dormant at the base of the spine, was activated.

Kundalini energy is the essence of life force. It is symbolized as a sleeping snake lying circled at the base of the spine. As we mature into middle life we arrive at a readiness to awaken this life force. However, if it accidentally awakens earlier than our ego structure can handle its fiery nature, we are in for a difficult and challenging ride. Activated, this energy shoots up the spine colliding with any blockages along the way. This can be very painful and dangerous. This is analogous to the caterpillar needing its required time in the cocoon. Premature exposure would abort and destroy its metamorphosis into the butterfly.

At my tender, uneducated age I was simply not prepared for the full impact of the rarefied vibrations circling around me as my mind opened to the energetic nature of this mysterious world. Dizzy, trying to get my footing, I grabbed onto a large urn covered with strange and beautiful images. The dark emptiness within the urn caught my attention. I lost all control as my energy body exploded within, casting my consciousness in all directions, fragmenting any sense of self, however freshly formed. Falling to the floor, sobbing, I held my head in my arms in an effort to ground myself. Scared and disoriented, I had no idea what was happening.

Suddenly the room became dark. There was a strange crackling sound like an eerie buzz getting louder and louder as I held my ears. The noise was an unbearable irritation sending chills along my spine.

The sound of fingernails scraping on a black board multiplied a thousand times barely approximates the torture to my inner ear from this electrical current. Curled up in a ball on the floor, crying from pain and terror, I saw a swirling dark mass about the size of a basketball materialize in the air and move toward me. It was oozing with negativity. Its swirling energy created a deep vortex that was powerfully magnetic. From within this dark vortex its horrible sound current emanated a shrieking tone.

Before I could even scream in horror this mass of darkness attached itself to me. Immediately it started seeping in through the pores of my skin sending burning sensations throughout my body. Then the bulk of it lined up along my spine from the back of my heart up to the top of my head. Some of it entered my crown chakra, lodging itself behind my left eye like a burning hot poker. The majority of it slithered into my heart chakra. Far worse than being stabbed in the back, it felt like the sting of a hundred scorpions sending its poison into my heart. As I lay on the floor, dying the slow death of having the life force literally sucked out of me, I knew that I had failed miserably. Faintly I remembered being warned not to rush into this incarnation. Filled with self-hatred and guilt for foolish ignorance, my consciousness surrendered to the darkness that closed in on me with its final embrace.

There was a tremendous struggle as I traveled down the death tunnel. The dark force was claiming me, pulling me back into a corridor within the death tunnel that leads to one of the many hells within the "evil" domain. At the same time, my teachers and beloved angels were drawing me toward the light at the end of the tunnel. The intense struggle between dark and light forces was psychically tearing me apart as my fate was suspended in that dreadful battle.

I knew I had allowed this to happen because of my need for revenge from the previous lifetime. I had called it my mission, but it was not for the highest and best cause that I managed to override my karmic counselors' caution. I wanted to stamp out this terrible distortion of Source's divinity, and I wanted to do it single-handedly. My rageful pride left me wide open to attack. Even a menial position as a woman servant could not teach me the humility I so badly needed in order to fight this powerful force.

Filled with grief at their inability to protect me from my own destructive hatred, my teachers and guides doubled their efforts to return me to them. This struggle seemed to go on for all of eternity. Suddenly I felt a tremendous blast of firelight as the magnificent presence of an Archangel joined its titanic force with my teachers. The sheer ferocity of his love instantly swept me out of the dark tunnel into the sweet golden-rose hue of the etheric plane, bypassing the lower astral plane in their efforts to raise my soul to the highest vibratory rate possible in order to neutralize the impact of the dark force.

Held within the arms of my beloved teachers I begged forgiveness for my stupidity and failure. They quieted me with soothing words of absolution reminding me that there would be future opportunities to work through this karma. They told me that I barely survived the ordeal and needed many lifetimes to completely heal. "You have not left this encounter unscathed," said my oldest teacher. "You will carry the embrace of the dark force within you until you are ready to understand the true nature of evil."

As he spoke he pointed to the left side of my heart. I felt an oozing, pulsing life form about the size of a grapefruit attached to the side of my subtle energy body. I could feel its poison contaminating me with every pulse of my being and knew that this was just the beginning of a long arduous purification. While the masters and angels could save my soul, they could not remove the karma I had created with these dark beings. They could only surround me in great healing love, doing all they could to raise my vibratory rate and keep me alive while I became strong enough to confront this parasitic, anti-life mass embedded in my side and banish it to the far corners of the universe.

Since my initiation with Vywamus fourteen years have passed. I have rarely reflected on Vywamus's tale of my horrific Egyptian lifetime. Occasionally it would cross my mind when I wondered how real that initiation was. I assumed that all channels probably give some terrifying past life scenario to the listener for sheer dramatic impact. I was still in the continuing struggle of convincing the psychologist within that I really was channeling an entity named Djwhal Khul and not just conjuring up some crazy "teachings" from an imagination gone berserk. In spite of the hundreds of individual readings and group classes that I have channeled over the past decade, my rational ego still struggles with releasing its skepticism of the phenomenon of mediumship

In September 1998 I finally began to deal with this ancient Egyptian trauma. My dear friend Nancy Howe had just returned from shamanic training with Alberto Villardo. I was eager to hear about all that she had learned, hoping that she might practice her latest magical tools and techniques on me, a most willing guinea pig! We have a soul agreement in this lifetime to help each other with whatever healing tools we have at our disposal. Our deep trust allows us to fully open to each other's healing "powers," letting the divine work through us, heightening our commitment to our mutual transformation. I can be fully myself with Nancy, free to allow all the strange aspects of my soul to be expressed without fear of judgment.

I knew that something was brewing inside, demanding my attention. My rational mind had no way to access these deep soul currents through "normal" psychotherapy or even meditation. In addition to the gifts of awareness brought to me through my dreams, I thrive on energetic healing approaches which circumvent my well-developed ego to access the deep rich material in my unconscious.

I tricked my ego by saying, "I'm only doing this work to give Nancy a chance to practice her new techniques." Resistance free, I dashed downtown to meet Nancy on a beautiful, warm, September afternoon. Thinking I would just try out her new shamanic methods and be on my way with many errands to run that day, I arrived at my office where we agreed to meet, in a playful, light-hearted mood. After delaying the work with lots of chit-chat, Nancy finally focused us into getting serious with the process.

As I stretched out on the floor pillows, looking up at the familiar wood ceiling of my office, Nancy told me to speed up and intensify my breathing while she placed stones on several of my chakras. Within a few moments of this altered breath work I started to feel energy streaming throughout my body. Initially I felt like jumping out of my skin, squirming on the floor trying to get comfortable. While Nancy worked on my energy body, invoking the assistance of the "Jaguar" and other power animals, I surrendered to this process in spite of my ego's fight for control.

After about ten minutes I was shaking from head to toe as electrical currents jolted through my body. I knew I was traveling through time to a place where distant trauma still resided in my causal body (the energy body carrying karmic records). Through the inner "eyes" of my subtle body I realized that I was back in Egypt in that fateful lifetime Vywamus had described. Although fearful of reentering that domain, it was too late to withdraw my consciousness. The breath work coupled with Nancy's healing abilities kept me moving through that lifetime as I relived, through my subtle energy body, the awful physical and soul violation I had endured. I clearly saw the face of the priest who had ordered this torture. My physical body was twitching and jolting as I accessed the cellular memory of the ordeal.

When I had completely traveled through the memory of the trauma, my body suddenly became still. As Nancy finished her energy work, thanking the "invisibles" for their assistance, I lay softly crying as I drifted into a state of deep inner peace. While my ego couldn't neatly explain this experience, I knew something major had just happened. My skepticism was unable to override the very real physical and emotional trauma that had been relived in my energy body.

Nancy and I processed the experience, trying our best to language this larger dimension. To ground and integrate our work she encouraged me to write about Egypt. I agreed, shakily leaving the office, feeling very weak and disoriented. Needless to say, I never ran my errands that Saturday afternoon. It was all that I could do to drive the few blocks home and sit on my front porch swing looking at the hills on the distant horizon wondering what "reality" I was in.

I never wrote about Egypt in the following months. Although it was on my list of things to do, I couldn't bring myself to write down my experience. As the months rolled by, I 'forgot' about it, chalking it up to a very strange event that hopefully was over and done with.

One month later I was talking on the phone to a client, sitting in my favorite wicker chair bathed in the October afternoon sunlight streaming into my bedroom. With large windows facing all directions, my bedroom feels like a porch. It's a wonderful place to do phone sessions as my mind travels out through the windows to meet the light reflected in the blue sky as it bounces off the Berkshire foothills surrounding my village home. Deep in the world of my client's dream work, I was surprised by a sudden sharp pain in my left side under my breast. I immediately felt disturbed by its presence. It passed as quickly as it came and moments later I was swept back into my client's reality.

The same pain stabbed me a few weeks later, again passing quickly. Pretty soon this pain was occurring on a regular, if not random basis. I managed to ignore this strange unnerving sensation for a full year. Steadily it increased until I could no longer pretend that nothing was happening. I knew I had to find a way to deal with it. My rational mind feared that I might have breast cancer. Intuitively I sensed that this pain was related to a psychic "disease," not a physical one. My body is extremely sensitive to my soul's process and often manifests "symptoms" that reflect the deep karmic clearing I am experiencing in this lifetime. The physical body is a vehicle for my soul's healing process. When I am releasing trauma from past lives, I can sense it on a cellular level. It feels as if my cells are being squeezed and wrung out.

My analytical mind immediately starting playing detective, searching for clues as to what was being cleared through my body, causing this pain. Reflecting back to first time I felt the stabbing pain, it was the same time that my husband, Zayne, and I had started our publication, *Transformational Times*. This alerted me to the awareness that the pain might be connected to my fear of public exposure.

The Tibetan has often urged me to clear out my resistance to bringing my full magnitude into the world. He reminds me that my belief: "I have to dim my light so that I can survive in this world without being attacked," is an illusion needing release. Djwhal Khul reassures me that it is safe to bring the extraordinary self into the ordinary self. The rightness of his message inspires me to move forward, facing the fears that would convince me to retreat into a state of mediocrity and self-diminishment, safe from the visibility that draws the dark force. However, often my forays into public exposure are accompanied by severe energetic releases such as migraines, nausea, fevers and chills as past life traumas surface for healing.

This exploration convinced me that *Transformational Times* was yet another stretch to go beyond lifetimes of conditioning. Once again I decided to visit my favorite shaman, Nancy, to accelerate this process of clearing in order to lighten my physical body's work of carrying pain and fear incurred a long time ago. Hearing my story, Nancy decided that I needed an "extraction." My only job was to lie on the floor as relaxed as possible, while she energetically pulled out the pain with her crystals. After working on this procedure for about twenty minutes she discovered a large round energetic plate lodged in the side of my subtle body, interpreting it as "jealous rage." Difficult to dislodge, Nancy was assisted by many "energetic hands" as she attempted to remove it from my field. These were the hands of the Masters, angels and power animals that support me through the transformation process. Only able to remove the surface layers of this negative mass, Nancy forewarned me that there was much more needing to be released. Acknowledging that this process was far from finished, we made another appointment to continue to tackle this strange energy lodged in my side.

After a few weeks reprieve I met with Nancy again. It was an unusually sunny November morning as I lay on the floor looking up through the skylights in my new office. The blue sky reflected such a beautiful current reality that I couldn't imagine why I even needed to do this work. A sharp pain in my side reminded me that there was still a deep disturbance going on in my energy field. Asking my body through muscle testing what the next step was in this healing process, Nancy decided we needed to delve very deeply into my soul. Once again she instructed me to begin the altered breath work to allow movement from the deep energetic currents of my causal body. Within moments I was traveling beyond time as my body attempted to find stability within the powerful electrical currents pulsing throughout. Although my physical eyes were closed, my inner eyes were opened, scanning the vague, ambiguous terrain of inter-dimensional travel.

Suddenly I was startled by a vision of tall bright green grasses swaying in the breeze in front of the great pyramid. I realized I was back in Egypt, long before it became a desert. Vividly real, I felt I could almost touch it. Within moments this vision was dispelled by intense energy coursing through my body carrying huge chunks of grief and despair as I wept for what seemed like hours. My rational mind was overwhelmed by the potency of emotions sweeping through me. I sobbed and moaned for no apparent reason. Mysterious as this process was, I trusted it. The release, although painful, felt profoundly satisfying like scratching a deep itch I hadn't been able to get to for lifetimes. After about forty-five minutes the torrential energy quieted down into gentle waves as Nancy finished her work of removing blockages

After she closed the sacred circle we sat quietly reviewing what had just occurred. As spaced out as I felt, I knew precisely what had happened. The Egyptian lifetime was demanding resolution. Although I hadn't written about it in the year that had passed since I first worked on it, it was still right there exactly where I had left off. The causal body exists out of time and space and can wait for eternity until we are ready to clear out our ancient wounds.

Feeling as if someone had blown the back of my head open, I thanked Nancy and stumbled back into my house. Painfully aware that the Egyptian lifetime had to be healed, I agreed to write about it during my upcoming family vacation in Bermuda. Although I dutifully took my laptop on the trip, I was soon lulled into complacency on the pink sands of Bermuda, pleasantly forgetting all about my agreement to write down my recent experience of profound karmic release. Ah, the resistance to making this process conscious is enormous!

Moving through Christmas festivities and gearing up to face the end of the millennium captured my attention leaving my soul wound, freshly opened from this psychic operation, to heal on its own. There was no time to write about it, reflect upon it or even notice that the pains in my side were still randomly sending piercing hot sensations through my left breast and down my arm. I told myself that the work was completed, and eventually I would get around to writing the story.

I had been concerned that I hadn't been able to do any creative writing on my book for seven months. I attributed it to being too busy with work and family life. Yet in my heart I was feeling jammed up, not understanding the cause of the blockage. The few attempts I made at writing new articles for "Transformational Times" ended in absolute frustration. I barely managed to squeak out a paragraph after two hours of writing and wondered whether my creative well was running dry. However, bigger concerns were on my mind. Would we have heat, food, etc. when the clock struck midnight, ushering in the year 2000? Would the world still turn? Although the Tibetan told me there would be nothing to worry about, I couldn't help but catch the "anxiety flu" contagious in the collective consciousness about the turn of the millennium.

Finally safe in my warm home, well fed, having made it through the porthole into the month of January 2000, I had a dream on a cold snowy night the week before my 51st birthday. In the dream a woman came to me saying: "This is about the pain in your side. We weren't concerned about you before, but now we are. It will be good and necessary to get on the other side of this. Get this behind you." After working on this in dream group, Nancy and I immediately set up a session to deal with this wound that wouldn't heal. We both respect the psyche's determination to catch our attention. We respond immediately when messages surface loud and clear from our unconscious.

The next evening Nancy and I met to deal with this "condition" once and for all! This time all I had to do was relax while Nancy employed all her shamanic skills to extract this dark stuff. Within moments, Nancy was hard at work trying to access this energy. The more she extracted, the more evasive it became. She said it had an intelligence that enabled it to slide away from her efforts to grab its illusive darkness. Like a worm, it fragmented when Nancy made contact with it, thereby making it impossible to pull the entire mass out in one lump. It broke off when she grabbed a piece of it, leaving the rest unattainable.

As Nancy performed the work, my breath naturally accelerated as I felt the battle between the dark and light forces taking place within my body. I was panting and sweating, as if running uphill. Even though she barely touched me with her crystal tools, it felt as if she was pushing them deeply into my body. The process was very painful. I was surprised to realize how keenly the physical body can register the impact of psychic surgery.

Nancy later described this energy as a black gooey mass the size of a bowling ball, like a leech that had claws embedded in the front and back left side of my chest. Working at superhuman level Nancy used her full shamanic power, coupled with the aid of the Tibetan and the angelic realm, to pull out this disgusting, repulsive emissary from the

TRANSMUTING THE DARK FORCE

dark force that had lodged itself within my soul in Egypt, not loosening its grip since.

After an hour and half of this struggle Nancy and I finally rested, feeling that most, if not all, of the leech—spirit sucker—had been extracted. Profoundly exhausted, my chest and back felt as if they had two bullet holes in them, so deeply did this energy imbed itself in my body. The removal of the mass took part of me with it. Profoundly grateful to Nancy for her willingness to do battle with the dark force, I said good night, barely having the strength to walk the thirty feet from my office to my bedroom.

The next morning I was scheduled to attend a weekend chi gong workshop. Dutifully I went in the morning, trying to ignore the acute weakness pervading my body. After two hours of attempting to move I left the workshop, spending the rest of the weekend in bed. My upper body felt as if I had been beaten up. It took a week to recover my strength and several weeks for the deep ache in my side to subside. I knew I had just experienced a profound impact on my causal body.

I met with Nancy one more time to do some follow up work. Still experiencing an occasional sharp pain, I wondered if we had not gotten it all out. Upon examination, her shamanic eye observed that its core intelligence was out, but that this dark energy's network of tendrils still remained in clusters. She patiently removed all the small stems to prevent a new mass from regenerating. Slowly as I healed, I was able to assemble the clues in my soul's story. Finally the puzzle pieces were coming together revealing the larger picture of my evolution. This is what it looks like:

My encounter with the dark force started in Egypt with the High Priest that tortured and executed me. Upon leaving that lifetime I vowed to battle the dark force and eliminate it from the planet. My next lifetime's attempt to destroy the dark force only resulted in my own destruction through possession by a dark being. This being was an extension of the dark intelligence determined to extinguish my light in my previous lifetime in the mystery school.

My vendetta to battle evil magnetized this destructive energy toward me. My weakness and rage enabled it to overtake me. This dark being was the leech energy attached to the side of my soul body. So great was its hold on me that none of my subsequent lifetimes were able to release this awful mass tenaciously glued to my soul. It was going to destroy me even if it took eons to do so. Regardless of the multitude of spiritual practices I employed to heighten my light factor, the dark mass slowly but determinedly devoured it. This insidious undermining of my spiritual progress was relentless.

My present lifetime is the arena for final resolution of this struggle with the dark force. My current relationship with the Tibetan springs from an agreement to release this darkness once and for all. In review of this life I observe that every time I have taken a step toward fulfilling my sense of mission, I have been brought to my knees in sickness and toxicity resulting in blinding headaches, sudden violent nausea, and a profound fatigue requiring hours of sleep before I can minimally function. It felt like a potentially lethal poison seeping into my blood stream. My personal stamina alone could not repel this vicious current. I am eternally grateful to Djwhal Khul and all the Masters for their alignment with my efforts, thereby allowing me to survive this battle and transmute the poison.

The sickness started at age thirty-four when I traveled to Boston from Ithaca, New York for an interview at Interface. I was applying to their sixteen-month graduate program in Holistic Counseling. This move represented the true beginning of my mission in this lifetime, although there were six years of preparation through my prior work in a variety of human service organizations working with people incarcerated in the local jail and nearby prison, juvenile delinquents, and hospice. After attending the interview, I spent the subsequent three days suffering from an extreme sense of poisoning, unable to leave my bed. Eight months later I started my first counseling work with anorexic women. Once again the sickness hit me as I was going through Copley Square to the movies, having to pull the car over to the side of the road amidst downtown Boston traffic to vomit. As the years unfolded the sickness increased with every step I took. Initially I thought that the headaches were symptoms of fear and insecurity reflecting issues with power. While this was true at a surface level, the intensity of the sickness in my cells made me wonder what was really going on at the soul level.

I supported myself during the Interface program by cleaning houses in Cambridge. I loved the program at Interface and called it "magic school." The witch within delighted in the exploration of the mysteries, depth psychology, sacred rituals and deep inner growth.

Cleaning houses was highly resonant with being a student in spite of frustrations with drudgery and an impatience to get to my "real" work. It was not simply a coincidence that I chose to be a cleaning lady going to my modern-day mystery school, just as I had been a cleaning lady at the ancient mystery school in which I was taken over by the "leech" energy. To counter my discouragement with having to clean toilets and messy kitchens, I motivated myself with the words: "Consider this a meditation just as monks would honor cleaning as sacred service." In those moments I felt high energy flowing through me as I unconsciously resonated with the environment in the mystery school attended thousands of years ago. Intuitively I was recreating these ancient circumstances to catalyze my karmic memory, allowing me access to the unhealed wounds of those pivotal Egyptian lifetimes. I am in awe of our instinct to precisely relive karmic circumstances in order to bring them to a conscious level.

I now understand the overriding agreement between myself and the Tibetan. When he first asked me to channel for him, I was honored in spite of struggling with unworthiness. The more I gave readings, the more I framed our work together as something I "had" to do for Djwhal Khul, for the divine plan and for other people's souls. I was not able to see that the channeling benefited my own soul. The service of channeling seemed a natural sacrifice that had to be made. I use the word sacrifice because channeling requires a tremendous amount of energy. This mandates a lifestyle adjustment to accommodate these energetic demands such as getting extra sleep, practicing chi gong and eating healthy foods. I longed for a normal life where I could get away with all the indulgences that regular people enjoyed.

By the time we opened the School of the Golden Discs and offered our first nine-month Core Program, I was feeling excited about my alignment with the Tibetan but also personally compromised. The Core Program was a channeled course in which Djwhal Khul worked with the students to heighten their soul alignment. It seemed that "Moriah" faded into the background, simply being used as a "radio station" to transmit his teachings. My individuality felt eclipsed by this great teacher. I hungered for personal recognition and attention. While I was honored to "give voice" to an ascended master, my own voice dissolved in this great merging within the channel.

These issues, coupled with the extreme energetic demands of channeling, heightened my belief that my work with Djwhal Khul was only for the benefit of others, a sacrifice to be made willingly and gratefully as a servant following instructions for the good of all. Martyrdom supposedly brings us closer to our spiritual nature, or so we are told. I don't wear the role of the martyr very well, chaffing against the annihilation of self. It is no wonder that the sickness associated with channeling accelerated to such an acute level that mercifully I was taken "off the hook" and allowed to close the doors of the school. For the second time I stopped channeling. During the following sixteen months I fell deeply into myself for a much needed rest and self-involvement.

As a result of the shamanic work, and finally viewing the big picture, I understand that the process of channeling Djwhal Khul was primarily for my own benefit, my own soul's salvation. Every time I channeled him, his energy was so potent that its force would push out and cleanse any karmic debris I was carrying. Over the fourteen years I channeled him, his energy merging with mine, I was able to access the very deep level at which this dark energy lived in my causal body. Just as white blood cells push out a splinter deeply lodged under the skin, so did the Tibetan's light factor extricate this dark force from its invisible but lethal cave within the walls of my soul.

It is no wonder that I felt so toxic from channeling. This is analogous to going on a strict cleansing fast that releases toxins into the bloodstream. It was an illusion that the channeling was making me sick. It was actually purifying me at a profound level. I now realize that the Tibetan had given his word to assist me 100% in this lifetime to release the "black monster" at long last. Rather than my serving him, he was serving me. My gratitude overruns at the incredible gift he has given in helping me to become conscious of this negative being and allowing his energy to be used to unearth this mass slowly over time. In this manner I could confront its dark impact on my soul's evolution and go beyond its negative impact.

I now understand a powerful dream I had during the first Core Program. This program was doubly challenging because I was taking it as well as teaching it. I had to go through all the clearing work the participants were doing as well as fulfill the role of channel, facilitator and teacher. Many times I wondered why I ever agreed to do such a rigorous task. My own soul material was gushing up. In spite of deep gratitude for the opportunity to surface to full consciousness under the guidance of the Tibetan, my personality was overwhelmed by the responsibility for the participants while I was "falling apart at the seams"—with the deluge of karmic debris clearing through my own psyche.

Midway through this endless nine-month program I had a dream in which I was shown a shell filled with pearls covered with slimy white maggots. This image was branded on my mind screen. Unable to push it out of my waking consciousness, I could not figure out what it meant. Years of dream work offered me little assistance with solving this enigmatic image. Consultations with fellow psychologists yielded minimal insight. Eventually I gave up trying to "crack" the dream, although I never forgot it.

At last, eight years later I experienced my "ah ha." The maggots on the pearls were representative of the dark mass attached parasitically to my soul. Just as the maggots obscured the beauty and radiance of the pearls, so did the dark glob, a possession from previous lifetimes, blot out my light and diminish my life force. "Pearls of wisdom" were pouring from my throat chakra during that nine-month course. But with the pearls came the awful sludge feeding off my soul's strength and beauty. My psyche, in its loving wisdom, provided an image of my core material needing to be released. I am deeply awed by the brilliance of the psyche and its integral part in our awakening process.

The dark force is persistent in its determination to overcome the light. The evil priest in the Egyptian mystery school who ordered my toes to be amputated reincarnated as the head priest in Greece who "translated" my oracle babblings into messages for the general populace. In the subsequent lifetime as a village witch that same dark spirit showed itself as one of the guards that dragged me down to the dungeon where the Inquisitors played out their diabolic games. It is no wonder that when opening up the channel and making contact with my soul, I dreamt repeatedly about being chased by Nazi's. For lifetimes I was on the run from this seemingly indomitable lightless force. The more I ran, the more it gained energy, feeding off my fear and disempowered rage.

The process of releasing this deeply embedded toxic material has clarified my issues with purity. How pure does self have to be in order to reach enlightenment? What does it mean to be completely pure? Is the need for purity a compensation for feelings of unworthiness? Does the purification process involve giving up everything that gives us pleasure? These questions have continued to bombard my psyche since my late twenties without satisfactory answers. No matter how many cleansing diets I tried or how much emotional debris I released, the need to purify was as urgent as ever.

I now realize how my soul's need to purge this dark mass was at the root of my obsession with purification. My past life as the village witch reflected the turmoil that this dark energy created. Driven to rid myself of this awful black parasite I willingly turned myself over to the Inquisition to be burned at the stake, a desperate attempt to sanctify my soul. After leaving that lifetime I realized how burning one's flesh cannot rid the causal body of its poisons. It only reinforced the profound feelings of powerlessness in the face of the dark force.

Feeling unbearably stained and contaminated by this energy feeding off my soul led me to believe that perhaps this "mark" was contagious. Not only was I a magnet for drawing the dark force to me, but I could also spread it to anyone with whom I had contact. In my lifetime as village witch my lover, a young wizard bursting with healing potential, succumbed to a dark possession that eventually sealed his heart shut, extinguishing our love. I felt that it was my fault. Not only couldn't I heal the dying babies in the village, but also had somehow transmitted the "mark" to my beloved resulting in his eventual demise.

In my current lifetime I have always felt a deep sense of responsibility for my mother's suicide. As an adult I rationally knew that a toddler couldn't drive his/her mother to self-destruction. However, I carried the guilt for many years. It is psychologically common for children to take on their parents' difficulty and pain, feeling as if they somehow are the cause of it. Regardless, my guilt persisted despite hours and hours in therapy working through accountability that is normal in children suffering from this kind of trauma.

As a result of the shamanic cleansing work I can track this self-blame to the following beliefs: "Being in my mother's womb contaminated her totality. The 'mark' attached to my soul couldn't help but permeate her being. Her own delicate psyche was all too susceptible to the poisons emanating from this viciously hateful leech, lodged seemingly for eternity in my soul. If I have the 'mark', so will anyone who loves me."

This belief system tormented me daily, leaving me unworthy to even consider my own magnitude. If I was responsible for my mother's death, I did not deserve to *really* live. I could only hope for purgatory, living in the gray area between life and death, never fully coming into my own.

I now see the illusion in these beliefs. My mother's karma was complex and difficult. As her being merged with mine in my conception and gestation, whatever past life wounds she carried were activated to be healed and released. It was not her destiny to be overcome by pain leading her to self-destruction. It was not my historic struggle with the dark force that pushed her over the edge. It was her own soul's pain that became unbearable. My communication with her on the spirit plane reveals her remorse and grief over the abandonment of her children. She is slowly healing from this, gradually working through the distortions that blinded her perception of herself and the possibilities for life.

Trusting Djwhal Khul in this lifetime has allowed me deeply open up to my soul. His instructions to remove the blockage in the back of my heart chakra in order to let him in challenged me to believe that I could receive higher energy from precisely the areas where I had been "stabbed in the back" (physically and emotionally) in past lives as well as in this one. Allowing the Tibetan to embrace me from behind when going into channel has been a shear leap of faith. Djwhal Khul's constancy, love, reliability and patience have repeatedly proven to me that I could really trust him. In trusting him, I can also trust the higher powers that orchestrate our ultimate enlightenment.

The Cosmic Janitor

Nancy and I "finished" our work in late February 2000. The dark mass was removed. All was well in the universe! In spite of the background intermittent pain shooting through my side, I eagerly jumped back into my busy life.

Reporting for a check-up with Nancy in mid-March, her penetrating shamanic hands traced my side, searching for any remaining vestiges of dark tendrils. She strongly sensed that we had fully cleared the black mass from my causal body. My physical body was having difficulty releasing the final imprint, reminding me of its presence through sporadic hot sensations just beneath my skin. Shaking our heads in puzzlement we wondered what *more* we could possibly do to rid my body of this nasty presence for once and for all. How do we give our physical bodies the message that chronic karmic conditions are finally resolved, releasing the need for our cells to carry the debris once it has been cleared from our subtle soul body?

Assuming that eventually the physical memory of this psychic battle would fade and these "ghost" pains would subside, we agreed to wait and keep a close watch on it. Two months flew by leaving me little time to reflect on this bizarre healing process. Quietly I hoped that full health would return, with my side free and clear from discomfort.

As the trees began to bud in late April I felt a sharp surface pain in the central region of the "mark." Assuming it was a pimple I decided to let it run its course. Perhaps my body was finding its own way of releasing the residual aftermath of all the shamanic extraction work. As four days passed this bump became reddened and sore. Six inches directly below my left armpit, difficult to view up close, I asked Zayne to examine it. "It's a tick," he blurted out, disturbed and concerned. In spite of our immediate efforts to suffocate the tick in rubbing alcohol, its mouth was deeply embedded in my side. Zayne patiently removed the engorged body. Since it was a wood tick, we weren't worried about Lyme disease.

Three days later I had a healing session scheduled with two very skilled energy workers. It was Zayne's idea for me to see these practitioners although at the time I was feeling no need for a healing. Chi gong practices coupled with a healthy diet keep me in good health. I rarely need healers. On the psychic/soul level, my work with Nance felt sufficient. However, responding to an inner nudge from my good friend Djwhal Khul, I acquiesced to Zayne's urging. He had set up an appointment two weeks prior to the tick bite. The timing of synchronistic events often amazes me. When my soul is ready to tackle difficult material, there is always a healer, an herb, a book, a dream, a workshop or other forms of support and guidance to move me through it.

My intention for this healing session was to assist my body in letting go of its attachment to the karmic memory of the dark force lodged in my side. I assumed it would be a mellow experience, involving sound work and deep relaxation. I should have known better!

The country road to the healer's house was devoid of its usual traffic. Alone on the road I responded to an inner voice telling me to slow down. Suddenly, out of the woods emerged a mysterious beautiful creature. Observing it walking very slowly across the road in front of the car, I tried to fathom what it was. Completely gray from head to toe, smooth skinned with sporadic patches of fur, it was absolutely wild. Arriving at the other side of the road, it turned and stared me in the eye for a suspended minute that felt like an hour. The ancient wisdom pouring from its eyes locked into a deep connection with my soul captivating me in a swell of excitement. I realized I was looking at a magnificent, molting, gray wolf.

The wolf is my power animal, an ancient allegiance developed lifetimes ago. To physically encounter my power animal in a geographic area where wolves are supposed to be extinct was an unbelievable honor. The wolf and I merged as one, filling me with strength and courage as I continued on the road to my date with the final clearing ground of the battle with the dark force.

Needless to say, my healing session was profound. We invoked the final layers of darkness. Deep sobs rippled along currents of energy streaming through me as I released layers of soul wounds inflicted through past life obsessions with fighting the dark force. My ego, baffled at the emotional intensity of what was pouring out of me, retreated into the background allowing surrender to this divine cleansing process. The wolf was internally aligned with me, providing the fortitude to say a final **NO** to anything that would compromise the light of my soul.

Exhausted, spaced out, rendered down to the bone, I barely heard the healer's words as he cautioned me that I might experience "fall-out" over the next few days from the intensity of our work. Mumbling my thanks, deep gratitude, I could barely drive the six miles home. Sleep was all I cared about.

Drying off from my shower the next evening while preparing to attend a concert, I noticed the tick bite site was getting larger and redder. By midnight it was burning hot. The next morning I desperately called Nancy for help. The inflammation was now the size of a football, huge blisters developing around the bite.

Nancy arrived in a flash, shaman's mesa in hand filled with crystals and stones. Trying not to touch the area, she painstakingly worked to cleanse the poisons spewing out. Nancy's determination to remove all the debris blocked out my moans. I could not bare the slightest contact with this boiling mass of corruption. Clutching Zayne's hand tightly, I attempted to breathe my way through this painful process. Forty-five minutes felt like hours as I struggled not to run out of the room, eager to end this entire ordeal. As Nancy finished her work I relaxed, filled with a strange sense of satisfaction knowing that finally this soul-laden material was surfacing through my body to be completely released. Throughout the following week Zayne devotedly applied hot compresses to the site, layering goldenseal, slippery elm and rain forest herbs to the inflammation. The wound reduced in intensity. Although I knew I was releasing major karmic material on a soul level, my anxiety grew about Lyme disease. Having exhibited the classic symptoms of the large red ring around the bite propelled me to see a doctor. The blood test confirmed my fears. Three weeks of antibiotics and intensive rain forest herbs purged my system of the disease with no side affects.

Yes, one can simply say that I had a nasty tick bite carrying Lyme disease. But I know better. Ticks and other parasites are metaphysically referenced as "cosmic janitors." They are "sent" to the very site on our physical body needing to release soul wounds. These janitors serve as the clean-up crew, drawing karmic debris to the surface that the body is having difficulty purging. Ironically, ticks look almost like scarabs, the sacred beetle of Egypt.

One last footnote on this mysterious process. When I returned to the doctor for a final check-up on the tick bite, she indicated that the infection was gone, although my side was still red and blotchy. She suggested a topical ointment. I offered that vitamin E might do the trick. Shaking her head, she said, "Why not try Egyptian Magic Lotion. You can find it at the local health food store." Visiting the health food store on a daily basis for my fresh produce, I had never seen this lotion. Sure enough, there it was tucked into the back of the shelf. The outside of the container was filled with esoteric symbols and statements of the mysterious healing methods employed by ancient Pharaohs of Egyptian magic. I could feel the Tibetan's eyes twinkling at me as I marveled at the wonder of the healing process, eventually all the pieces coming together over thousands of years, integrated at long last.

Djwhal Khul elaborated on my process:

> *This is the time for final resolution with your ancient battle with the dark force. There is no longer any need to fear these negative energies. Your soul has learned the futility of losing its precious life force through an undue attachment to conquering the destructive forces within the universe. Perhaps it is time to reconsider the entire issue, taking it to a higher level. At this heightened level of awareness you can arrive at a place of forgiveness. This forgiveness illustrates Source's compassion for all creation, even the great illusion that continues to support the dark force.*
>
> *This is not to deny the truly destructive aspects of the dark force and its painful impact on humankind. Consider the*

possibility of neutralizing this unilluminated energy through Love. Fear only feeds its anti-life appetite. Rage, springing from fear and powerlessness, fires it up, fueling its power. To travel down the road of fear and rage is to hand one's power over to the dark force. This act of disempowerment invites futility, despair and lovelessness.

We greatly appreciate your efforts to annihilate the dark force and are sympathetic with your burning need to contribute to the return of peace on planet earth. However, to continue to struggle against this negative current is no longer necessary. This battle dissipates tremendous energy. In past lives your fight against these dark currents contributed to the elimination of some of the many crimes perpetrated by "evil." This heightened your own sense of light. However, it cost your soul its joy of being. Your work as warrior is over. Now it is time to consider the role of universal peacemaker.

The paradigm is shifting on planet earth. As humankind goes beyond the duality, the dark force loses its purchase on the ambivalence that undermines faith. The dark mesh that reinforces the illusion of separation is dissolving, unable to withstand the heightened vibrations of the new millennium. The dark force responds to this threat with a determination to tighten its hold on the collective soul of humankind. However, its futile efforts cannot withstand the emergence of the "New Cosmic Day.

To continue to fight the dark force is to continue to energize the third dimensional paradigm of polarities, good vs. bad. It is time to experience the true spiritual nature of life— Oneness. Within this Oneness is an eternal peace that extends itself far beyond the domain of the dark force. As humankind releases its fear of the dark force these negative energies wither and die, unable to sustain themselves in an energetic field of compassion. Teach this to others, passing on the word that it is truly SAFE in the universe!

The Masters shower self with gratitude for your willingness to face the dark. Now it is time to experience the release from lifetimes of adversity and severity. Trust the Garden of Peace that flowers within the heart chakra extending itself forth into your outer life. This is the true place of magic that eliminates all energies attempting to undo the Great Life Force that is Source. Allow self to deeply relax. Trust grows. Nightmares fade. The Light prevails. And so is the way of all things Divine.

Addendum

Exactly one year later, on our anniversary, Zayne woke up with a tick embedded in his side. Yes, the same left side, exactly six inches below his armpit in the middle of his side. We removed the tick with some difficulty. Thankfully, he did not get Lyme disease. Was this a reminder from the dark force of its persistent presence? My understanding tells me that this was Zayne's time to release his share of our mutual karma around negative forces. The cosmic janitor knows exactly where to go and how to get our attention. We are now both cleansed of attachments to ancient lifetimes of struggle with dark energies as we merge together into a higher, light-filled consciousness.

Evil

For many years I have hidden my issues with the dark force from all but a few close friends. My psychologically sophisticated ego/persona is embarrassed to reveal such a concern. It believes that the concept of evil is something explainable through theories involving the collective unconscious (unintegrated aspects of the human condition) known as the shadow. This belief collides with the notion that evil is an entity, a great dark force, that exists only to destroy the essence of life. I have struggled with this confusion around evil throughout my adult life. Many times I, as well as others, have asked the Tibetan for his teaching about evil.

I finally accept that evil exists (although a part of me still quivers with ambivalence as I write this). Accepting that the issue of "evil" falls into the terrain of the Greater Mysteries, paradoxically I allow my self to speak about evil as a definite reality.

Dear reader, please make this leap with me so that together we can explore the dimension of the struggle between the dark and light forces as I have perceived it over lifetimes. This has been an effort to illuminate an attunement to the Great Mystery that encapsulates our human experience.

Stories about evil are told in all the worldly religions and spiritual teachings. This leads me to believe that at a collective level we are attuning to some negative force that appears to have a life and perhaps intelligence of its own. Maybe this is not such a far-fetched notion when we consider that Source is an immense being of inconceivable intelligence who created our intricate and complex world. Few of us are yet at the level to be able to imagine ourselves creating this earth plane, not to mention our galaxy. From Source's level of brilliance our plane of duality was created and expressed at a beyond-genius level. Therefore, all aspects of the duality, the full range of positive and negative energies, have the same potential for heightened intelligence.

The negative, or dark, aspect of our world appears to have many levels. The basic levels are manifested through experiences such as bad moods, negative thinking, fear, poor physical health, loss of faith, etc. This is the negative polarity as it impacts the physical, emotional, mental and spiritual bodies. The negative polarity can express itself from a basic to a very complex and advanced level. At this developed, highly intelligent application of the dark, it appears to have a potency of being that is equal in opposite counterpart to our saints and experiences of the miraculous. Just as we reference the heightened light factor in beings such as Master Jesus, we also reference the heightened dark factor in beings such as the "devil" or "Lucificer." Does this mean that there is no end to the dark force just as the light force seems infinite?

Djwhal Khul reassures me that ultimately Source is a Being of complete Light. It is only in the dimension where life is bifurcated that we experience the darkness. He adds:

> *It is correct to assume that the dark aspect, often called evil, is imbued with an intelligence of its own, and therefore a consciousness of its own. The White (light) Brotherhood has dedicated itself to neutralizing the dark force through its efforts to assist in the collective awakening process in humankind. It is through humanity's attunement to the duality that the dark force attaches itself.*
>
> *The dark force at its origination point is a distortion of the light—the result of a bend in the frequency of creation that, through the free will imbued in all of Source's creation, developed into a "monster." Its instinct (energetic matrix) was to devour light, just as most of humankind's impulse is to be drawn toward the light—generate light—through love and creativity. Energies multiply themselves. Their very being is their purpose. The more that humankind absorbs and reflects light (its essential Divine nature) the more that light is multiplied. Equally, the more that the dark force devours light, the more it wants. Darkness multiplies. Intelligence at this level, barely removed from its origination in Source, is powerful enough to create universes. This implies that the dark force could create its own, or establish a hold on the universe, especially the earth plane, that could potentially rule out all light. However, the Light Force is equal to it and ultimately more powerful because it is not a distortion of Source's essence.*

TRANSMUTING THE DARK FORCE

All distortions of the divine eventually even themselves out—smoothing out the illusions resulting from the frequencies that offset their original matrix. While this process seems endless to humankind, it does have a finish line. This is the endpoint where this original distortion of Source's Being returns to Its true nature. Light prevails in all aspects of Source's creations.

As humankind evolves beyond its attachment to duality, it is no longer fertile feeding ground for the light-devouring dark force. Because humankind expects to be bifurcated, it is highly susceptible to the magnetic draw of the original dark force. The more humankind infuses with light, the more it expects to be undone by the dark. The Masters have worked devotedly toward assisting humankind in eliminating the illusion that it is possible to lose one's connection to the light. It has been within this illusion that the dark force has zealously taken over the minds and hearts of many.

As humankind awakens, it realizes the distortion, and therefore the lie inherent within the dark force. The magnetic attraction breaks down. The dark force simply has to go elsewhere in order to feed. As all of humankind opens up, the entire earth is enlightened. As the earth plane is enlightened, the light factor of the universe heightens exponentially which then heightens the light factors of other universes which lead to fewer feeding grounds for the dark force. This becomes a form of extinction.

The universal environment no longer can support the dark force in its habit of devouring light. As this occurs, its potency weakens, shrivels and resolves itself into the void where it then rediscovers it original matrix, one of Love. Not only is this process do-able, it is already done and simply waiting for the actual events to catch up with Source's original response to this distortion, (this inverted ripple of Source's intention)—which was to send out a corrective Force to re-establish the Sacred Order of the Divine as It knows Itself to be. The masters, angels, and many other helpers have been a part of this corrective Force for eons.

My Soul's Response to Letting Go of Evil

"Thank you, thank you, thank you from this point of infinity to your human plane of apparent limitation. Oh, so grateful am I to you, my extension on the earth plane, who braves the rigors of multidimensional cleansing. Know that you alone did not incur or create this karma but rather simply agreed to carry it forth into a lifetime designed for resolution, closure, healing and illumination.

Aside from bouts of resistance and negativity, you have courageously faced the dark pockets within me that have been too volatile to exorcise, too painful to touch, and too unfathomably deep and extensive to uproot. Your entire being, astrological configuration, childhood experiences, gifts, talents, wounds, and wisdom have all been designed to make you the vehicle; the instrument of triumph over loss, to help break the attachment to an ancient battle initiated thousands of years ago and truly of no good purpose to the world.

Your work has given me, your soul, a new paradigm into which the divine Joy is able to flow. This paradigm cares not for battling darkness and experiencing pointless agony for the sake of endurance and wisdom. My being now has the clear space to explore itself through a light dimension never yet known, as blinded as I have been by my engagement with the Great Battle of the Forces. This light dimension is just beginning to shower upon me like sunshine warming one's brittle bones, allowing them to regenerate a new level of strength not dissipated by allowing self to be the victim of intergalactic vampires.

I know ever more clearly my essential right to BE. I am releasing the struggle for existence as I have dissolved much confusion about needing to display to Source my worthiness through heady, gallant battle against all beings who would devour the great Light that unites all. Still torn am I about who will fight this battle if I step beyond the front where light clashes against dark. Yet my beloved teacher Djwhal Khul reminds me that the old paradigm, grid that has sealed our universe into a zone of self-destruction is lifting, like a dark cloud dispersing under the impact of sunshine.

My fire emerges stronger because I am more complete—free to simply create

Self in magical forms reflecting the true universal nature—Love. I burn as myself a great fire that lights the hearts of others as I weep tears of gratitude and joy that wash away the last days of darkness, as they recede from the consciousness of all who dwell in our universal family."

BREAKING THROUGH

Resistance

What are we supposed to do with the inevitable resistance that surfaces for all of us as we approach our magnitude? Djwhal Khul teaches that resistance increases proportionately to the potency of energy needing to emerge. That's like saying that as we get closer to reaching the top of the mountain, the mountain gets higher and steeper. How frustrating and disheartening! Djwhal Khul explains:

The plane of duality embodies a dynamic tension resulting in a profound push/pull in the creative process. This is the tension in bringing forth one's greatest aspirations as they interface with the opposite impulse to negate these desires. This negation of emergence is called resistance.

My hungry mind frequently chews on that teaching. Why do we push away, resist, the very things in life that give us our greatest satisfaction? How many of us fall just short of fulfilling our goals, allowing "life" to snatch away our victories at the last minute? We offer ourselves the usual excuses: "No time to get to what I really want to do. I don't have the money to realize my dreams. It's too much effort to do anything beside the basic demands of daily life. Maybe when I am older I'll be able to give myself what I really want. Other people's needs are more important right now. I don't deserve to be *that* happy." None of these rationalizations really sheds light on this strange phenomenon of collective self-sabotage that is rampant in the human condition.

I am amazed that the prevalent feeling usually experienced as we get close to self-fulfillment is *fear!* Rationally, it makes no sense to fear having something, or achieving a state of mind, that we have desired for so long. However, most of us cringe in awe and resistance as we encounter the life we have always wished for. The Tibetan responds:

> *Get used to resistance. Acceptance of resistance allows the student to use it as a tool to work with the dynamic tension inherent in the creative process.*

How are we supposed to use resistance as a tool? Customarily, I battle my resistance, trying to overpower it with my will, usually resulting in an exhausted surrender to this strange undertow to my good intentions. Impatience with Source flares up in response to this difficult assignment of working with resistance. It is like trying to hold sandcastles in place as great oceanic waves pulverize them. Djwhal Khul smiles at my frustration, reminding me:

> *The potency of resistance issues guidance toward the core of one's soul's intention for this lifetime. Yes, resistance is formidable. But it is a powerful counterpart to the speed of the mind and imagination. It allows a level of difficulty to emerge requiring heightened intentionality, determination, and faith. These qualities create a great vehicle through which the soul emerges. It is useless to try to overpower resistance. The attempt to dominate simply adds more energy to the resistance. One must acclimate to the resistance and gently, but persistently, move forward within its energetic field.*

This reminds me of mountain climbing. Initially when I have hiked for as little as fifteen minutes I feel exhausted, as negative thoughts swirl through my mind: "This is too much. I don't have the stamina for this. I'm too tired. I hate this hike. I hate nature. I want to go home and have a cup of tea, put my feet up and be lazy!" Yes, resistance grabs my original inspiration to seek a vision from atop a 360 degree vista and smashes it into little pieces left along the ever-steepening trail. The resistance gathers energy forming a thick, seemingly impenetrable, wall that seeps into my muscles and joints, clogging up free-flowing life force. This heavy force-field reaches its height as I hang on for dear life refusing the seduction of the resistance as it encourages me to give up and turn back. Resigning myself to be miserable, I plod along shutting my ears to the voices of resistance.

Suddenly my energy shifts. I've broken the resistance barrier and energy is streaming through me. I'm hiking fluidly, joyfully, as inspiration returns, eager to seek the messages from the mountaintop. Sitting at the peak and reviewing my hike, I am deeply grateful to myself for persevering through the inevitable "wall" of negation. This wall came very close to robbing me of my vision quest. I am struck by the mystery that carries this strange process of hitting the wall and going beyond. What is it in us that allows us to shift through the wall?

The process of hitting the wall evokes all of our false beliefs about ourselves and our lives. In those moments of seeming impossibility we re-experience our greatest illusions. These illusions spring from early childhood conditioning, unresolved past life material and the collective pool of delusion indicating that we are separate from our divinity and therefore separate from our true magnitude. The wall is everything that negates our truth. Therefore, resistance is really a flushing up of all perceptions that would stop us from moving into our enlightenment. Yet the Tibetan says that resistance is integral to the creative process on planet earth. Why? To me it is only a "show stopper"—an energy drain that leaves me 100% convinced that there is no point in "going for it." Djwhal Khul responds:

Resistance is basically a cleansing process. It brings up all the karmic debris needing to be released in order for true liberation to occur. Yes, resistance is a negating counterpart to life itself. This negation dynamic scours the soul of its impurities. These impurities are the result of accumulated false beliefs.

The field of polarity is an arena in which to explore one's divinity through the interplay of opposites. However, it is not the truth of one's essence. Spiritual essence lies beyond the field of duality and cannot be contaminated by negativity. Therefore, humankind plays and creates within the field of duality in order to ultimately realize the illusion within it. To be caught in this illusion is to be caught in the web of resistance. Resistance allows all aspects of the negative polarity to surface through which self becomes better acquainted with the soul.

As self realizes the illusion of duality then self can detach from the "reality" of it. At that point self is able to dance with resistance, rejoicing in the understanding that resistance is a clearing process of accumulated toxins stored within negative false beliefs. At any point in the soul's history that has played out the illusion that it is possible to be separate from Source, a pocket of resistance develops. This is the resistance to full awakening. Any action that self takes toward wholeness and full integration of one's divinity stimulates these pockets of resistance to allow past illusions and false conclusions to be cleared.

The Tibetan's words soften my frustration, allowing me to more clearly understand the divine function of resistance. When I consider it an opportunity to flush out and purge any buried material within self that might prevent or postpone my liberation, I drop to my knees in gratitude. Of course I have to be willing to engage karmic debris creating blockages in my soul-alignment—how obvious! The resistance "wall" allows me to exercise my strength and determination. It also points out that I am on the right track. When there is little at stake, the resistance evaporates—it's smooth sailing. When my soul is at stake, the resistance towers like a giant monster daring my intention to challenge all limitations dominating my life.

So, I invite the resistance—rolling up my sleeves—preparing for a wild ride as I break through the resistance wall into true liberation— knowing that my freedom has been hard-earned and well-deserved!

Striving

"Stop striving!" insists the Tibetan. He gives me this message over and over again. Dutifully I try to obey his guidance but find it harder than I thought. I realize how automatic my striving is. I am forever trying to get "there" without even knowing where "there" is or when I have arrived "there." Djwhal Khul teaches that "there" is an illusion. My mind knows this but impulse overrides understanding as striving takes over like an unleashed stallion charging into the oblivion of accomplishment.

Of course I can never accomplish enough, having a never-ending list of things to achieve in order to arrive at a sense of completeness with my life mission. I tell myself, "Today is not a good day to die because I have not yet achieved all that I am meant to in this lifetime. It would be a failure if I left the earth plane before fulfilling my calling." This thinking backfires as each accomplishment leads to another perceived karmic demand. Like the mountain climber who reaches the peak only to get a better view of the yet unclaimed higher peaks in the distance, I am driven by ambition. This ambition, while spiritual in nature, plays itself out in the external world through the pursuit of high level work, ultimate health, potent creativity, deep relationships and complete liberation. To sum it up, I want to be perfect!

These goals are not inherently negative. Quite the contrary, they are reflections of advanced spiritual work. However, the attitude and energy brought to these pursuits are not exactly high level! I carry a belief system indicating that Source's love is conditional based on achievement. It implies that my beingness alone is not enough to get me through the fifth dimensional gate of enlightenment.

I have difficulty discerning the difference between energy used to compensate for inadequacy through striving, and energy used to express my soul's passion for full expression of its magnitude. Djwhal Khul reminds me that the two energies feel very different from each other. The former comes from a place of fear, tension and anxiety woven within it, while the latter explodes out of me in an uncontainable exuberance of life. Stepping back from my own compulsion allows me to distinguish between the two approaches. However, much of the time my face is right up into the quest. One result stands out above all the rest—a cellular feeling of deep exhaustion, probably lifetimes old, resulting from a tension-driven striving to please a God who would judge me as lacking if I didn't produce, produce, produce!

I often envy "laid back" cultures. Vacationing in Jamaica was a wonderful culture shock. I had to step down my insane pace to avoid jumping out of my skin as I yielded to the "no problem, man" attitude and rhythm so richly expressed in the Caribbean. The Jamaicans know much more about "being" than I will ever know, madly driven that I am by my cultural expectations. As I looked out on the clear turquoise waters of the Caribbean, I wondered what it would be like to know that my divinity was well served and well expressed through that moment of simple beingness, without concern about what it was that I was becoming.

I ask Djwhal Khul how I can embrace my magnitude without becoming attached to goals of greatness and accomplishment. I know that our internal reality is eventually mirrored in our external experience. It seems inevitable that in opening to my soul's magnitude internally, my outer life would become larger or more successful. Djwhal Khul responds:

> *The soul's magnitude is not reflected through accomplishment or outward success. Rather it is an increased vibratory rate that reflects a quality of experience, not a quantity of successful achievements. You will have arrived "there" when you have completely forgotten any impulse to get "there." When you are so fulfilled by your very breath that anything extra feels superfluous you will be dwelling fully ensouled in your magnitude of being. This is not something that you can try to make happen. It is the result of allowing your being to exist free from the pressure to be more than you are in that moment.*
>
> *Striving is based on the fear of not being enough. These karmic fears, carried for lifetimes, result in exhaustion, self-criticism, guilt, and a deep sense of failure. No amount of striving has ever brought one closer to Source. It certainly does not earn extra credit when appearing before the karmic board in between incarnations.*

As he speaks my fears surface. How will I motivate myself to do anything if "nothing" needs to be done? What would I do with the inevitable emptiness that would result from releasing endless striving? What would make me feel important or special? All these agendas that I carry apparently have little or nothing to do with the divine plan.

I thought I was on a mission requiring major output of energy into forms—counseling, teaching, writing, healing, etc. Is Djwhat Khul telling me that none of it matters, that all of this push has been for nothing? Talk about getting the wind knocked out of your sails! Releasing these imaginary "requirements' for enlightenment leaves me in a mush state.

Djwhal Khul puts his etheric arm around my shoulders encouraging me to celebrate the freedom brought forth by this new awareness. But, I don't trust this freedom. It feels too vacuous to celebrate. I want my striving back! It is so familiar and comforting, even if it is exhausting and life-shortening. It gives me a sense of progress that I am getting "somewhere." Djwhal Khul reminds me that my need for progress reflects insecurity about being enough. The false belief is that progress equals enoughness.

As I attempt to breathe his teachings into my solar plexus, a deep sense of fatigue surfaces revealing how tired I am of pushing for Source's approval. Fear has fueled striving for lifetimes, robbing the precious present as it continually propels me into the illusion of a future worthy self. My present self and future self could never be enough regardless of all that I might accomplish.

In this moment of apparent emptiness, the agenda wiped clean, I take a moment to let go of all my projected future selves. Djwhal Khul reminds me:

> *There is nothing in nature that needs to strive in order to grow. Growth is automatically programmed into the Divine Matrix inherent in all of Source's creation. Ironically, striving slows down true growth as it creates a countering force to the natural cycles of evolution.*

As I soak in his perspective I can feel my cells relaxing and opening. What a relief it is to know that I am enough. To shortchange self is to shortchange Source. Djwhal Khul suggests:

> *Exchange striving for cooperation. The student does not have to strive to assist with the Divine Plan. Simply cooperate with it. Let self open, trust, and rejoice in your birthright which is inherently filled with gifts of enlightenment and liberation. From that point on, all outward achievement is*

simply the soul's creative passion and play. The student takes to the cosmic playground called planet earth and expresses self in endless forms as a child plays in the sand creating spontaneous mandalas that unite all beings.

Magnitude

The Tibetan often challenges us to move into our magnitude. I am struck by our instinctual impulse to think and be smaller than we really are. In the past my magnitude was only expressed in fantasy and daydreams. If other people offered reflections about my potential I inwardly blocked out their vision of my significance.

I have worked very hard to be ordinary. I thought that ordinary meant small and that normal meant invisible. If I had displayed my magnitude to my parents I would have been quickly punished, silenced. I grew to believe that magnitude was a dangerous thing. I thought that if I allowed myself to perceive my glorious capabilities my ego would inflate with self-importance. I would lose control of my humility. I would be obnoxious. I would overshadow others. I would get carried away with power and self-reflection. I would be a narcissist.

I now understand that to resist my magnitude is to waste precious time. While I fully believe in immortality and the mastery of death, I also recognize the gift of life on the earth plane. Every moment is to be cherished. Every moment that I hold back or diminish my light is a wasted moment. Being incarnate provides the opportunity to experience magnitude in form. This opportunity is not to be taken for granted. So, I have to face the unbearable task of embodying and expressing my greatness. The time for hiding has run out. This is true for all of humankind. The accelerated energies do not allow for diminishment.

As I allow myself to become larger I can feel the old self breaking off in pieces. I can no longer bite my tongue, holding back my truth in dangerous situations. I can no longer "space out," disassociating from my passion. I can no longer wile the time away fantasizing about the future. I can no longer make other people's needs more important than my own. I can no longer say yes when I really need to say no. I can no longer tell myself that I am not yet ready to pick up the torch of my purpose. I can no longer tell myself that greatness is for others, not for me. I can no longer hide my temperament and impatience. I can no longer swallow my fire to keep it from burning others.

I have reshaped my understanding of what it is to have a spiritual life. It is not total dedication to others. It is not martyrdom. It is not utter devotion to the Masters. It does not require complete self-purification. I can still be angry, sexual, confused, lost, dependent on others, and fearful. I don't have to have answers or brilliant visions of Source. Rather, salvation/enlightenment lies right in the *heart* of my human condition.

An exquisite treasure nestles within the richness of the paradox of the human soul. That treasure is only retrievable if we accept who we are at a fundamental level. Source wants us to embrace Its creation in form. How can we possibly do that if we are so focused on transcending who we are. The task is to hold steady to our humanity as it evolves itself.

We are the keepers of the human condition. We weave all of its facets together within our individual being. We must find the courage to allow the fullness of our light to penetrate all the dark corners of our psyche and unconditionally rejoice in what we discover.

My life is more "spiritual" than ever. I have discovered that the ultimate spiritual practice is to allow more and more space for myself to fully emerge. In that I honor Source. My spiritual life is my awareness. As that increases so do the blessings and gifts shower upon me.

Gratitude is unavoidable even in my most cynical moments. It is startling to realize how much of Self there is inside. The more I pour out, the more I fill up. There is no end to Moriah. With that awareness I can release the false belief that I won't make it in this lifetime or that I am not enough. Yes, I can embrace my extraordinary Self. Yes, I can tolerate my magnitude. I eagerly step upon the Pathway of Greatness. My soul rejoices at long last. I am free.

This is the process we all face—the greatest challenge of all—to dare to substantiate our outstanding importance, gifts, strengths and sheer potency of being in honor of the Great Loving Force that has made our existence possible. To embody our magnitude is to heal the world.

GLOSSARY

Affirmations: Specifically worded statements, spoken repeatedly, to energize and enhance positive thoughts and to reprogram negative thinking.

Akashic Records: Records stored in a non-physical library on the causal plane which is an etheric dimension. These records hold the soul's entire karmic history including all lifetimes on planet earth.

Alchemy: A process used in medieval times to turn lead into gold. This term is used symbolically to describe the transformation process in the soul.

Astral Plane: The next dimension beyond the earth plane, the energetic field surrounding the earth plane. It is the initial place our spirit goes after death, the place where ghosts reside.

Chakras: Seven energy centers in the body, described as vortexes that receive and emit cosmic energy.

Channeling: Attuning and opening to receive wisdom, guidance and teaching from the higher self, and/or spirit-plane teachers and guides.

Chats: Monthly groups sponsored by the School of the Golden Discs when the Tibetan is channeled by Moriah Marston for teaching metaphysics.

Eleusinian Mysteries: An ancient Greek ritual of initiation, attended by thousands of people, to explore the meaning of life, death, and beyond.

Etheric Plane: A non-physical higher dimension where refined and evolved beings from the spiritual plane reside.

False beliefs: False conclusions made during times of trauma and difficulty, usually based on experiences in previous lifetimes that hold negative patterns that limit our openness to our present life potential.

Higher Self: The essential, eternal level of self that exists beyond the earthly realm. The Higher Self extends itself to earth as a human being with an ego and personality.

Hu tone: From an ancient Hindu system of sounds—it is a powerful, penetrating sound that aligns, opens and stimulates the physical, emotional, mental and spiritual bodies.

Kundalini: The central life force that runs through all beings. It lies curled up like a snake at the base of the spine while dormant. When activated, it rises up the spine and sparks the electrical system of the body that catalyzes awakening.

Medium: Someone who communicates with the spirits and allows that spirit's energy to blend with his/her own; may allow that spirit to speak directly through them.

Oracle: A person who receives revelations/divine wisdom from a higher plane to be offered as guidance to humanity.

Shadow: The unclaimed, unintegrated, unconscious aspects of self.

Self: A shortened term for Higher Self.

Soul-alignment: The process of self-realization. The integration of the Higher Self and one's karmic history into full conscious awareness in this present lifetime.

Source: God, Goddess, "All that is," the Ultimate Supreme Being, the Creator.

MORIAH MARSTON AND THE SCHOOL OF THE GOLDEN DISCS

In 1990, Moriah journeyed with a group of people to the sacred sites of Greece in a reenactment of the Eleusinian Mysteries. It was in Delphi that Moriah had a vivid dream of the Golden Discs. This dream inspired her first vision of this school. The Golden Discs are objects found in ancient Greek art. They are covered with symbols the meaning of which has never been discovered. It is in the domain of the Greater Mysteries in which the human spirit dwells that this school is founded.

The primary binding influence of this school is Ascended Master Djwhal Khul, the Tibetan. Djwhal Khul guides from the spirit plane the overall program with wisdom, compassion, humor and inspiration.

The acceleration we are feeling at the onset of the third millennium brings us increased chaos, crisis and opportunity. We have a choice to creatively work with these heightened energies rather than be overwhelmed by chaos. We live in a period of history where there is a major paradigm shift occurring on the planet as we move from a model of individualism to a different form of consciousness—a group consciousness. The paradigm shift is occurring through a collective awakening experience. The school provides a vehicle for opening to the great potential of these times.

OFFERINGS

COURSEWORK

The School of the Golden Discs offers the following processing and channeled group exploration sessions facilitated by Moriah, including channeled discourses by Ascended Master Djwhal Khul. These events are held in Shelburne Falls, Massachusetts and are offered to interested groups throughout the nation. Contact Zayne @413-625-6754 for information about hosting an event.

"Chats with the Tibetan" are held monthly on Sunday afternoons. These sessions inspire the group with the Tibetan's wisdom, compassion and humor as he explores themes pertinent to the new millennium and the collective transformation that is occurring on the planet. Join us in this special communion as the Tibetan explores the spiritual process of integrating and applying the higher perspective into daily life.

"Seminar Intensives with Moriah Marston and the Tibetan" These half-day and weekend long workshops address the psychological and metaphysical process of transforming core issues we all experience in order to evolve our consciousness. As facilitator of the group, Moriah applies her psychological background to assist the participants in exploring and working through current issues and past experiences related to the seminar's theme. Then Moriah channels the Tibetan who provides the spiritual perspective on the work. This helps the participants to release false beliefs and to expand their awareness of the topic, leading to greater self-acceptance and insight. Bask in the Tibetan's transformative energy as he heats up this alchemical process with his original insight, compassion and humor.

The Transformational Times Show with Moriah Marston and the Tibetan: An Internet based interactive Talk Radio show with Moriah

Marston including a channeled discourse by the Tibetan which addresses a range of topics covered in *Earth School* (see publications below). Visit www.transformationtimes.com to check the schedule, link to the weekly, hour long show and to access the show's archives.

"Inward Unbound" Correspondence Course: Keep the heat turned up on your transformational process in the privacy of your own home! This is an opportunity to work with tapes/CDs and journaling questions related to the topics in *Earth School*. Rolling enrollment allows you to begin the program at any time. The program will offer you the following:

*An inexpensive and convenient way to accelerate your spiritual transformation on the path to full soul alignment and awakening.

*Heightened awareness of your soul's journey, false belief systems, childhood wounds, past life material, unconscious patterns and blocks.

*Tools for working through the karmic material that surfaces as a result of accelerating your process through this program.

AUDIO CASSETTES AND CDs

80 minute audio tapes/CDs of the Tibetan's general discourses from the School's monthly "Chats with the Tibetan" as well as 60 minute seminar tapes that cover most of the topics in this book. CDs of future topics will be available in the Fall of 2006.

CDs of Moriah's narration of *Earth School.*

PUBLICATIONS

EARTH SCHOOL: A Fresh Perspective on the Human Condition, a treasure chest of articles published in a widely acclaimed column in *Wisdom Magazine* provides penetrating psychological guidance, stimulates awareness of the terrain of the soul, fosters self-acceptance through deepened understanding of the human process and provides uplifting original insight. This unique essay series couples the author's candid personal exploration of each topic with her professional expertise of mapping the unconscious. The synergy of this powerful combination is then ignited by the Tibetan's profound wisdom and cosmic perspective on these puzzle pieces of the human condition. This interface of psychological and metaphysical inquiry is penetrating, condensed and potent.

WORDS OF PRAISE FOR *EARTH SCHOOL*

"In **EARTH SCHOOL**, Moriah and the Tibetan take you on a guided tour of the subterranean levels of consciousness, shining a bright healing light onto all aspects of the human condition. Deeply psychological, informative and transformative, this powerful work is destined to be the standard text for all students of the earth plane."
—Mary Arsenault, Publisher, *Wisdom Magazine*

"I've been a student of Moriah Marston and the Tibetan since about 1995, and the lessons have altered my perception of the world, intensified my awareness of how I spend my energy…completely changed my life. It's as if the essence of different "religions" has been distilled into a powerful elixir, infusing my days with a simpler, more direct sense of spiritual connection—to the cosmos and to my fellow creatures. I've come to see that each of us has a part to fulfill in the Divine Plan that is unfolding and by sharing our unique gifts, inborn and learned, we can experience the infinite mysteries, wonders and pleasures of Earth School. For that I will always be grateful…and always ready for the next lesson."
—Ellen Lovinger Eller, Shelburne Falls, MA

"I just wanted to let you know your article in *Wisdom* magazine spoke to me first hand. As I continued reading, I was struck and amazed at how insightful and real the words became to me personally. Years of searching, reading, counseling could not have uncovered such an empowering truth as your article did to me, in minutes, and at such a place and time in my life that required just that knowledge, just then to clear a path along my journey. A true soul connection. Thank you!"

—a grateful reader, TC –MA (Cape Cod)

TRANSFORMATIONAL TIMES, the School of the Golden Discs' quarterly publication is an alternative media, dedicated to building community and group consciousness through the exploration of digestible metaphysics. The metaphysical perspective expands our awareness beyond ordinary day-to-day reality. It brings us to a place of heightened creativity, self-responsibility, wisdom and self-love. This allows us to recognize and embrace our true potential as spiritual beings.. Yearly subscriptions are $15. Complementary issues available.

Contact Zayne 413-625-6754 for Chats and Seminar Intensive schedules, book purchases and list of topics on CDs and audio cassettes or visit our website: www.transformationaltimes.com.

PRIVATE COUNCELING SESSIONS WITH MORIAH

INDIVIDUAL

Moriah, in private psychotherapy practice since 1983, offers individual ongoing soul mentoring sessions either by phone or in person at her office in Shelburne Falls, MA. She works with your astrological chart to help flush out your "life lessons." Moriah includes dream analysis in her session because dreams offer an uncensored glimpse into your unconscious which will assist the process of soul "uncovery."

In her sessions Moriah intuitively links with the Tibetan, who offers the larger perspective on your soul's process. The sessions are deep, rapid and penetrating as you explore false belief systems from past lives, early childhood wounds/patterns, life purpose, relationships and any other areas that are calling for your immediate attention. You will be sent a tape of the session to assimilate the information from the session. Usually people have an initial session and then take some time to integrate the material. You will be sent a tape of the session to assimilate the information.

COUPLES

One of Moriah's specialties is couples counseling. She works with the astrological charts of the couple to examine the underlying issues that might create power struggles, blocks to communication and projections on one's partner stemming from childhood wounds and karmic patterns. Once again, the work is very deep and penetrating.

To find out more information about her soul-mentorship, healing work and/or couples sessions or to set up an appointment call 413-625-6754 or contact School of the Golden Discs, 26 Monroe Ave., Shelburne Falls, MA. 01370 or visit www.transformationtimes.com.

CREDITS

Book Cover:
Concept and Design: Zayne Marston
Front Cover Photo: Peter MacDonald
Back Cover Photo: Zayne Marston